POPLARISM, 1919–1925

Poplarism, 1919–1925

George Lansbury and the Councillors' Revolt

NOREEN BRANSON

LAWRENCE AND WISHART

London

Lawrence and Wishart Ltd
39 Museum Street
London WC1A 1LQ

First published 1979
Copyright © Noreen Branson, 1979

First issued as paperback 1980
Paperback reprinted 1984

1001474287

Printed and bound in Great Britain at
The Camelot Press Ltd, Southampton

0 8 5 3 1 5 5 3 6 4

Contents

Abbreviations

BGM	Poplar Board of Guardians Minutes
DH	*Daily Herald*
EEN	*East End News*
ELA	*East London Advertiser*
ELO	*East London Observer*
MAB	Metropolitan Asylums' Board
MCPF	Metropolitan Common Poor Fund
PBC	Poplar Borough Council Minutes
PRO	Public Record Office
THL	Tower Hamlets Library, Local History Collection

Acknowledgements

I would like to thank all those who helped me in the writing of this book. Mrs Margaret Morris made many constructive observations after reading an early draft. At a later stage, Mrs Yvonne Kapp made numerous suggestions which were of great value to me. Finally, the manuscript was read by Miss Margot Heinemann, Mr Roger Simon and Dr Brenda Swan all of whom gave me the benefit of their expert knowledge.

My thanks are due to Mrs Patricia Ryan who advised me on sources and enabled me to read her own essay on the poor law in Poplar before it appeared.

I must express my appreciation of the unfailing help I received from Mr Bernard Nurse, the local history librarian at Tower Hamlets; it was from him that I first learned that the word 'Poplarism' was in the dictionary. I am most grateful to Mr Albert Cressall who sent me interesting information about his parents and to Councillor William Guy of Tower Hamlets for supplying some biographical details about other people involved. I am much obliged to Mr Robin Thompson for the loan of his father's presentation album of photographs.

I wish to thank the London Labour Party for giving me access to their archives at Herbert Morrison House, and the British Library of Political and Economic Science for access to the Lansbury Papers, and for granting me permission to quote certain passages in Chapter 9 of this book.

It will be apparent to readers that much of the material in this book has been derived from three local newspapers as well as from the *Daily Herald* of the period. In this connection I would like to express my appreciation of the service provided by the British Library's newspaper library at Colindale.

Too little has been written on the subject of this book to warrant a detailed bibliography but I must record my debt to the essay on 'Poplarism' by Professor B. Keith-Lucas which appeared in the journal *Public Law* in 1962. Those who wish to explore the field further should note that there was also an essay entitled 'Herbert Morrison and Poplarism' by G. W. Jones which appeared in *Public Law* in 1973. For general background there is, of course, George Lansbury's own memoirs published in 1928 under the title of *My Life*, and Raymond Postgate's *Life of George Lansbury* published in 1951.

Finally I must make clear that none of the people mentioned here are responsible for anything in the book, and views expressed in it are my own.

Noreen Branson

I

'Something Like a Miracle'

Every public seat in the council chamber was filled and the gallery was overcrowded. It was 10 November 1919 and Poplar's newly-elected councillors were meeting for the first time, watched by an enthusiastic crowd of supporters. Labour had just won a majority in the borough council elections, something which had never happened before. Tonight they were choosing their first Labour mayor and George Lansbury, who described himself as a 'pacifist and out-and-out socialist', had been nominated. Now turned sixty, he had been one of a small minority group on the council for many years. As he came in they stood up and cheered. Like everyone else he found it hard to believe that Labour had won through at last. 'When I first came on to the council, the last thing I thought was that I would ever be Mayor of Poplar' he said in reply to speeches of his friends. 'I thought I should always be in opposition and fighting a forlorn hope. But something like a miracle has happened, and here I am!'[1]*

Poplar was not alone. Throughout London, Labour candidates had won seats and on twelve out of twenty-eight metropolitan borough councils they had now a majority for the first time, or formed the largest party. Before the war scattered groups of Labour and socialist candidates had failed to make much impact. Their success had been confined to a handful of areas; elsewhere they had been ignored and even derided by the workers for whom their message was intended. But now, as the Labour paper the *Daily Herald* put it, 'The sky is brighter and we can all join in a shout of triumph that at long last, the workers are coming into their own.'[2]

Less than a year before, such an event would have seemed far off. A hasty general election had followed the 1918 armistice and Lloyd George, Liberal Prime Minister in the wartime Coalition Government, had asked for a mandate to continue with an all-party coalition in time of peace. The Labour Party had refused to collaborate, had fought as an independent party

* See notes at the end of each chapter.

and had been denounced by its opponents as unpatriotic, pro-German and pro-Bolshevik. Although Labour supporters had been at it night after night, speaking at street corners and under lamp-posts, their words did not appear to reach beyond a limited circle, any more than they had done before the war. On polling day a Conservative-dominated coalition was swept to power on a wave of patriotic fervour.

But after the general election the tide began to turn. Returning soldiers expected life to be better than before. Workers were demanding shorter hours and higher pay, while the unorganised were flocking into the trade unions. All these movements went hand in hand with a shift in political attitudes. For the first time decisive sections of working people began to identify themselves with the labour movement, to think of themselves as 'Labour'. In the spring of 1919 quite a number of Labour candidates won seats on local councils and local boards of guardians and by November it had suddenly become clear that a majority, even in Parliament, was no longer a utopian dream but a practical possibility.

As soon as this happened socialists were inevitably faced with a totally new question: what do you do when you get a majority? How far does the existing legal and administrative framework allow you to bring about the changes for which you stand?

The answer to these questions could never be simple. In any case there were not many issues on which the Labour Party could speak with a single voice. Though it had changed significantly during the war, it was still a federal body in which affiliated trade unions dominated the decisions and affiliated socialist societies were a minority wing. On the other hand, in 1918 it had at last broken free of its Liberal ties and had made clear its socialist aim in a new constitution which had as one of its stated objects 'the common ownership of the means of production'. Moreover its programme, also adopted in 1918, and entitled *Labour and the New Social Order*, envisaged radical transformation rather than tinkering. 'We need to beware of patchwork,' it said. 'What has to be reconstructed . . . is not this or that Government department or this or that piece of social machinery but, so far as Britain is concerned, society itself.'

Brave words, but capable of many interpretations, just as the Labour Party comprised people with many different points of

.w. There were, for example, those who thought in trade union rather than political terms. And these same trade unionists ranged from those who believed in collaboration with the employers to promote prosperity and maintain industrial peace, to those who believed in uncompromising struggle for immediate improvements in pay and working conditions.

But even among those who looked beyond the satisfaction of present working-class demands and who, as conscious and dedicated socialists, believed in the transformation of society, there was every variety of approach. This was illustrated in the three main socialist societies affiliated to the Labour Party. Members of the Fabian Society stood for the gradual extension of public services and social reform brought about through parliamentary and municipal activity. The British Socialist Party, like its forerunner the Social Democratic Federation, was avowedly Marxist; its members believed in the class struggle, extra-parliamentary action, workers' control of industry and the forcible overthrow of the ruling class. The Independent Labour Party, much the largest of the three, included individual socialists of every shade of opinion; unlike the Fabians and the majority of the trade unions, it had opposed the war, and both pacifists and internationalists were numerous in its ranks. For all socialists the 1917 Russian revolution had proved a turning point, inspiring many, filling others with misgivings.

With such a diversity of views it was inevitable that as soon as Labour looked like achieving political control, either at local or national level, there would be profound disagreements concerning both ultimate aims and immediate tactics. One such division was between those who believed in working within the legal and administrative framework laid down by their predecessors and those who thought that if you accepted this framework you would get nowhere.

At the same time the growth in Labour representation created alarm among those who supported the existing social order. To them it seemed that these directly elected local councils and boards of guardians had far too much power; that the constitutional framework was not nearly restrictive enough.

Poplar was to be at the centre of this conflict. For the newly-elected Poplar councillors, with George Lansbury as their leading spirit, were unusually determined that Labour rule should mean a significant change for those who had elected them.

Indeed the need for change stared them in the face. The voters
of Poplar were among the most poverty striken in East London.

To a great extent their poverty was related to the docks and
all the activities associated with the waterfront which dominated their environment. To the south, Poplar was bordered by
the river Thames which encircled the territory known as the
Isle of Dogs. Here lay the West India Docks and Millwall Docks.
A little further east was Blackwall and the East India Docks.
Down the borough's eastern side flowed the river Lea and
across it a canal known as Limehouse Cut. Machinery and
manufactured goods were brought daily to the docks to be
shipped for export, while cargoes of timber, sugar and grain
were unloaded and stored in warehouses or moved into transit
sheds. Associated with this perpetual movement were the railways, still the main link between the coast and the interior. In
the railway goods yards, men were always lifting, pulling,
checking and loading goods which had arrived by water in
preparation for the next stage of their journey overland. A
growing amount of freight was being transported by road, and
the East India Dock Road, which crossed the borough from
east to west, was fast turning into a major artery for the haulage
of goods.

Over one quarter of Poplar's male population was employed
in what the 1921 census loosely described as 'transport', which
usually meant work at the docks, the canals, their associated
warehouses, the railways, or in road haulage. Mechanical aids
were not yet much developed and the work was heavy. More
important for the lives of Poplar's inhabitants, much of the work
at the docks was casual. Unemployed men from other parts of
London drifted into the area hoping to pick up a few hours
work, competing with the regular dockworkers whose lives were
already insecure, since they never knew whether they would
have a full week's work or not.

Apart from the docks there was in the borough a heavy concentration of general industry whose owners found proximity to
the means of transport a convenience. Ship repair works, engineering and chemical factories clustered along the riverside.
Inland there were furniture and paint works. In the north of the
borough were some big factories including Hayes Cocoa Works
and the match-making firm, Bryant and May.

There were 162,000 men, women and children living in

Poplar and their living conditions were pervaded by industrial sights, sounds and smells. Attempts to segregate residential areas from industrial zones were still something for the future; at that time houses and industry were in close proximity. The overcrowded dwellings, many of them insanitary and fit only for demolition, were sandwiched between goods yards and canals, or huddled up against gasworks or under tall chimneys. Their inhabitants took it for granted that their lives would be dominated by the incessant clang and clatter, the smoke, the fumes and the ugliness that went hand in hand with industrial activity. The children played in the street, unless they were lucky enough to live in the north of the borough with access to Victoria Park.

'When one knows the conditions of life in our slums, one stands in admiration of the great struggle which is put up against their environment by thousands of men and women,' was the comment of John Scurr, who was to play a leading part in Poplar's struggle during the nineteen-twenties. 'Cramped together under overcrowded conditions in dark mean streets and alleys; overworked at miserable wages; never enough to eat; seldom able to buy a new dress or suit of clothes; content to purchase cast-offs in the pawnshop or on the stall in the street market; subject to disease from conditions of work and conditions of living. What chance have they or their children? They have been cast into the abyss of ignorance, and our society passes them by and abuses them for their dirt and their ignorance which our social system has thrust upon them.'[3]

'The greater number of Poplar people live always on the verge of destitution' was how another local figure, Charles Key, summed it up.[4] Such findings were corroborated by well-known investigators. A *Survey of London Life and Labour* in 1928 found that 24 per cent of Poplar people were living 'in poverty',[5] much the highest proportion of any London borough. There were also a larger number of unskilled, low-paid and casual workers. Conversely only 2·5 per cent of the residents were described as 'middle class'. Their homes were largely concentrated in the northern part of the borough where pockets of better-quality houses were to be found. The employers and managers of local industry tended to live elsewhere. Edgar Lansbury amused his supporters when he said of Poplar: 'People who can afford to live out of it wouldn't be found dead in it.'[6]

In the years up to 1919 this better-off minority had nevertheless dominated the Poplar Borough Council and the Poplar
Board of Guardians, under the leadership of an organisation
known as the Poplar Municipal Alliance. The Alliance had
been set up in 1905 by a group of local industrialists, who were
resentful of rising rates and had met to consider action to keep
them down. Among the thirty-three firms represented at this
initial meeting were Bryant and May, the Great Eastern Railway Co., Yarrow and Co., J. Westwood and Co., Millwall
Docks Co., Brown's Dry Dock Co. The representative of Bryant
and May was elected president,[7] and ever since the Alliance had
sponsored or supported candidates in local elections, whether
Conservatives, Liberals or Independents. Most of the candidates
had been small businessmen, shopkeepers, company secretaries,
or professional people, including clergymen. Some of them had
business addresses in Poplar but lived outside it.

When the war ended in 1918 it had seemed as though there
was nothing to stop the local employers continuing to dominate
the scene through their sponsored councillors, as they had done
for so long. For in the general election just after the armistice,
Poplar had followed the national pattern. The Labour candidates were defeated in Poplar's two parliamentary constituencies, their opponents alleging that German money had been
used during the war to finance pacifist propaganda in the
borough, and asserting that Poplar 'wants no Bolsheviks.' A
favourite slogan was: 'The men who won the war should be the
men to make the peace.' One of two seats (Bow and Bromley)
was won by a Coalition Conservative and the other (Poplar
South) by a Coalition Liberal. Less than half those entitled to
vote did so.

But within a few months the mood had changed, and this was
reflected in the results of the London County Council elections
in March 1919 when all four Poplar seats were won for Labour.
A month later the Labour candidates gained a majority on the
Poplar Board of Guardians for the first time. These unprecedented developments were enough to cause dismay among those
who had hitherto controlled the local borough council. In some
anxiety the local employers revived the Municipal Alliance
which had suspended operations during the war. They selected
a new committee with the managing director of Bryant and
May still president, and issued a press statement about 'the

danger that threatens the community if at the next local elections the public is led by specious promises and unscrupulous misrepresentations to return men of extreme and revolutionary views to power'.[8] Claiming to be 'strictly non-political and non-sectarian, uniting all shades of opinion', the Alliance issued a manifesto stressing the 'paramount importance of maintaining fair and reasonable administration in the interests of all sections of the ratepayers'.[9] This appeal fell on deaf ears. In the November borough council elections Labour won control of Poplar. Moreover, the magnitude of the victory – a labour win in thirty-nine out of forty-two seats – had surpassed all expectations.

It was noticeable that the majority of newly elected Labour councillors came from a different social class from that of their predecessors. Industrial workers predominated for the first time. Seven of the councillors were directly connected with the docks, including three stevedores, two dock labourers, a corn porter and a man who had until recently been a dock labourer, but was now full-time secretary of the largest dockworkers' trade union branch in the area. There were also seven railwaymen among the councillors, an engine driver, a signalman, two railway vanmen and three who worked in the railway goods yards. Four councillors described themselves as 'labourers', one of whom worked in the building trade. There were two postmen, a road engineer, a toolmaker, a boilermaker, a leadworker, a journeyman bootmaker and a farrier. And there were four housewives.

Those in non-manual jobs were a minority and included some who had previously worked in manual occupations but were now trade union or party secretaries. Among these were a former railwayman, a former carman and a man who had worked in a paint shop. Otherwise the non-manual element consisted of an editor, a schoolmaster, a grocer, a timber merchant and two clerical workers. In contrast the six remaining non-Labour members on the council – three councillors and three aldermen – consisted of a butcher, a jeweller, a manufacturer, a solicitor, a non-conformist minister and a Church of England parson.

In their occupations, the newly-elected Labour councillors were thus much more typical of the Poplar electorate than their predecessors. But in other respects they were not typical. The older among them had all been pioneers, seeking to preach socialism when few would listen, trying to establish branches of the Social Democratic Federation or of the Independent Labour Party, helping to form trade unions where none had existed, or to recruit into unions those who had never been organised. Some had been active in support of the struggle for Irish independence; others had been involved in the fight for women's suffrage. Some had been victimised, some had been arrested for their activities; all could have chosen a more orthodox and therefore easier path through life, but had rejected it because of their principles. As for the younger ones, most of them had already shown qualities of leadership, particularly as active trade unionists at a time when building the unions was uphill work.

George Lansbury was the natural choice for their first Labour mayor. Christian pacifist and left wing socialist, he had been a leading figure in the old Social Democratic Federation before the turn of the century, and for thirty years had been prominent both in Poplar and beyond it as the champion of those who suffered under the Poor Law. He had even been MP for a brief period for the Bow and Bromley division of Poplar before the war, but, a passionate supporter of votes for women, he had resigned his seat in protest after failing to persuade the Parliamentary Labour Party to vote against *all* measures sponsored by the Liberal Government until they brought in a Bill to enfranchise women. He was now the editor of the *Daily Herald*, to which he had recruited a team of young writers who conveyed the paper's socialist message with a crusading fervour seldom seen in after years.

Lansbury was proposed and seconded as mayor by two of his oldest colleagues. Charlie Sumner, a heavily built man in his fifties, had spent thirty years as a labourer firing boilers in chemical factories. A well-known member of the old Gasworkers Union, and of the local Social Democratic Federation, Sumner had been on the borough council since 1900 where he had spent year after year doggedly moving amendments only to see them rejected.

Sam March, the seconder, had been on the council almost as long. Now white-bearded, he had been a carman, or driver of horse-drawn vehicles, in his youth. From 1889 he had been active in the London Carmen's Union which had since changed its name to the National Union of Vehicle Workers. It had

28,000 members, and Sam March was its full-time general secretary.

After the mayor had been installed, the councillors went on to choose four aldermen. To avoid by-elections, they did not appoint them from among themselves, but brought in four people who would be powerful reinforcements in the difficult times ahead. And to some extent they illustrated the diversity of background to be found in the movement.

Susan Lawrence had been Labour representative for South Poplar on the London County Council since 1913. A woman in her late forties, her origins were very different from those of her colleagues. The daughter of a wealthy solicitor, she was one of the few among them who had been to a university. She had begun her political career as a Conservative, having been elected as a Municipal Reform candidate to the London County Council for Marylebone in 1910. As a member of the London Education Committee she had been horrified at the conditions of work of the school cleaners. Having failed to persuade her Conservative colleagues to take action in the matter, she had made contact with Mary MacArthur, become an organiser for the National Federation of Women Workers and in 1912 gone over to Labour. A friend of the Webbs, she was by now a Fabian Society nominee on the National Executive of the Labour Party. 'Susan never believed what she was told but always went to see for herself,' a colleague recollected years later after her death. When she was made alderman she was already widely known for her devoted work both as a women's organiser and a councillor and was affectionately referred to as 'our Susan'.

John Scurr, a tall spare man in his middle forties, was of Irish descent, and his first experience of public life had been with the United Irish League. At the age of twenty-one he had joined the Social Democratic Federation and then the Poplar Labour League, of which he became secretary. 'He is a thinker and a scholar rather than a ranter,' was how one local reporter described him: 'He speaks in a quiet cultivated voice and few people would guess that he is an East Ender, bred in Poplar and received his education at the George Green school.'[10] After various office jobs, Scurr had run his own hardware store, then been taken on as a journalist on the *Daily Herald*. He had been president of the London district committee of the dockers union at the time of the great strikes before the war. In coming on to the council as an alderman, Scurr was joining his wife Julia who, before her election as a councillor, had already been on the Board of Guardians for many years. She had also been active in the suffragette movement and played a leading part in a campaign against sweated female labour. Julia was a few years older than her husband and was, like him, of Irish origin and a Roman Catholic. She had been a close colleague of George Lansbury's for many years before the war, and was renowned for having organised the feeding of 7,000 dockers' children throughout the 1912 dock strike.

The third alderman to be appointed was Robert Hopwood, a toolmaker by trade. A small silent man, he was secretary of the Bow branch of the Amalgamated Society of Engineers (soon to change its name to the Amalgamated Engineering Union) and as such was highly influential among a fast growing section of workers. He had formerly been employed at Bryant and May.

The youngest of the four aldermen chosen that evening was Minnie Lansbury who was thirty. Born in Whitechapel of Jewish parents, she had been a school teacher before her marriage in 1914. During the war she was assistant secretary of the suffragette organisation led by Sylvia Pankhurst. She was well known among the war disabled and bereaved for her work on the local War Pensions Committee which, among other matters, had responsibility for some 500 war orphans in the borough. Minnie's husband was Edgar Lansbury, George's son. He was partner in his brother's small timber firm and had been a councillor since 1912. Minnie and Edgar were left-wingers, and were soon to become members of the newly-formed Communist Party of Great Britain. At that time and for some years to come there were no bars against Communists being also members of the Labour Party.

After the election of the four aldermen, the councillors went on to decide the composition of the council's various committees. Much of the business transacted that evening was routine; yet already at this, their first meeting, it was clear that the councillors were filled with determination to do what was possible to alleviate the poverty in the borough. George Lansbury said as much in his speech. In carrying out his duties as mayor, he said, he would do what he had always done: try to improve the lot of the people at the bottom. And he attacked the injustice of the rating system under which 'the poor had to keep the poor' and suggested that the council should take drastic steps to compel the central authorities to deal with the matter. No one outside Poplar noticed these words nor, had they done so, would they have grasped their implication.

At the end of the meeting the councillors assembled behind the local Irish drum and fife band, and together with some five hundred supporters marched round the borough, ending up at George Lansbury's house with more cheers.

NOTES

1. ELA, 14 November 1919.
2. DH, 4 November 1919.
3. *Socialist Review*, September 1924.
4. *Red Poplar* (pamphlet by Charles Key), 1925.
5. See *New Survey of London Life and Labour*, 1932, vol. III; Survey of Social conditions, I, The Eastern Area. The definition of 'poverty' was the same as that used in the Booth Survey in 1889 when 36·5 per cent of Poplar people were found to be 'in poverty'.
6. ELA, 24 June 1922.
7. An account of the formation of the Poplar Municipal Alliance appeared in the *Municipal Alliance Quarterly Bulletin*, March 1955, No. 6.
8. ELA, 16 August 1919.
9. ibid.
10. ELA, 6 May 1922.

2

The Road to Confrontation

Newspapers other than the *Daily Herald* were in the habit of suggesting to their readers that Labour was unfit to govern and there is no doubt that among the middle classes this belief was widely accepted. For although there were some formidable intellects in the leadership of the Labour Party, its main strength rested on the uneducated. This was exemplified on the new Poplar council. It was easily seen that John Scurr and Susan Lawrence had trained minds. The same could be said of their colleague, a 36 year old schoolmaster named Charles Key who had just become a councillor for the first time. But most of the councillors were not like this; they were, or had been, manual workers who had left school at an early age to earn their bread in some occupation for which facility in reading and writing was of no particular advantage. The idea that public affairs could be managed by semi-literate dockers or railway-men was hard to accept.

Some of Poplar's new Labour councillors did indeed have difficulty with paper work, but this was not the major problem. A more formidable one was how to find the time and energy necessary for council work (which was, of course, unpaid) on top of the hard grind of earning their living. Thus Albert Baker, a councillor in his early thirties, frequently found himself clocking on at six o'clock in the morning at the railway goods yard after an evening meeting which had gone on till midnight. Baker was not only a councillor, but a member of the Board of Guardians; he was one of a new breed of Labour men and women who were voluntarily to devote most of their waking life for years on end to what is sometimes condescendingly referred to as the 'parish pump'.

The Poplar councillors set about their new tasks with energy. They inaugurated their first house-building programme; they put pressure on landlords who neglected repairs; they extended and developed the electricity undertaking which the Council owned; they launched a scheme for free and cheap milk for expectant mothers and babies; they appointed a full-time

tuberculosis officer and opened a new tuberculosis dispensary
for the treatment of what were termed 'consumptive' patients;
they expanded their library services; they arranged for the
public baths to open on Sundays; they enlarged the recreational
facilities in the parks and held dances on Saturday nights at the
town hall. Summing up the experience at the end of his year in
office, Mayor George Lansbury observed amid laughter that it
was 'not a bad record for a council which was suspected of
Bolshevik tendencies'.[1]

This speech was made soon after British military intervention
against Soviet Russia had come to an end, largely, it was
believed by socialists, as a result of the opposition of the labour
movement, which had culminated in councils of action and the
threat of a general strike to stop the war. To this movement of
protest one Poplar councillor had made a notable contribution.
He was David Adams, a Poplar born man, who had been taken
to Wales as a child and had started work in a coal mine at the
age of twelve. He had been 'shanghaied' (as he put it) at the age
of fourteen to become a sailor, had then enlisted as a soldier, and
some years before the war had begun work as a casual labourer
in the London docks. Now he was secretary of the 4,000-strong
Export Branch of the Dock, Wharf and Riverside Workers
Union. In May 1920 a boat known as the *Jolly George* was at the
East India Dock being loaded with munitions for use against the
Russians and Adams played a leading part in the refusal to
continue with the loading. In the end, the ship left without its
cargo of munitions, an episode which caused a great stir, and
not only in Poplar.

A few weeks earlier, George Lansbury, as editor of the *Daily
Herald*, had paid a visit to Soviet Russia; on his return he
gave a detailed report on the working of the Moscow Soviet to a
borough council meeting. All this was certainly outside the
normal confines of the parish pump and was treated by
Labour's opponents as confirmation of their accusations of
Bolshevik influence.

However, the action which aroused most indignation among
the Poplar employers during that first year in office concerned
the councillors' treatment of their own employees. Only a
month after they had been elected, it was announced that a 4s
war bonus which had been awarded to vehicle workers was to be
extended to all other employees *provided* they belonged to a

trade union.[2] To the local employers this action had serious implications. It was raised in the House of Commons by Sir Reginald Blair, Conservative MP for the Bow and Bromley Division of Poplar. Shortly afterwards a court case was brought against the council on behalf of a watchman who objected to joining the union; on this occasion the council, as defendants, won the case.

Another action of the council concerning its employees was to have repercussions which would reverberate for many years to come. Early in 1920 a conference of London local authorities agreed to recommend a minimum wage of £3 10s 6d for municipal employees. But on 27 May, Poplar council took a decision to bring the lowest grades among their employees up to a £4 minimum. In future this minimum would apply to both male and female employees. Most of the employees concerned were men; they included sweepers, dustmen, sluicemen, gullymen, baths and wash-house attendants. All had been getting £3 4s per week and were now raised to the £4 minimum. But there were also some women involved, including seven lavatory attendants and twenty-six baths and wash-house attendants who had been getting only £2 9s 9d. They too had their wages raised to £4. Thus, though the men received a 25 per cent increase, the women got one nearer to 70 per cent.

The background to this step was the decision of the Labour Party in 1918 to adopt the principle of 'equal pay for equal work' as part of its stand for the emancipation of women. Yet though the principle had been accepted, it was difficult to find any sphere where it was being operated, or indeed to find a trade union campaigning for it in any serious fashion, apart from one or two professional organisations.

These actions were taken at a time when Poplar was enjoying relative prosperity. Earnings were higher than they had ever been, or were likely to be again for the next twenty years; there was unprecedented activity at the docks and the dockers achieved a rise in pay to 16s a day. But half way through 1920 Britain's post-war inflationary boom came to an end and the scene began to change rapidly to one of declining trade and mounting unemployment. Within a year the country was engulfed in the worst depression in living memory.

The impact on Poplar was more devastating than elsewhere owing to the decline in foreign trade and the resulting drop in work at the docks. The majority of dock workers were not employed by the week but hired by the half-day. A dock registration scheme had been recently introduced in the Port of London so that unemployed workers from other trades would not be taken on and only regular dock workers would get the jobs that were going. But jobs became so scarce that by mid-1921 less than half those registered were employed on any one day. At the dockside men struggled with one another for work; it reminded people of the bad old days. Other firms in Poplar were laying men off as well; the building trade was slack; engineering and ship repair firms were short of orders; furniture firms were discharging their employees. At the offices of the Poplar Board of Guardians queues of unemployed asking for poor relief began to appear. There were men who were exhausted with tramping the streets in search of work; mothers who had pawned their wedding-rings for money to feed the children.

Already in September 1920 the Poplar Borough Council had called a special meeting to discuss the situation. It received a deputation of ex-servicemen and other unemployed which was introduced by Councillor Chris Williams, who had been active in the old Gasworkers Union since the early 1900s. He had fought in the war and was now in various ex-service organisations and a member of the local War Pensions Committee. In response to the deputation the council adopted a number of resolutions. One of these, moved by John Scurr, attributed the crisis to the Government's foreign policy, demanded the cessation of war against Soviet Russia, the withdrawal of the army from Ireland, and the revision of the Treaty of Versailles. This last point reflected the growing view in Labour circles that the economic crisis was due to the elimination of Germany as a trading centre.

Another resolution, moved this time by Charlie Sumner, demanded that the Government make grants to poor districts like Poplar to enable them to employ men on road-works. It was also decided to send a deputation to the Ministers of Health and of Labour to tell them of conditions among the unemployed in the borough. And, on a proposal from David Adams, the council resolved to open its own register of unemployed at the town hall; the people who signed it would be offered any jobs which the council itself could make available.

The councillors were convinced that the Government bore a

heavy responsibility for the economic crisis. Such a situation has sometimes been used in politics as an occasion for apportioning blame and suggesting that the solution is to vote differently at the next election. The Poplar councillors, however, were not prepared to confine themselves to speeches and resolutions; they wanted immediate action. From that time on their major concentration was on practical schemes to create jobs for the workless in their borough. Only a little later they were to be denounced for encouraging idleness by their 'lavish' scales of relief for the unemployed. Yet the ironical truth was that the first step which ultimately led to confrontation with the central authorities was the initiation of a big local public works' scheme to provide employment.

This was a road and sewerage scheme which had been prepared soon after the September meeting at an estimated cost of £31,000. Its preparation coincided with a statement from the Prime Minister on 19 October promising to provide employment for large numbers of ex-servicemen on road-making and road improvement under the auspices of the Minister of Transport; for this purpose grants from the road fund would be made available. In December it was reported that financial help had been approved for a number of such local authority road schemes.

The Poplar councillors were not unnaturally hopeful that their £31,000 scheme would rank for a grant under one or other of the new arrangements. They went on several deputations both to the Minister of Labour and to the Minister of Transport to discuss the possibilities. The Minister of Labour appeared sympathetic and told one deputation that he would try to persuade his Cabinet colleagues to give them such a grant. On the strength of this assurance the councillors decided to take a chance and at their December meeting they authorised work to begin on the £31,000 scheme. Three hundred men were taken on almost at once. Shortly afterwards the councillors were overjoyed to receive a letter from the Ministry of Transport which appeared to offer a 50 per cent grant towards the cost of resurfacing roads.

Their joy was short lived, however. Early in January 1921 they were told that the grant was only available for schemes where job preference was given to ex-servicemen. But the council had given preference to the men with the largest families, knowing that those with several dependent children were in the greatest distress. It was nevertheless discovered that about half those who had been given work on the new Poplar scheme were indeed ex-servicemen. However, the councillors were told that, since their scheme had not conformed with the regulations, the government grant which was already being dispensed for a number of other schemes would not be forthcoming for theirs.

No doubt the Ministers were convinced that it would be hard to justify expenditure of public money to their supporters, both in the House and outside it, unless they could show that it was going to a cause everyone recognised as deserving – that of the returned soldiers. But in Poplar they saw it differently. At a council meeting held on 27 January 1921, Councillor Joe Hammond, a railway signalman, expressed his indignation that the Government should turn down a grant for a scheme because men who were not ex-servicemen were employed on it. Like other railway employees he had not been allowed to join the army, he said, and had been told that the work he was doing was as valuable as fighting. It was not right that men who had not been in the army should now be penalised.[3] Councillor Chris Williams was bitter. He said he thought that the condition in favour of ex-servicemen was an attempt to set civilians against them.

The debate had been opened by Councillor Heales, a journeyman bootmaker who, speaking on a report concerning a local committee to organise relief, asked whether work was to be provided, or whether relief was to come through charity. He thought it degrading to see able-bodied men going about with collecting boxes. The Government, he said, had not only done nothing itself to create employment, it was tying the hands of others. He added that the only thing which could prevent unemployment would be 'the abolition of interest and profit and the ending of the whole capitalist system'. George Lansbury was immediately on his feet. They had passed pious resolutions, he said, but had got no further. If Labour had been in a minority on the council they would have been worrying for something to be done. But now they were in a majority they ought to be worrying themselves. He moved that they should appoint another deputation to try and persuade the minister to modify his grant regulations and this was agreed.[4] At the same meeting it was reported that the number of men employed on the new scheme had risen to five hundred.

The debate that night was a depressing one. Lansbury's year of office as mayor had expired the previous autumn and Sam March who had succeeded him was in the chair. The meeting was thinly attended by the public. The heady days of 1919 were over. Then Labour supporters had packed the gallery anxious to watch their representatives running their affairs for the first time. Now the novelty had worn off. The councillors were very conscious of the growing distress in the district. Charles Key talked about the children at his school. He told of a thin little boy who had caught scarlet fever and had gone into hospital where he had been well fed and had come back quite plump. But now he was thin again; his father was out of work and there were five children in the family. Charlie Sumner, who looked at all problems in terms of the conflict between capital and labour, was convinced that the rise in unemployment was caused by a conspiracy between the Government and the big firms to bring down wages. Susan Lawrence expressed fears that the London County Council's new housing scheme in Dagenham was about to be abandoned, though 'an army of men' could be employed on it if it were started.[5]

The debate provoked some gentle sarcasm from a writer in one of the local newspapers, the *East London Advertiser*:

> The predominating impression which the meeting left on my mind was the intense earnestness of the members . . . Another impression was the lack of economic soundness which lay beneath many of the arguments. The speakers obviously had the best intentions in the world, but so far as practical possibility went, they might have been administering the affairs of Utopia.[6]

The councillors were indeed up against a situation which was new at the time, but which has faced many dedicated socialists since. Convinced of the need for fundamental changes in the system, such people have believed that if elected they will be in a position to make a major impact on the lives of those they represent. But once elected, whether in local or national government, they have found that their opportunities are smaller than expected. They are hemmed in by the structure of property relations which in turn is reinforced by administrative ties and legal props. They are bound down by the financial fetters imposed from on high. The existing framework is too strong for them.

Many such people become sidetracked by the practical details of administration; unconsciously their sights are lowered, the achievement of small things becomes a substitute for the great things they once envisaged. Others become profoundly disillusioned. The significance of the Poplar councillors during these years was that, as one of the first groups of socialists to achieve a working majority, they were also among the few who refused to remain confined within the limits of the system in which they found themselves. They believed that it was their responsibility to bring about major changes in the conditions of life of their electors and in so doing help to build a movement which would one day lead the country to socialism.

In February 1921 they were looking for any action open to them which would provide immediate relief to the poor of their borough, while simultaneously forcing the central authorities who had rebuffed them to take notice. In the course of such action they would be making clear to the world the injustices of the system, and would demonstrate Labour's determination to change it. The action they chose took the form of a refusal to levy the rates on behalf of other central London bodies.

The choice of action was, of course, dictated by the pattern of local government in London which was like that of no other city. At the top was the London County Council which covered a population of some $4\frac{1}{2}$ million.[7] Within its territory, and forming a lower tier, were twenty-eight metropolitan borough councils, ranging from the very rich – Westminster, to the very poor – Poplar. Parallel with these boroughs were twenty-eight directly elected boards of guardians administering poor relief.[8] In their turn these boards appointed most of the members of the Metropolitan Asylum Board which ran the Poor Law hospitals. There was also the Metropolitan Water Board whose members were appointed by all London local authorities and finally the Metropolitan Police Authority which, alone among these bodies, was not elected but came directly under the Government, via the Home Office.

A little of the expenditure of all these authorities was borne by government grants or subsidies, but most of it fell on the local rates. These were levied by the metropolitan borough councils, who collected them on behalf of themselves and the outside authorities and paid over to the latter the sums due to them, keeping the rest for their own purposes.

When central authorities like the London County Council spent money the costs were pooled for London as a whole, the richer boroughs contributing more than the poorer ones. But the opposite was true of those services provided directly by the borough councils and boards of guardians which were financed mainly by the populations they served. It was precisely on these local bodies that the new financial burdens arising from the growth in unemployment largely fell. The Poplar councillors knew that with the rise in jobless men and women demanding poor relief, they would be obliged to impose a big rate increase at the end of March 1921. Yet in the previous four years the rates had already doubled.

It had long been argued that part of the costs of these local services should be pooled like those of the LCC so that the richer boroughs contributed towards the costs of the poorer areas. The need for pooling had indeed been recognised officially by the introduction of two special funds. One was the Metropolitan Common Poor Fund which pooled certain workhouse costs. But this scheme had been restricted since 1916 when the amounts received out of the fund by poorer boroughs such as Poplar had been frozen despite a vast rise in costs. The Poplar Board of Guardians estimated that the failure to update the scheme was costing them £38,000 a year. The previous summer the Minister of Health had promised to update the fund's arrangements but the Bill under which this was to be done had been subsequently withdrawn and since then nothing had happened despite protests.

The same inertia had been displayed in connection with the Rate Equalisation Fund. Under this, a 6d rate imposed throughout London was redistributed among the poorer boroughs. There had been a demand that this arrangement should be extended, and as recently as 5 May 1920 the House of Commons had actually adopted a resolution urging further equalisation of London's rates. Like all other such expressions of opinion, nothing had come of it.

And nothing, of course, came of the further deputation which went once more to see the Ministers after the January meeting of the Poplar council. A grant for the work scheme was again refused. But unlike most local authorities in such a position, the

Poplar councillors decided that they were not going to submit. They were going to make a protest which would force the central authorities to pay attention.

They did not take their decision without consultation with their supporters. The local Labour Party called a conference of representatives of local trade union branches to thrash out the matter. To this conference Lansbury put the proposal that the Poplar Borough Council should continue to levy the local rate for its own purposes and for those of the local Board of Guardians, but should stop collecting rates for the outside bodies whose precepts (i.e. orders to levy a rate at a certain level) normally made up their total rate demand.

It was not the first time that Poplar councillors had considered the use of this method of protest; indeed afterwards nobody could quite remember who had first suggested it. A few months earlier, on one of the innumerable deputations concerning the road scheme, they had told a government representative that unless they got relief they would refuse to pay their quota to the central authorites.[9] Now at this conference of local trade unionists there was a long discussion about the legal implications of such a refusal and its possible consequences. In the end, the conference delegates agreed that if such action were taken they would support the council by all means in their power. After this, the councillors finally took a decision to go ahead.

Their belief in the necessity for some desperate action was reinforced in the middle of March by the decision of the London County Council to shelve the Dagenham building scheme in obedience to a recommendation from the Ministry of Health. In vain Susan Lawrence urged the LCC to go on with the scheme 'both to supply the housing needs of London and provide useful work for the unemployed'. Her amendment was defeated at the London County Council meeting by sixty-one votes to twenty-two. During the debate, Charlie Sumner who, like Susan, was one of Poplar's LCC councillors, said angrily that if the council did not do justice to the people in working class constituencies, those people would stop their money. 'After next Tuesday, Poplar will show you how to fight,' he declared. 'We are not going to give you any Asylums Board or police precept. We will not levy any rates for you, and you can get on with it.'[10]

At last, on Tuesday 22 March 1921, Poplar took its formal

decision at a specially convened meeting of the borough council.
It was almost time for the fixing of the local rate; the borough
council did this once a quarter at a figure which would bring in
enough money to cover expenditure for the next three months.
On this occasion Sam March, the mayor, was unable to be
present, so George Lansbury took the chair. By this time there
was no sign of the despondency of previous months; as Edgar
Lansbury later recalled: 'The air was electrical.'[11]

The councillors did not want their finance committee to bear
the responsibility for any illegal action; it must be shouldered
by the full council. So the finance committee's estimates were
brought before the council meeting as though nothing unusual
was planned. But after they had been formally presented, a
resolution was moved to refer them back so that the precepts for
the London County Council, the Metropolitan Police, the
Metropolitan Water Board and the Metropolitan Asylums
Board could be deleted.

The resolution was moved by Charles Key who was chairman
of the public health committee. He said that their responsibility
towards local needs demanded that they should make the most
effective protest they could against the studied indifference of
the Government. Desperate conditions compelled their action,
he said. At every turn their poverty stared them in the face.
Sumner, who seconded, said that for over a year they had tried
to deal with the matter on constitutional lines, but their resolutions had been ignored and their deputations met by 'windy
and wordy statements of government officials meant to hood-
wink them'. It was time the ratepayers knew about the hypoc-
risy and criminal indifference of the central government. If
other councils took similar action the authorities would soon be
brought to their senses.[12]

There was only one dissentient voice, that of the Rev. H. J.
Kitcat, the Rural Dean, who had been elected as an independent with the support of the Municipal Alliance. He said that
although he fully appreciated the difficulty they were in, mostly
owing to the grave distress that prevailed as a result of unemployment, he could not, on conscientious grounds, see how they
were justified in refusing to meet their obligations.

Edgar Lansbury rose to answer him, pointing out that Poplar
was going to spend the money it raised on its own people. It was
a form of direct action well within the province of the council.

From the chair, George Lansbury said their action might put them in the bankruptcy court. 'Well, let it be so.' If the central bodies came down and levied the rate, those who had to pay would be no worse off than if it were levied now.[13] The resolution was carried with only Kitcat voting against.

The decision came into effect on 31 March 1921 when the regular borough council meeting took place, this time with Sam March in the chair. The valuation committee reported that if the estimates of the LCC and the other bodies were omitted, those for the borough council and the Board of Guardians only would require a rate of 4s 4d in the pound for the next three months. This compared with a rate of 6s 10d which would have been levied had the precepts of the central bodies been included. The council then agreed without discussion to fix the rate at 4s 4d.

Thus was launched the protest action in support of the demand for 'equalisation of the rates' – not on the face of it a particularly appealing slogan – nor one likely to set fire to the imagination of the poverty-stricken masses, it might be thought. Yet it was around this action and this slogan that a great popular movement was to develop in the East End of London.

NOTES

1. ELA, 6 November 1920.
2. PBC, 27 November 1919.
3. ELA, 5 February 1921.
4. ibid.
5. ibid.
6. ibid.
7. The London County Council covered only part of the population of Greater London; a large part of the rest was in Middlesex, or formed part of the territories of Herts, Essex, Kent and Surrey. As part of Greater London there were also the county boroughs of West Ham, East Ham and Croydon.
8. The geographical boundaries of the boards of guardians were not in all respects similar to those of the metropolitan borough councils, but as it happened the territory administered by the Poplar Board of Guardians was identical with that of the Poplar Borough Council.
9. ELA, 4 December 1920.
10. ELA, 19 March 1921.
11. *My Father*, by Edgar Lansbury, 1933, p. 72.
12. ELA, 26 March 1921.
13. ibid.

3

A New Form of Strike

The reaction to the Poplar council's decision was mixed, but on one question orthodox opinion was unanimous: the Poplar councillors could not win. The *East London Observer* an independent local newspaper which, like the Rev. H. J. Kitcat, was sympathetic to the aim of equalisation of the rates, put the prevailing view:

> Nobody supposes that this new form of strike can be successful, because no Government could possibly allow a local authority to set the ordinary law at open defiance. It would bring about a complete breakdown of the metropolitan system of local government. It will not be beyond the wit of the Law Officers of the Crown to discover a practical means of bringing the recalcitrant local authority meekly to heel.[1]

This prophecy was in the end to prove wrong in every particular. But initially Poplar's action was dismissed as a mere gesture intended to draw attention to the plight of the borough. The assumption that the matter need not be taken too seriously was reinforced by a correspondence with the police which ensued within days of the March meeting. In addition to the decision not to levy the police rate for the next quarter, the Poplar council had already withheld payment of £25,000 owing to the police for the last quarter, admitting that although this money had been raised for the purpose, it had been spent on the unemployed instead. The council received a slightly incredulous letter from New Scotland Yard, asking whether it had correctly understood that the money owing to the police had been diverted to other purposes and that the council definitely refused to pay. Since the debt referred to the previous quarter and not to the current one, Poplar decided to return a soft answer and Scotland Yard was told that the council hoped to pay over the money as soon as possible. The matter was raised in the House of Commons on 6 April and the Home Secretary was able to give a similarly reassuring reply.

Those who attended the well-filled public meetings in Poplar throughout April 1921 when the councillors explained their policy, can hardly have believed, however, that it would be easy to bring them 'meekly to heel'. Sam March, the mayor, raised loud laughter when he told a meeting that they were all waiting for the police to take them into custody.[2] Sumner confessed to another audience that he did not know what the authorities would do. 'I don't think that they quite know themselves,' he said. 'They sent for old Skeggs, our Town Clerk, and when he got to the office of the Receiver for the Metropolitan police, he found the officials busy reading the *Daily Herald* (*laughter*). Oh yes, they are all anxious to know what George Lansbury has to say about it (*renewed laughter*).'[3]

Most working class families paid their rates together with their rent and the decision therefore meant an immediate reduction in the weekly sum demanded by the rent collector. For local firms it meant a substantial fall in the quarterly rate demand. It is not easy to mobilise opposition to such a measure and this put the Municipal Alliance in a quandary. It had originally been formed by local firms and had lower rates as its main object. The secretary of the Alliance was at this time Sir Alfred Warren who had been mayor of Poplar from 1913–18 and was a prominent freemason. In 1918 he had become Conservative MP for Edmonton. From time to time in the past, Warren had urged that the costs of certain services, such as the Poor Law, should be a national rather than a local charge. At the same time the necessity of bringing up to date the arrangements under the Metropolitan Common Poor Fund was accepted by all concerned.

In these circumstances, the approach of Sir Alfred Warren was to attack the councillors for their form of action rather than their aim. 'There is a right way and a wrong way, and the Socialistic majority on the Poplar council have chosen the wrong way.'[4] On 6 April he made a speech in the House of Commons saying that Poplar's action was unconstitutional and if carried out throughout the country 'would reduce us to a system comparable with Bedlam'. This phrase gave Sir Alfred so much pleasure that he repeated it in a letter to the *East London Advertiser*. ('It has been rightly observed that "Poplar is wrong and has adopted a course which if followed would reduce London's life to Bedlam".')[5] And he told a public meeting early in May that 'he must repeat what he had often said, that if the action of the council was persisted in it would reduce the district comparable with Bedlam'.[6]

At this public meeting, which had been organised by the Municipal Alliance, the representatives of many of the bigger Poplar firms were present. On the other hand, the aldermen and councillors who had been elected on the Municipal Alliance ticket were conspicuous by their absence. They were criticised by Warren who said: 'When the vote was taken in the council, only one of them had the courage to vote against the proposal not to levy a full rate.' Actually two of the councillors concerned, Cowl and Cohen, had absented themselves from the council meeting and two others, Aldermen Brandy and Knightbridge, had voted with the majority. As we have seen, it was only the Rev. H. J. Kitcat, who had been elected as an independent, who had voted against the decision not to levy the rate.

Sir Alfred Warren's strongest card was the argument that ultimately more money would be taken out of their pockets as a result of the borough council's action. He put this to his audience, asking them whether they thought that the LCC would take the matter lying down, or whether the police would write off the account as a bad debt, and was emphatic that, on the contrary, steps would be taken to assert the rule of constitutional government. In the long run the borough would not only have to pay what it owed but, if payment had to be enforced by law, there would be heavy legal costs in addition. In other words, by failing to pay now they would all be forced to pay more in the end. The following resolution was then passed:

> That this meeting including most of the largest ratepayers of the Metropolitan Borough of Poplar, enters its strong protest against the unconstitutional action of the present members of the Borough Council in definitely declining to levy a rate sufficient to meet the legitimate liabilities of the borough, therebye occasioning great difficulty and confusion, and ultimately involving the ratepayers in additional charges in respect of costs etc. And demands that the full amount required to discharge the Borough's obligations for the current period be immediately levied.[7]

Under the guidance of this meeting, several large firms wrote to the borough council returning their rate demand notes and asking that the precepts of the central authorities be included. They received in reply letters from the council pointing out that the rate demand conformed with the rate made, and that in case of non-payment the council would take the usual steps to enforce it. Thereafter this particular rebellion fizzled out.

It was, however, widely assumed that the Poplar ratepayers would ultimately be obliged to pay even more than they would have done had the councillors levied the rates in full. At an all-London meeting of ratepayers associations held in Westminster early in May the chairman observed that the only effect of Poplar's 'ill-judged action' would be 'to involve Poplar rate-payers in a still heavier burden because naturally the county and the other authorities will ultimately collect the monies for services they are compelled to perform, and in enforcing the law doubtless heavy costs will be incurred.'[8]

But it soon transpired that enforcement of the law was going to be easier said than done. The first instalment of the London County Council precept was due to be paid before 28 May, and in the middle of May the LCC's solicitor wrote to the Poplar council asking whether the County Council was to understand that Poplar did not intend to honour it. He added that unless he heard that Poplar intended to pay up before 25 May, the LCC would without further notice 'take steps to enforce payment'. The amount due to the LCC was £33,944, part of a total of £135,778 owing for the half year. The general purposes committee of the Poplar council decided simply to acknowledge the LCC's letter, an action which was endorsed at the full council meeting on 26 May.

But the threatened 'steps to enforce payment' were not going to get the LCC very far, as it discovered after taking counsel's opinion. Indeed, the legal system has not on the whole been designed to deal with those who break the law from high-minded motives. And the LCC rapidly began to realise that it was embarking on a long course of legal action which, though no one could deny its rights under the law, was unlikely to bring redress unless the councillors could be persuaded to change their minds.

Originally the fear that the LCC might be able to step in and seize the council's funds to reimburse itself had been voiced in Labour circles in Poplar. But the councillors had taken legal advice and knew the answer: the LCC had no such power. The confident predictions that Poplar could be brought meekly to heel were for the most part based on the assumption that some such power existed. It was only during the ensuing long-drawn-out legal proceedings that it became clear this was not the case.

Alternative remedies were hastily explored. Could the Government suspend or dismiss the council if it broke the law? Again the answer apparently was 'No'. Could the Government set up alternative machinery for levying the rate in Poplar? Curiously enough, such a power had once existed: under the Metropolis Management Act of 1855 the central authority could appoint persons to levy rates in defaulting parishes. But by some oversight this provision had been left out of the 1899 Local Government Act which had created the Metropolitan borough councils. Only in the case of the police rate could special overseers be appointed to collect the rate. This was under an earlier Act. But the police rate was only a fraction of the money now being withheld, and there was no way of putting in collectors to levy the rest.

It appeared that it might be possible for the LCC to get a court order empowering it to seize some of the Poplar council's property, sell it and so raise the money owed. This however was not a course of action which appealed to the LCC at all. The complications and trouble such a move would entail filled their administrators with dismay.

The LCC's legal advisers came to the conclusion that their only course was to apply to a court for a writ of *mandamus*. This is a term unfamiliar to laymen. It means an order directing some person or body to do some particular thing relating to its office or duty. It has always been regarded as an exceptional remedy in circumstances where there is no alternative.

Accordingly, on 3 June application was made on behalf of the LCC to the King's Bench Divisional Court for a 'rule *nisi* for a *mandamus*', requiring the Poplar council to pay to the LCC the money due: £33,944. The application came before Mr Justice Lush and Mr Justice Sankey. Alexander Macmorran, KC, one of the country's leading experts on local government law, appeared for the LCC. Macmorran explained that the Poplar council 'for some reason that was not very apparent' had struck out of its estimates the moneys owing to the precepting bodies, and had levied a rate for its own purposes only. He knew that a *mandamus* would not be granted if there were an alternative remedy, but in this case the alternative remedy was a curious one, deriving from the County Rates Act of 1852, under which the LCC had the right to distrain on the Poplar council by the sale of its goods. To do this would be obviously futile. Macmorran also said that the matter was of great urgency and he would like to have a date fixed for the case to be heard as soon as possible. The court fixed 20 June.

A week later Macmorran again applied to the court for a *mandamus*, this time on behalf of the Metropolitan Asylums Board, to which the Poplar Borough Council now owed two instalments of £7,000 each out of a total of £28,143 payable for the half year. The court granted this application too, one of the judges observing that the life of the community would be imperilled if this attitude were adopted.[9]

The Poplar councillors had meanwhile made a last attempt to persuade the London County Council to change course. At a full council meeting on 7 June, Sam March said that there were many Poplar women who had pawned the pictures on their walls, and even their wedding-rings, to get money to pay rates. He knew families with twenty to forty pawn tickets who had been compelled to go to the Board of Guardians for relief in the end. The council was now spending £4,600 a week in out-relief, he said, and it was impossible to ask the people to pay higher rates. Susan Lawrence said that Poplar was in a position of 'absolute desperation'.[10] She stressed the poverty and the low rateable value of the district. But the Labour Party had only fifteen councillors out of 124 on the LCC, and the Municipal Reform Party (Conservatives) had a majority over Labour and Liberals combined, so no one was surprised that the Poplar members failed in their attempt.

The councillors had long since been preparing their legal defence. Their solicitor was W. H. Thompson, a young man who had been imprisoned during the war as a conscientious objector. He was not only an exceptionally able lawyer, but held socialist views and was convinced of the political importance of the case. With Lansbury and others he discussed the legal problems. The councillors knew they had little chance of winning the battle in the law courts, and in preparing their defence, they had one main object in view: delay. While they kept the legal argument going, Poplar people would continue to benefit from substantial rates relief. At the same time the need for a fairer rating system, which would remove some of the burden from the poorest boroughs, would be publicised. Until they took action the desperate position of Poplar and the other poor London boroughs had been virtually ignored. Now at last they were news; they wanted the publicity to build up so that, as support for their case grew, other Labour-controlled local authorities would take similar action. Provided the movement was strong enough, they were convinced that a change in the law could be won.

It was this objective which guided them when the case first came up in court on 20 June. The proposal made on behalf of Poplar to the court would hardly have helped the situation in the borough. But it offered a legal problem which the judges had some difficulty in resolving. Poplar's lawyers argued that a writ of *mandamus* could only be issued if there were no alternative remedy, but in this case there was such an alternative; under the 1852 County Rates Act the LCC could obtain the money owed by 'distress', i.e. by seizing Poplar's goods and selling them.

Thompson had briefed Henry Slessor, KC for the defence. He was Standing Counsel to the Labour Party and was later to become a Labour MP and hold office under the first Labour Government. The court was composed of the Lord Chief Justice, Mr Justice Sankey, and Mr Justice Branson. Slessor told the court that the reason why Poplar had not honoured the precepts was that the borough was 'practically insolvent'. He read an affidavit signed by March, Sumner, Lansbury and Scurr saying that it would be useless to levy a higher rate on Poplar's ratepayers. They explained that Poplar had suffered the loss of £38,000 a year owing to the wartime alteration of the arrangements under the Metropolitan Common Poor Fund, whereby wealthy boroughs contributed to poorer ones. They referred to the poverty of Poplar's inhabitants, large numbers of whom had always been either unemployed or underemployed. They stressed that the council's funds had had to bear most of the burden caused by the abnormal unemployment. 'The council, relying upon promises of assistance from the Government, have spent between £30,000 and £40,000 upon schemes for relieving the unemployed. These promises have not been carried out and no assistance (beyond £3,000 from the Prince of Wales Fund) has been supplied.'[11]

Slessor went on to say that the council had no desire to be 'contumacious', but that the limit of its resources had been reached. He therefore urged that the alternative remedy should be adopted, and that the LCC should distrain upon the borough council's property. 'That would have the effect of depriving the borough council of all its available assets and so dislocating local government entirely,' objected the Lord Chief Justice. To which Slessor replied, 'It is probably inexpedient for the County Council at the moment to ask for their pound of flesh in any way'.[12]

There followed a long discussion on the feasibility of Slessor's proposal. He himself suggested that Poplar's recreation grounds, libraries, baths and electricity plant could be distrained upon, but Macmorran for the LCC objected that there was nothing to take except the tables and chairs in the council house and the horses and dustcarts, and they would certainly not yield anything like the amount owed. The Lord Chief Justice observed that if the council had £33,000 worth of goods and the whole were taken, it would have to buy fresh goods in order to carry on, and levy a rate for that purpose. 'That is a circuitous method of procedure.' Precedents were quoted on either side, and at one point the Lord Chief Justice said he could not imagine the reasons for Poplar's action, 'unless it be popularity', to which Slessor replied: 'No, my Lord, I am afraid it is poverty.'

The court went on to consider the case of the Metropolitan Asylums Board, which was, as we have seen, responsible for the Poor Law hospitals. However, the Lord Chief Justice raised a laugh by referring to 'the lunatics of Poplar', a comment which irritated one of Poplar's local newspapers, the *East London Observer*: 'It is really easy for a man with ten thousand a year to describe poor devils out of work for ten weeks as lunatics because they can't pay the rates.'[13]

Towards the end the Lord Chief Justice asked Macmorran what would happen if the *mandamus* were issued, but the councillors refused to give in. 'Suppose they disregard the order?' he said, to which Macmorran replied that the LCC would then have to take proceedings against the councillors for contempt of court, and he quoted the case of some councillors in Worcester who had been brought to court for contempt. 'But,' he said, 'it may not be necessary to take such proceedings in the case.'

'They may be more reasonable?' asked the Lord Chief

Justice. To which Macmorran replied, 'They may be', and added: 'Even the Poplar Borough Council will think twice before they disregard an order of this court.'

In the end the judges said they would order the issue of the *mandamus* in both cases, but in view of the importance of the case they proposed to put their reasons in writing. Slessor said his client would appeal. Interviewed by a local newspaper, Sam March observed that the necessity for the judgement to be in writing showed that Poplar had raised a very intricate question. As to the possibility of being had up for contempt of court, he did not think the councillors would have insomnia over it.[14]

In the event, the judgement was not delivered until 7 July, on this occasion by Mr Justice Sankey. He said that the court could not issue a writ of *mandamus* if the alternative remedy were equally appropriate, beneficial and convenient. But the remedy suggested in this case was to levy the sum by distress, and their Lordships did not think it would be appropriate, beneficial or convenient to sell on one day goods which the borough council would have to replace immediately, probably at an enhanced price.

Thus ended the first stage of the court proceedings. The judgement was issued on the eve of a visit to dockland by the King and Queen, who were coming to the East End of London to open a new extension of the Royal Albert Dock. Salutes were fired as they sailed past the Tower of London; they were to disembark at the Victoria Dock and return by car. Poplar council had already agreed to a proposal from Sumner that a placard should be exhibited for their majesties to see as they passed down the river: 'Poplar Borough Council expects this day the King will do his duty by calling upon His Majesty's Government to find work or full maintenance for the unemployed of the nation.'[15] But a suggestion from John Scurr that a special memorial be presented to the King drawing attention to the burdens from which the borough suffered was dropped following disagreement on the wording between those, such as Charles Key, who said he was a loyal subject of the King and others, including Edgar and Minnie Lansbury, who said they were nothing of the sort. So the mayor and councillors absented themselves from the reception party which greeted the King and Queen on their arrival. However, as their Majesties drove back through the borough on their homeward journey, they were much gratified by their reception; cheering crowds lined the roadways and flags hung from tenement dwellings.

Poplar council had been celebrating some minor achievements of its own. Very few houses in the borough had baths, and the three ancient council establishments which offered facilities (6d, first class bath, 2d, second class bath, children half price, unemployed free) were inadequate to meet demand. Indeed on Saturday evenings there were long queues waiting outside the Bow Baths in Roman Road. The chairman of the baths committee was Councillor Alfred Partridge, a large man in his late fifties, a blacksmith by trade and known as a pillar of the local congregational church. He had been one of the minority labour group on the council in the years before the war, and when he was made chairman of the baths committee he was aware that the need for more baths had been talked about for thirty years. So he announced that there had been enough talking, now they would have some action; so persistent had he been that temporary baths had been opened in Violet Road, to be followed by some permanent ones in Wick Lane in the North Ward. For the opening celebration the building was decorated with bunting, and boys from Shenfield Training School played the band. 'I hope that one day every house will have a bathroom,' said Partridge to an applauding crowd, 'or failing that, then every other house.' Meanwhile he hoped people would use the baths to the utmost.[16] They did. It was a long hot summer and the numbers mounted.

In that same month of June at the annual conference of the Labour Party both George Lansbury and Susan Lawrence were reelected to the national executive committee of the Party.

It was in June too that the first signs of doubt began to show among one or two of the councillors. Councillor John Suckling, a boilermaker, resigned from the council 'owing to pressure of business'. It was not difficult to find a successor who was eager to join in the battle and, in the by-election held on 23 July, William Lyons polled 1,064 votes, an increase on Suckling's original vote of 822 in 1919.

The majority of the councillors had no doubts at all, or if they had did not show them. By the end of June the rates strike had gone on for three months; on 29 June when they already knew that they had lost their case in the courts, they decided to continue their action for another three months. It was time to

fix the rate for the ensuing quarter to end on 30 September and
once again the council held a special meeting with Lansbury in
the chair. Again the estimates of the finance committee on an
orthodox basis were brought before the council showing that in
the coming quarter the council's requirements, combined with
that of the Board of Guardians, would amount to £235,318,
while the amount owing to the central authorities for the
quarter would be £103,511. By this time there was a similar
sum owing to them for the previous quarter. To meet the total of
£442,340 the valuation and rating committee recommended a
rate of 9s 11d in the £ for that quarter.

Thereupon Charles Key moved that the council once more
decline to collect the money for the central authorities and that
a rate of 5s 3d be levied to meet local requirements only. Key
said he felt he had to do this in order to continue with the protest they had made in March. He reminded the councillors that
the Government had failed to carry out its promises to provide
money for relief work for the unemployed; moreover, he said,
the Ministry of Health had also failed to keep a promise to
refund half the money spent on free milk for poor families. The
reasons for not paying the central authorities were indeed
stronger than they had been three months earlier. The rate
burden was just as heavy, but wages had gone down.

It was after Councillor Sloman, a stevedore, had seconded
Key, that Councillor J. H. Jones raised doubts, not about the
refusal to pay the central authorities the money owing to them,
but on the wisdom of omitting to collect the money. Jones, now
in his sixtieth year, was another pioneer trade unionist. He had
formed a local branch of the carmen's union in the 1880s; he
was now a member of the National Union of Railwaymen,
having worked for the Midland Railway for over twenty years.
He was also a churchwarden. He was deeply worried about the
situation of Poplar tenants who, he felt, would have to pay the
precepts sooner or later and would face great difficulties. He
suggested that it might be better for them to pay the full amount
in their weekly rent now rather than let arrears accumulate.[17]
That the ratepayers would one day have to pay had of course
been an opinion reiterated in the newspapers and, behind the
scenes, by certain Labour leaders. However, in the council
chamber, Jones's proposal was met with indignation. Minnie
Lansbury said she hoped they were not going to advise people to

pay the rates to their landlords. She asked what was the use of taking the action they had if, after all, they would have to pay. Edgar Lansbury said he did not believe there would be any paying on their part; he thought they had 'got the Government on the run' and that it would have to bring in legislation for equalisation of the rates. Susan Lawrence thought it would be a bad policy to collect the money if they were not going to hand it over, and Sumner said he would not vote for it until the Government had done its duty. After which the resolution not to levy rates for the central authorities was carried with only one dissentient, Councillor Cowl, a solicitor, one of the few Municipal Alliance councillors, but who had been absent on the first occasion when the decision not to levy the rate had been taken.

Throughout July, Slessor did his best to get the courts to postpone action against Poplar. When the judgement was given on 7 July he asked for a stay in issuing writs until the matter had been before the Court of Appeal, but Tindal Atkinson, for the LCC, protested that by now the money owing was not £33,000 but had mounted to over £60,000 and further delay was undesirable. Sankey refused any postponement and said there would be an order for Poplar council to pay the costs of the case. The council had given notice of appeal and on 20 July Slessor, appearing before Lord Justice Warrington and Lord Justice Scrutton, asked for a stay of proceedings pending the hearing of the appeal. Macmorran who again appeared for the LCC said that if the matter were allowed to continue, 'all local government would be in chaos'. Warrington agreed that it was a matter of urgency and decided that the appeal could be heard on the following Friday, two days hence. The appeal was dismissed after Herbert Smith, the barrister acting for the Metropolitan Asylums Board, had emphasised the need for haste. He said that members of the Poplar council had already been served with writs, and his clients wanted to enforce them before the long vacation. The arrears were growing month by month and 'things were getting into a chaotic state'.[18] Slessor's request for a stay so that an appeal could be made to the House of Lords was rejected.

On the following Monday, 25 July, Tindal Atkinson for the LCC, and Herbert Smith for the MAB applied to the court for a rule calling on the mayor and councillors to show cause why they should not be committed for contempt of court since they had not obeyed the order to levy the rate. 'Have they done nothing in the matter?' asked the Lord Chief Justice. 'No, except take steps to delay the proceedings,' complained Atkinson. 'I believe there is to be an application to the House of Lords for a stay of execution. The matter is urgent because at end of August the sum of £133,000 becomes due to the London County Council.' He again referred to the financial aspect as 'chaotic'.[19] The judge granted the applications.

Herbert Smith, for the MAB, said that four opposition members of the council had said they were willing to levy the rates, and the board did not intend to add to the expense by serving them with a notice to appear. At which Atkinson remarked: 'The London County Council intend to take no risks and will serve the lot.' In court this remark was greeted with laughter, but in point of fact it turned out to be untrue. The LCC served writs on 31 only out of Poplar's 49 councillors and aldermen, and included among them five out of the six non-Labour members. They also served a writ on the Town Clerk. The MAB on the other hand served writs on 29 councillors, but their group excluded the Municipal Alliance councillors, and included five Labour councillors not served by the LCC.

The distinction between those served with writs and those not was to cause much mystification among the councillors. Albert Easteal, one of those omitted, suggested in a letter to the *Daily Herald* that the LCC and the MAB must have given instructions that prominent members of the Poplar Borough Council only should be served, and the others omitted 'in the hope that they will rat against their leaders. . . . To say the least, it looks very fishy.'[20] Yet it turned out that one very prominent leader had been left out: Charles Key, chairman of the public health committee, who had twice been personally responsible for moving the resolution in the council chamber not to levy the rate. Equally incomprehensible was the omission of Councillor Jack Wooster, chairman of the works' committee. Wooster was a bricklayers' labourer by trade; like a number of his colleagues he had started political life in the SDF and moved on to the ILP later. To his dying day he never understood why he had been left out.

On the other hand, there was one Labour councillor, John Clifford, who had regularly voted with the majority, but when matters seemed to be coming to a head had changed his mind, and had written to the council resigning his seat. This move did not stop him being served with a writ, much to his dismay and the ironic amusement of his former colleagues.

The discrimination over the writs was a symptom of the dilemma in which the leaders of the London County Council had found themselves. Realising that there was no direct way in which they could collect the money owed to them, their aim had been to persuade the Poplar councillors to change their minds. It now appeared that they would go to prison rather than do so. This meant that unless a sufficient number of councillors were left outside to form a quorum, all local government in Poplar would come to a halt. This would bring the LCC no nearer to getting the money, but the chaos so freely talked about would become a reality.

At last persuaded that their legal action was unlikely to bring about the desired result, the LCC sent a special deputation to the Ministry of Health on the morning of 28 July. They explained that though proceedings for contempt were to be taken against the councillors the next day, they anticipated that the councillors would persist in their rebellion whether sent to prison or not. Morever, they were conscious that the case was being carefully watched by other borough councils of the same character as Poplar, notably Shoreditch, Bethnal Green and possibly Fulham, and that unless drastic action were taken, these borough councils might follow Poplar's example. They therefore urged that a short Bill be passed at once enabling the ministry to appoint a commissioner to exercise the functions of a council which defaulted.[21]

That afternoon the matter was brought before the home affairs committee of the Cabinet. But its deliberations were to bring no joy to the London County Council. For the committee was told that it would be impossible to get a Bill of this nature through the Commons during the present session; moreover such a Bill would be very controversial and would involve a discussion on the need for the equalisation of London's rates. So it was decided merely to call for opinions on whether any, and if so what, legal remedies could be enforced, and to give further consideration to the question when these opinions were available.[22]

That evening the councillors faced the fact that their delaying action was at an end. Thirty-six councillors had been served with writs and were summoned to appear in court the next morning. At the council meeting, Cowl, one of the six opposition councillors, made an eleventh-hour attempt to persuade them to reverse their decision. He moved that the orders of the court be obeyed. The Labour majority had no hope of getting the legal decision reversed, he said, and he did not believe that illegal action would result in a change of government policy. If they went on they would be piling up expenses for nothing, and the burden would eventually fall on innocent shoulders. In the long run the inevitable would happen and the council would have to make the rate and levy it. He appealed to the council to accept his motion as a 'golden bridge' by which they could escape from their difficulties. Alderman Knightbridge seconded. He admitted that he had voted with the majority at the start because he had thought it was time to make a strong protest about the plight of the borough. But now he thought the council should realise it had been beaten.

John Scurr opposed him, supported by Sumner. Susan Lawrence said she believed that, whether the council was wrong or right, they should see the business through to the bitter end. George Lansbury declared that there were times in the affairs of men and nations when it was necessary to take a stand on something that was above law, and that was right in equity and justice. 'We have got nothing by being passive and quiet,' he said 'and we are going to be passive and quiet no longer. If we have to choose between contempt of the poor and contempt of Court, it will be contempt of Court.'[23] Cowl's proposal was defeated by 36 votes to four, the four being Cowl, Cohen, Knightbridge and Kitcat.

The gallery was packed, but the proceedings were quickly over. The councillors had a long day ahead of them. They were not sure whether they would not find themselves in prison the following night. The August bank holiday weekend was coming and Sam March and his wife had arranged to go to Clacton; they now wondered whether they would get there. Lansbury went off and wrote a special article about the meeting for the *Daily Herald*: 'Nobody who has served in public life so many years as I have done could but feel proud of the splendid band of men and women councillors who, in face of all the threats of Courts and Judges, decided once more to burn their boats and tell the Court in plain unmistakable terms that, so far as they

were concerned, the poor of Poplar should not be forced to pay',
he wrote. 'The Courts may send us to prison,' he went on, 'but
this will not get the money, for whether our period of detention
be short or long we shall not give way. Here and there a com-
rade may for one reason or another, fail us, but the mass is as
solid as a rock'.[24]

Early on the morning of Friday 29 July the members of the
council assembled outside Poplar Town Hall, intending to
march the five miles to the Law Courts. After George Lansbury
had appealed to the crowd to march with them, what was
described in a local newspaper as 'an imposing procession' set
off headed by a banner which proclaimed: 'Poplar Borough
Council marching to the High Court and possibly to PRISON
to secure EQUALISATION OF RATES for POOR BOROUGHS'.
Other banners carried the words: 'Let Justice prevail though
the Heavens Fall'; 'Poplar is paying £4,500 a week on Out-
Relief'; 'Westminster get £29,000 for a penny rate; Poplar get
£3,200.' Mayor Sam March had gone on ahead to be present
for the opening of the proceedings, so the procession was led by
the deputy mayor, Charlie Sumner, who had beside him the
official mace-bearer; it was accompanied by a drum and fife
band and followed by banners from dockers, vehicle workers
and general workers' trade unions. According to the *Daily
Herald* over 2,000 participated in the march, many having
given up a day's work to do so. Large crowds gathered in the
Strand opposite the Law Courts to cheer the arrival of the
procession.

Inside the court the proceedings had already begun in front
of the Lord Chief Justice, Justice Bray and Justice Sankey. The
arguments used by the Poplar council's defence lawyers (Disturnal and Slessor instructed by W. H. Thompson) were again
technical. They said that the original writ of *mandamus* had been
directed to Poplar council as a corporate body and not to the
individual councillors; the latter could not now be served with
summonses for contempt for refusing to comply with a direction
they had never been given without evidence that they had
individually done something they ought not to have done. 'You
could not say,' argued Disturnal, 'that the Corporation is in
contempt; you are a member of the Corporation; therefore you
are in contempt.'[25] The three judges did not accept this
argument by the defence, though it was one which, in the end,

enabled Poplar to deprive the LCC of the only advantage it might have gained.

A barrister named Hilberry appeared for the four members of the Municipal Reform Party, Aldermen Brandy and Knight-bridge, Councillors Cowl and Cohen, who had been served with writs by the London County Council though not by the Metropolitan Asylums Board. He said (untruly so far as Brandy and Knightbridge were concerned) that they had been anxious all along to levy the rate, but as they were in a hopeless minority they had been unable to act reasonably or legally. The Rev. H. J. Kitcat, the Independent member of the council who had also been served, spoke in his own defence, simply stating that he was in favour of levying the rate, though he sympathised with the motive animating the majority.

Another lawyer, W. P. Donald, appeared for the Town Clerk, J. B. Skeggs, who had also been served with a writ. After the LCC's lawyers had explained that this was a formality, Donald asked for the town clerk's costs. The Lord Chief Justice told him that the town clerk could recover his costs from the Poplar Borough Council. 'Your Lordship is more optimistic than the Town Clerk', observed Donald, to which the Lord Chief Justice said 'Oh cheer up', and there was laughter.

At this point George Lansbury rose to his feet and asked whether the councillors were to be allowed to say anything before judgement was delivered. The Lord Chief Justice said he hoped not all forty members of the council would want to speak: 'The time of the court is valuable.' 'Your Lordships' time I know is valuable,' responded Lansbury 'but thirty or forty of us may be sent to prison without being heard, and our liberty is as precious as the time of the court.'

A number of the councillors then spoke. Sam March said there were from 10,000 to 15,000 unemployed in Poplar; rates were already 22s in the £ and if they paid the precepts for the outside bodies would be 38s in the £. They were providing maintenance for the unemployed whereas it was the Government which ought to support them. They had been to one government department after another for help without success. George Lansbury asked the court to visualise Poplar with its thousands of unemployed and its hungry children. 'Unemployed men, like animals, become dangerous when they are not fed,' he said, 'so that for 15 months we have done nothing less than keep the peace under difficulties.' Susan Lawrence said that conditions of life among the poor in Poplar were appalling; John Scurr explained the financial difficulties of the council and why they were demanding equalisation of the rates. Williams asked that no more burdens be put on Poplar's ex-servicemen. One councillor invited the Lord Chief Justice to spend a week at the docks and watch the daily struggle to get taken on. 'Men scramble for work like dogs after bones', he said. Another councillor spoke of children who fought for crusts of bread in an ashbin.

In his judgement the Lord Chief Justice confessed that he had been moved by the descriptions of distress in Poplar. 'We have been very much impressed by the honesty and earnestness of the men who have addressed us,' he said. But he went on to say that their action was misdirected. They had looked through a microscope at the distress around them in Poplar, forgetting that they were part of a community of five million people and that such conduct as theirs ended in anarchy. The question of equalisation of the rates was a political one of great difficulty, and the court was not the place to discuss it. They had simply to consider whether the council had done its duty; the councillors admitted that they had consciously failed to do it. So if the rate were not levied within the next fortnight the councillors must go to prison with the exception of the minority who had committed no contempt. He made clear that the Poplar council would bear the costs of the case. Lansbury asked for a stay of execution pending appeal to the Lords but this was refused. Finally John Clifford, who had earlier resigned from the council, asked what his position was, to which the Lord Chief Justice replied unhelpfully: 'You supported the resolution and your position is a very unpleasant one.' This caused some merriment.

Legally speaking it looked like the end of the road. However, even now the councillors managed to find another turning. Lansbury and the solicitor W. H. Thompson went to the clerk of the Master of the Rolls and asked that an Appeal Court should be constituted that afternoon to hear an appeal. This was refused at first, but eventually they prevailed and a hearing was arranged for 10 o'clock the next morning.

By this time it was the Saturday of the August bank holiday weekend (then at the beginning of the month) and normal court sittings had come to an end. But in front of the Master of the Rolls, Lord Justice Warrington and Lord Justice Younger, Disturnal and Slessor once more put the argument: since the writ of *mandamus* had been directed against the council as a corporate body, and not against individual councillors, the latter could not be committed for contempt for disobeying it without evidence that they were personally guilty. After much argument Warrington admitted that had it not been the last day of the sittings he would have said that there was sufficient grounds to grant a stay of execution. But he did not want the case held over until next October. He therefore announced a special sitting of the Court of Appeal during the vacation and fixed the date for the Thursday after the bank holiday, 4 August. This decision provoked a leader in *The Times* praising the courts for speeding up judicial proceedings in general and being prepared to sacrifice a week of the long vacation in particular. 'The Trinity Sittings of 1921 will be remembered for their proof of business-like efficiency and an adaptability to the needs of the hour.'[26]

At the Court of Appeal on 4 August it turned out that Poplar's legal advisers had achieved something more than further delay. For the judges found that there had indeed been an irregularity in the procedure adopted by the LCC. Where the individual councillors were concerned it was an irregularity which could be waived: the councillors must go to prison. On the other hand the judges found that the appeal by the council as a corporate body must be allowed, which meant that after all the council would not have to bear the costs of the case. Meanwhile the time allowed to the councillors to change their minds and levy the rate was extended until the end of August because, said the Master of the Rolls, he did not want anybody to go to prison without time for due reflection.

In a subsequent article Lansbury rubbed in what he took to be the lesson of the judges' decision to send them to jail despite the irregularity of the proceedings:

These judges, paid to administer the law have, on their own confession, not merely stretched but smashed all law in ordering us to prison. . . . It is well that organised labour should understand that in the Courts of law all the scales are weighted against us because all the judges administer class-made laws, laws which are expressly enacted, not to do justice but to preserve the present social order. The Poplar case will be remembered most because of the fact that three High Court judges deliberately set themselves to help the LCC and the MAB out of the hopeless mess in which they had landed themselves by making a new law of their own.'[27]

But the news that the London County Council was to be compelled to pay the costs of the case was greeted with applause at a special meeting of the Poplar council held on the evening of the appeal hearing. For on this issue at least, the prophets of doom had been confounded. All those who had said that Poplar would not only have to levy the rate in the end but would have to find, in addition, large sums for costs, had been proved wrong.

Moreover, during that week they had registered one major victory. On 2 August, Sir Alfred Mond, Minister of Health, told the House that he was taking steps to end the temporary wartime 'stereotyping' of payments from the Metropolitan Common Poor Fund. 'This will afford substantial relief to the poorer boroughs, including Poplar. I may add that I trust that the Poplar Borough Council having made its protest, will obey the Order of the Court.'

At last one of Poplar's demands was to be met. The Government had in fact promised such a measure long ago; yet now it was being said that Poplar's action had won it. Thus the clerk to the Whitechapel Board of Guardians suggested to his board that 'in all probability the extreme action of the Poplar Borough Council was responsible for the readjustment of the Fund'. 'Let us give credit where credit is due' observed one local newspaper, the *East London Advertiser*.[28]

The relief that Poplar would get from the readjustment of the fund was only a small part of what it needed. It would mean the saving of approximately 10d on the rates. Nevertheless if the Government's announcement had come during the previous winter, the Poplar councillors might never have started their rates strike. For it had been partly the fact that their representations had been continuously brushed aside or stone-walled that had provoked their action. An earlier sign that those in power were listening and prepared to concede something might well have prevented the issue coming to a head. Now it was far too late.

Sir Alfred Mond may have thought that he was offering Poplar a way of climbing down without losing face. If so such a hope was quickly dispelled. For at their meeting on 4 August the councillors not only reaffirmed their decision not to levy the rate but took steps to see that the rate strike should be prolonged into the far future. Well in advance of normal custom they fixed the rate for yet another quarter – that beginning on 30 September and ending on 30 December. Again for the third quarter running only enough was to be collected to pay for the council's own expenses and those of the Board of Guardians. The rate fixed was even lower than before: 4s 3d. They thus made sure that the rates for the central authorities would continue to be withheld up to the end of the year. And by this action of course they finally made clear to all the world that despite the decision of the court they were not going to give in. Which meant that prison at the end of the month was now a certainty.

NOTES

1. ELO, 26 March 1921.
2. ELA, 16 April 1921.
3. ibid., 7 May 1921.
4. EEN, 8 April 1921.
5. ELA, 9 April 1921.
6. EEN, 17 May 1921.
7. PBC, 26 May 1921.
8. EEN, 6 May 1921.
9. ELA, 18 June 1921.
10. ELO, 11 June 1921.
11. PBC, 26 June 1921.
12. See EEN, 24 June 1921 for ensuing report of these proceedings.
13. ELO, 25 June 1921.
14. ELA, 25 June 1921.
15. EEN, 28 June 1921.
16. ibid., 21 June 1921.
17. ELA, 2 July 1921.
18. *The Times*, 23 July 1921.
19. ELA, 30 July 1921.
20. DH, 30 July 1921.
21. PRO, Cab 24, CP 3176, Memorandum by Minister of Health on Default of Poplar Borough Council.
22. PRO, Cab 23/26, 28 July 1921.
23. EEN, 2 August 1921.
24. DH, 30 July 1921.
25. For ensuing report of these proceedings see *The Times*, 30 July 1921, EEN, 2 August 1921, DH, 30 July 1921.
26. *The Times*, 1 August 1921.
27. DH, 2 September 1921.
28. 27 August 1921.

4

Critics in Disarray

The councillors had never believed for a moment that their battle could be won in the law courts. The aim there had simply been delay and publicity. They had always been convinced that if they were to achieve their object, which was a fairer deal for poor boroughs, they must mobilise support, first and foremost from among their own people in Poplar and secondly from the labour movement outside. In aid of this the *Daily Herald* had been running a campaign to inspire solidarity.

However, there were members of the Labour Party who were profoundly uneasy about Poplar's action and some, particularly in the leadership, who disagreed furiously with the whole tactic. Among these was Herbert Morrison, secretary of the London Labour Party.

Morrison had watched the development of the Poplar drama with growing consternation. The *Daily Herald* was conducting propaganda in terms which appeared to identify the Poplar struggle with that of the labour movement as a whole. The Poplar Trades Council had sent a circular to other local trades councils asking them to bring pressure to bear on their Labour councillors 'to support the action of Poplar by all means in their power'. On the other hand, the councillors had not approached the London Labour Party leadership for any discussion on the matter, nor had they raised it at any of the London party's municipal conferences. Had they done so before taking action, Morrison and those who thought like him could have done their best to dissuade them. But in the absence of any approach from Poplar, Morrison had been deprived of the opportunity of using his influence to stop it.

Then had come the lengthy court proceedings, and until their outcome was known any intervention was clearly out of the question. So it was not until August that Morrison at last called a joint meeting of the London Labour Party executive and the London Labour mayors to discuss Poplar. He placed before them a draft declaration which, he suggested, should be sent out privately to Labour parties and trade councils. In this draft,

which was over two foolscap pages in length, the Poplar action
was subjected to detailed criticism.[1]

The meeting called to consider it took place at Shoreditch
town hall on 4 August, the very day on which the final Court of
Appeal hearing was held and nearly four weeks before the
councillors were to be imprisoned. George Lansbury was at this
meeting by special invitation; so were Susan Lawrence and
John Scurr, both members of the London executive, and Sam
March who was present in his capacity of Labour mayor. The
majority of those present shared Morrison's view of the Poplar
action, and certainly did not want to see their own boroughs
involved. But in response to a strong appeal on behalf of Poplar
in which fears were expressed that the press might get hold of
the statement even though it was marked 'private and confidential' and use it to damage the Poplar case, it was decided that
for the time being the statement should not be issued. Instead
the meeting contented itself with a private circular merely
advising municipal Labour parties and trades councils that, in
the opinion of the executive and the Labour mayors, it was not
desirable for them to follow Poplar's lead. This circular went
out on 5 August. Though the *Daily Herald* reported indignant
reactions to it from some localities, the other newspapers
appeared unaware of its existence. It was before the days when
the scent of a rift in Labour's ranks would bring newshounds to
a quivering alert. Indeed most newspapers were inclined to
suggest that all Labour men and women were tarred with the
same Bolshevik brush.

The Poplar action had, however, raised in an acute form the
differences within the Labour Party. Though these disagreements appeared to centre round the issue of immediate tactics,
in reality they went deeper, embracing two closely related
questions: what was meant by socialism and how to achieve it.
On the second of these there had been hot debate, particularly
since 1919, between those who wanted the Labour movement
to limit itself to 'constitutional' action and those who believed
they should try to mobilise the workers for 'direct action'. The
latter was a term of syndicalist origin; it meant, among other
things, taking industrial action for a political purpose. Specifically it had meant, in 1919–20, taking strike action to stop the
war of intervention in Russia. The dominant leaders of the
Labour Party and the TUC had resisted pressure for such

action, asserting that it would be undemocratic and would probably lead to violence, whereas Labour could, and one day would, win power through the ballot box. But in August 1920 the pressure of events forced the Labour leaders to take the very unconstitutional action they had previously resisted and to set up a council of action to stop the war on Russia. It was an isolated instance, however. On other subsequent issues the Labour leaders had adhered to their previous position.

That Poplar was a case of 'direct action' could not be gainsaid; the local councillors had taken illegal and unconstitutional steps to coerce Parliament into changing the law. In his declaration, which never went out but which was published in amended form in November 1921 after the whole event was over,[2] Morrison made seven points of criticism: (1) the way to win equalisation of the rates was by educating people to vote for Labour candidates at elections; (2) the rates which Poplar had declined to levy were the very rates which were already equalised over London; (3) if Labour conceded that one local authority was justified in rebelling against the legally established rights of other local authorities, Labour would be placed in a morally indefensible position in the case of a Tory council which might rebel against a future Labour majority on the London County Council; (4) Labour had nothing to gain by appearing to create financial chaos in a borough for whose local government it was responsible, but everything to gain by building up a reputation for efficient administration, particularly in the department of finance; (5) it was probable that in the end the people of Poplar would have to pay, and if not, the other boroughs, including Labour ones, would have to pay for them; (6) 'by accepting office on the various borough councils we accepted the responsibility of discharging the functions and liabilities of those councils'; (7) the Poplar policy was likely to play into the hands of those who desired to strengthen central control over local government.

These seven points illustrate Morrison's attitude which was in many ways the antithesis of that of Lansbury and his friends. During the war Morrison had finally discarded his earlier Marxist views and, as mayor of Hackney, had become a dedicated local government man. An exceptionally able administrator, his main interest and activity was concentrated upon the possibilities in the town hall; central to his outlook was the systematic winning of Labour control on local authorities throughout the country and above all control of the LCC. To do this, in his view, Labour must prove to the electorate that it would act 'responsibly' and this, among other things, meant acting lawfully. 'Personally I am very determined in this question or any other question, only to uphold constitutional action and action within the law,' he told the Hackney Borough Council when it discussed the growing unemployment crisis.[3]

He was also determined that Labour should prove itself more efficient than its opponents; his charges against the Conservatives and Liberals who formed the majorities on most national and local bodies were not so much that they were safeguarding the free enterprise system which was the cause of the poverty around them, as that they were incompetent. Morrison not only wanted Labour councillors to *look* efficient; conscious of the fact that many of those newly elected were manual workers with little formal schooling, he put in a great deal of work trying to teach Labour councillors to be good administrators. He set out his general approach in an article in June 1921 in the *London Labour Chronicle* in which he said:

> A machine without high principles is a machine of no real value. And high principles without an efficient machine constitutes but a voice crying in the wilderness. We have to make an efficient machine for a high moral purpose.

Now it could not be denied that the Poplar councillors were imbued with a high moral purpose. Moreover, as administrators, quite a few of them were a good deal more experienced than Morrison, having served on their local council since long before the war. But they had found the machine at their disposal totally inadequate for putting their principles into practice; indeed it might have been expressly designed for hindering the very purposes for which they believed they had been elected. So they had deliberately refused to man the machine any more and had stopped it working. Such behaviour was guaranteed to outrage all those with views such as Morrison's.

The Poplar councillors and their supporters had, of course, been energetically defending themselves against the arguments of their 'constitutionalist' critics. To the assertion that laws made by a democratically elected Parliament should not be broken, Sam March had a simple answer. 'The master class has made the laws,' he said.[4] He did not elaborate on this statement, but it was one with which all Marxists and many trade union activists could at that time agree. To them the enemy was the capitalist class and the government its creature. George Lansbury used a simple moral argument. He held firm Christian beliefs and was convinced that 'wicked' laws ought to be broken. 'The question is not whether what we are doing is legal or illegal, but whether it is right or wrong,' he wrote in a special article in the *Daily Herald*.[5] He reminded readers that 'all reforms came from those who are ready to break bad laws'. 'The established Church in Ireland and Wales, with all its tithes and rents, was abolished because people refused to consider it obligatory on their part to support a Church they despised.'

To the argument that illegal action by Labour would encourage its opponents to break the law should Labour come to power, Lansbury pointed out that these opponents never hesitated to break laws with which they disagreed. 'Carson, Smith the Galloper, Bonar Law and others contemptuously defied and broke all law in Ulster and gloried in doing so, reaping the reward of their treason by the creation of an Ulster Parliament.'

A less sophisticated argument was one used by a Hackney councillor during a discussion on unemployment. He told Morrison that 'when men are hungry they do not care much about constitutionalism.'[6] And indeed this was always the strongest argument for those who saw hunger close at hand.

Such were the answers made to the 'constitutionalists' in the labour movement, though at this stage the latter's voices were hardly heard except behind the scenes. Out in front the councillors were making clear to all the world that they had no intention of abandoning their stand. They had a letter from the Receiver for the Metropolitan Police asking if they intended to pay the police precept; at the borough council meeting on 18 August it was decided to reply that the police rate had not been levied so there was no money with which to pay.

Unknown to the councillors, the Home Affairs committee of the Cabinet had been considering the matter once more. Their law officers had told them that although they had no power to step in and levy the rate for the LCC, when it came to the police rate they did have such a power under the 1829 Act, and Edward Shortt, the Home Secretary, asked the Cabinet whether they thought the power should be used. He said that he himself doubted the wisdom of making use of an obsolete Act for such a purpose. Sir Aubrey Symonds, who was present as a permanent official of the Ministry of Health, was asked what would be the likely reaction in Poplar to such a course. His forecast was gloomy: 'The inhabitants of Poplar, even the more prosperous classes, were inclined to sympathise with the Borough Council, and resistance was therefore not unlikely.'[7] Sir Ernest Pollock, the Solicitor General also thought it would be unwise to proceed under the 1829 Act, particularly since the police rate formed a very small part of the money owing. The committee then agreed that the Home Secretary should not try to collect the police rate.

Sir Alfred Mond, the Minister of Health, was unable to be present at this meeting which took place on 17 August, but Sir Aubrey Symonds made a long statement on Mond's behalf. He said that it was clear the Poplar councillors about to be imprisoned 'were quite determined to be martyrs', and only a complete concession of all their claims would change their decision. Some of their demands had already been met. For example, the war-time arrangements under the Metropolitan Common Poor Fund had been abandoned resulting in relief to Poplar of some £30,000 a year. The council had complained that they had received no grant from the Unemployment Grants Committee. It was impossible to meet them on this. The committee had rejected their application owing to their refusal to give preference to ex-servicemen. For further equalisation of the rates, legislation would be required. The Royal Commission on Greater London was to consider it. The figures showed that the heavy rates in Poplar were due to the policy of its own borough council which included amongst other extravagances, the payment of £5,000 a week on out-relief. The number of out-door paupers per thousand was 92·5 in Poplar while in Whitechapel it was 0·2.

Continuing, Sir Aubrey Symonds said that, 'Dating from the time before the Poplar enquiry in 1906 up to the present time, it was known to be the policy of Mr Lansbury to make administration of the borough impossible in order to secure complete equalisation of London rates.' The question now was 'whether any effort should be made to prevent the members of the Council from going to prison'. The Minister believed that 'on the whole it seemed desirable to let matters take their course'.

The Cabinet committee thereupon agreed that nothing should be done to prevent members of the borough council from undergoing imprisonment.[8] (In view of the reiterated public statements later that the Government had no power to get the councillors out of jail, it is noticeable that such doubts were not raised in this Cabinet committee meeting. It was not whether they *could* do anything to stop them going to prison, but whether they *should* which was under discussion.)

Meanwhile, the leaders of the London County Council had at last realised that the Government was not going to help them. For them nothing at all had yet been achieved. They were no nearer collecting the money owed than they had been before they embarked on legal proceedings. On the contrary, although they had employed the country's leading experts in local government law, Poplar and its lawyers had to some extent outwitted them, so that a mistake in the procedure they had adopted had involved them in heavy costs. Earlier assumptions that the law could and would be enforced had turned out to be wide of the mark.

Incredulity and frustration were expressed by the two MPs for the borough, Sir Reginald Blair and Sir Alfred Yeo, who cross-questioned Sir Alfred Mond on the very day that the Cabinet had taken its final decision not to intervene. Yeo asked Mond what steps he proposed to take to 'put an end to this iniquitous Government which is running the show in Poplar', and said: 'Has the Right Hon. Gentleman's Department no power at all, or is the whole of local government to be held up to ridicule in the eyes of the world?' And Blair asked if the Minister was taking any steps at all 'to enforce the law and have constitutional local government in Poplar'? To which Mond replied: 'The Hon. Member assumes there is some law of which I am not aware giving me power to act in the matter.' Challenged by another MP to bring in a short Act to give himself such power, Mond refused to commit himself.[9]

Two days later Parliament adjourned for the summer recess.

NOTES

1. London Labour Party, folios 685–687.
2. ibid. and *London Labour Chronicle*, November 1921.
3. *Hackney and Kingsland Gazette*, 16 September 1921.

4. DH, 30 July 1921.
5. ibid.
6. *Hackney and Kingsland Gazette*, 16 September 1921.
7. PRO, Cab 23/27, 17 August 1921, Home Affairs Committee of Cabinet.
8. ibid.
9. House of Commons, *Hansard*, 17 August 1921. Col 1411.

Prison

Towards the end of August the councillors held a series of town's meetings explaining their action all over again. A special event, 'Ye Old English Fayre', was put on in the recreation ground in the East India Dock Road to raise funds for the legal costs of the defence. It made a profit of £334.

In private the councillors had much to do. They were not a very youthful group, only seven of those who had been served with writs being under forty. Minnie Lansbury, thirty-two, was the youngest. Thirteen were in their forties; seven in their fifties and three – George Lansbury, March and Jones – over sixty. The men were all breadwinners and their families would need money for rent and food, and indeed a little later, appeals for donations to a maintenance fund brought in considerable help from well-wishers. A group of the councillors' children were taken to stay at the holiday home of the Fellowship of Reconciliation in Kent.

Among those who had to make special arrangements were George and Nellie Cressall, both of whom had been committed to prison. Forty-one-year old George Cressall had been full-time secretary of the South Poplar Labour Party since 1918. Born in Stepney, he had previously been employed as a labourer in a paint works. He had once been in the Liberal Party, but had become dissatisfied when the Liberal councillors on the LCC refused to support a wage of 30s for employees. In 1907 he left the Liberals and helped to form the Limehouse branch of the Independent Labour Party. Nellie had worked in a laundry in Whitechapel Road; her father had been a carpenter and her mother a parlourmaid. She had married George in 1904, and with him joined the ILP.[1] In 1912 after they moved to Poplar, she became active in the left-wing suffragette organisation led by Sylvia Pankhurst, often speaking at meetings at the dock gates at Blackwall Tunnel. The Cressalls had five sons between the ages of seven and seventeen, and Nellie, who was thirty-eight, was expecting her sixth. They arranged that the youngest should be cared for by their grandmother, while two of the boys joined the group of children taken to Kent.

Prison came at a most inconvenient time for Councillor Rugless, a leadworker and vice-chairman of the finance committee, whose wife had just presented him with a son after an interval of eleven years. It was even more complicated for Walter Green, a dock labourer who was chairman of the libraries committee; his wife had recently died and he was left with three little children. He arranged for his sister to care for them.

The final meeting of the borough council took place on 31 August. By this time the affair was attracting much attention. Poplar, which had been utterly ignored when using orthodox methods to try and alleviate its misery, was now the focus of nation-wide publicity. Normally, when a council meeting took place, a couple of local reporters had the press table to themselves; now it was crowded with the representatives of the national dailies. The meeting started late because the councillors were besieged by photographers at the entrance; others took flash-light photographs from the gallery. The business of the meeting lasted only half-an-hour and was confined to arrangements for the borough council to continue functioning. Formal leave of absence was granted to the thirty who were to go to prison; Charles Key was appointed deputy mayor to act in the absence of the mayor; eight important committees were reconstituted so that those Labour councillors left at liberty – in particular Blacketer, Easteal, Hammond, Hegarty, Hubbart, C. J. Kelly, Rawlings, Wooster and the new recruit Lyons – should form a majority on all of them. The borough treasurer was authorised to settle certain bills likely to fall due; a resolution was passed to ensure that the wages of council employees would not be reduced for the next six months. At the end of the meeting the members stood up and sang 'The Red Flag', delivering with special emphasis the words: 'Come dungeon dark or gallows grim, this song shall be our parting hymn.'

They then repaired to the town hall where their supporters were packing the alleyways and standing on the window sills. Outside, some 6,000 people who could not get in waited patiently for councillors to come out and address them. Sam March told the meeting that Poplar's action had already had some effect on the Government, as was proved by the change promised in the Metropolitan Common Poor Fund. Councillor Rugless, who told the *Daily Herald* reporter that 'all the prisons in the country will not alter our determination to win',[2] suggested to the meeting that those who were taken to prison would at least be better off than some of Poplar's unemployed, since they would get enough to eat (in this respect, as it turned out, he was unduly optimistic). John Scurr insisted that the Government was on the horns of a dilemma. If it sent the councillors to prison it would not get its money, and if it didn't it would bring the law into contempt. Every speaker was greeted with tumultuous applause. 'We are going in', said Lansbury. 'It is up to you to get us out as soon as possible, but not until a thorough victory has been obtained.'

In the later afternoon of the following day, Thursday 1 September 1921, the arrests began.

The authorities had clearly decided that the process of arrest should be conducted with courtesy in order to avoid disturbances and accusations of ill-treatment. The councillors were also anxious to discourage violent resistance to their arrests. This was not only because George Lansbury, their leader, was a pacifist; they knew from experience how fights with the police could be used by the newspapers to distort their purpose. At the same time the councillors wanted their arrests to be given the utmost publicity. The result was a long drawn-out and somewhat ceremonious affair which lasted for many days.

The first to be arrested was George Cressall. Two motor cars, (described as 'luxurious') drew up outside the Poplar Labour Hall where he had his office and he was driven off to the cheers of a large crowd. Next the cars arrived at the home of the mayor, Sam March. The family had just had dinner and March's sister-in-law was in the middle of a song. The sheriff's men obligingly waited until the song was ended. After this the cars drove to the home of Russell, one of three railwaymen who had been served with writs, and waited half an hour for him while he washed and finished his tea. Chris Williams, the ex-serviceman, was the fourth to be taken into custody. The night before he had told the *Daily Herald*: 'I should be a traitor to those left behind on the battlefield if I did not stand against the attempt to overburden soldiers' widows with heavy rates.' Appropriately enough, he was attending a meeting of the War Pensions committee when arrested.

Two others were picked up that evening. They were Ben Fleming, a labourer in his forties, who had told the *Herald* that 'there can be only one end: a win for Poplar', and James Jones, the railwayman who had previously had doubts about the wisdom of declining to collect the rates, though he had strongly supported the council's action in refusing to hand the money over to the central authorities. The night before he had said, 'I am proud to belong to a council which is doing a real Christian action.'

The sheriff's men also went to Scurr's house, but Scurr had got bored with waiting and had gone for a walk; they then drove to the Dockers Hall to look for David Adams but he wasn't there. In the end the sheriff's cars departed for Brixton with only six of the councillors. Meanwhile, crowds had surrounded the homes of most of the other councillors and it was suggested that no arrests should be permitted after dark, so detachments of men remained on guard for the rest of the night. In the event throughout the week that followed the sheriff's men never tried to arrest anyone after dark.

The next day, Friday 2 September, Councillor Oakes, a toolmaker, dashed to Woodstock Street where the Scurrs lived to warn them that the sheriff's men were on their way. By the time the men arrived the street was thronged with supporters whose attitude became so threatening that it was only thanks to John Scurr's own efforts that he was taken away. 'Don't forget what I told you,' he said to the assembled crowd. 'No rioting on any account. You have one weapon; that is passive resistance.'[3] On the same day, Joe Banks, the local Labour Party agent, was arrested. Banks had been on the borough council since 1903 and had been the secretary of the pre-war Poplar Trades and Labour Representation Committee; he had been dismissed from his job on the railways in 1910 for taking time off to help in Lansbury's election campaign. Now a grey-haired, balding man, he usually preferred to let other people do the talking. But he had told the *Daily Herald* reporter: 'Our fight will be the forerunner of a complete change in the social conditions of the people.' Also arrested on that day were James Rugless and Thomas Kelly, the grocer, who had said: 'We are determined to stand by our principles no matter how long we may be in gaol'; the two stevedores, Henry Sloman, who asserted that he was 'prepared for anything that comes along so long as we can do the people some good', and Joe O'Callaghan who addressed the crowd outside his house saying: 'We will never give in. If they keep us for twelve months and a day, when that time expires I am willing to go back for another such term.'[4]

On Saturday 3 September George Lansbury telephoned the Sheriff for an appointment. Having fixed 11.30 he got in touch with his son Edgar, with David Adams and Albert Baker. The three met Lansbury at his home in Bow Road and after making speeches and being photographed they were driven away. Also arrested on that day were Alfred Partridge and J. E. Oakes. Despite the councillors' intention that the arrests should pass off peacefully, several men were fined at Thames Police Court that Saturday for disorderly conduct, obstructing and assaulting the police during the arrests. The magistrate said: 'Assuming that the mayor, aldermen and councillors have a good case, men like you will only bring discredit and disgrace upon it. If these disturbances do not end, those taking part in them will be dealt with very severely.'[5]

Sunday was a day off for the Sheriff's men and no one went to prison. The high point came on Monday 5 September with the arrest of the five women, Susan Lawrence, Julia Scurr, Nellie Cressall, Minnie Lansbury and Jennie Mackay. That morning the newspapers published an announcement from Key, temporarily deputy mayor, that the event would take place at 3 o'clock at the town hall. Key explained that this arrangement had been made with the Sheriff's officer 'in view of the intense feeling that has been aroused by the arrests already effected. We have appealed to the people of the borough to allow the official to carry out his duties without hindrance or interference. But this will be possible only with the cooperation of the police authorities, and we trust they will appreciate the great resentment felt by our people and refrain from any action likely to intensify the strong feeling that already prevails.'[6]

Naturally the town hall was crowded an hour before the appointed time and supporters gathered in their thousands outside; a detachment of mounted police arrived and stood by but made no move. Susan Lawrence spoke to supporters inside the hall and one man shouted: 'Why let the women go at all?', to which she replied: 'We are here representing a principle which we have the right to defend as well as the men. If you prevent us going you do us the worst turn you can.' Julia Scurr spoke to the crowd outside and begged them to be peaceful. She told them to organise the borough for a 'No Rent' strike to be started

when the word was given. Minnie Lansbury brought grim news
from Brixton where she had that morning been allowed to pay a
last visit to both her husband and her father-in-law. She declared
that George Lansbury 'looked ghastly' and that Scurr and
O'Callaghan had already been transferred to the prison infirmary. The food was uneatable and the only reading matter was
the novels of Mrs Henry Wood, and that, she considered 'is
torture in itself'.[7] She had sent a telegram that morning to the
Home Secretary protesting against the 'disgraceful treatment of
the prisoners'. Minnie was chairman of the War Pensions Committee and for several days her home had been surrounded by
patrols of unemployed ex-servicemen who were very unwilling
to allow her arrest. Now she and her four female colleagues were
rewarded with the largest demonstration yet seen. After they
had delivered farewell messages from the balcony outside the
hall, they were presented with bouquets and then driven at
walking pace away down the East India Dock Road, escorted
by a procession of 10,000.

The only man arrested that day got little publicity. He was
J. J. Heales the bootmaker who had said to reporters: 'When
Mayfair does its bit the people of Poplar will be able to do
theirs.' Within twenty-four hours of his arrival in Brixton, he
too had to be removed to the prison infirmary.

On the next day, Tuesday 6 September, Councillor Albert
Farr, a postman, returned home from duty at five o'clock to
find the sheriff's officer having a cup of tea with Mrs Farr and
friends. He was arrested and driven in a car to pick up another
postman, T. J. Goodway, who had been for years secretary of
the local branch of the Postman's Federation (later the Union
of Postal Workers). Goodway had been sacked from the Post
Office for taking part in a strike in 1890 but reinstated in 1893.
Now a man in his fifties, he had been on the borough council
since 1912. His message to supporters was reminiscent of a
popular war song: 'We don't want to leave you but we think we
ought to go.' Now his home was surrounded by a crowd of 2,000.
'Stand firm.' he told them. 'No violence and we will win.'[8] The
car then drove to Walter Green's home; he said goodbye to his
three small children who kept on asking where their mother was.
Also taken away that day were the docker Charles Petherick
and Robert Hopwood, the engineering branch secretary.

By this time only one of the thirty, Charlie Sumner, still

remained at liberty. It was not that he had been trying to hide. On the Sunday after the arrests began he had addressed a public meeting. He had then gone to Cardiff where the Trades Union Congress was in session and where, on the Tuesday afternoon, there was a prolonged debate about unemployment, the Poplar councillors receiving praise for their stand. But Sumner had not agreed with the policy of making appointments with the Sheriff; it was against all his instincts and moreover he feared that once they were all in jail they would be tricked in some way. Now, however, he got in touch with the Sheriff because, as he put it, 'rather than see my colleagues imprisoned and myself outside I think in justice to them it is better I should surrender.'[9] The appointment was for 10.30 on Thursday 8 September at his home in Knapp Road. After delivering a farewell speech from his bedroom window to the assembled crowds below, Sumner was driven away to Brixton. The thirty arrests were complete.

Sumner's imprisoned colleagues had already discovered that the consideration and courtesy shown to them when being driven to gaol vanished with the clang of the prison-gate behind them. Indeed prison life was a great shock to most of them; their feelings were summed up in a statement issued on their behalf by Sam March on the day they were finally released:

> In spite of the so-called privileges granted us and taken by us, we are of opinion that prisons are hells. No one is bad enough to be treated as men and women are treated in these modern Bastilles, and no man or woman is good enough to be given such power over the life and liberty of their fellow creatures as is given to the governor or doctor and other prison officials.[10]

They were filled with pity for the other prisoners they encountered. 'There are young boys here who make your heart ache,' Partridge said to a visitor. He was deeply concerned about 'the little chance they'll have of leading a straight life after.'[11] For Nellie Cressall in Holloway, the worst thing was 'the dreadful screaming of the poor women in the padded cells'. 'Think of it, you mothers,' she said in a talk to some women after her release; 'Young girls taken from a life of freedom and locked up in cells with doors as thick as the doors of a pawnbroker's safe'.[12]

Despite the arguments of reformers that the aim of imprisonment should be the reform and rehabilitation of the prisoner, the system was still essentially punitive. For most of the time the prisoner would be locked in a dark, badly ventilated cell. Sanitary arrangements were based on the chamberpot and daily 'slopping out' routine, individual visits to the WC being severely limited. The diet was no longer expressly designed as an instrument of punishment (as it had been in the nineteenth century) but the quality of the food caused digestive difficulties to most prisoners, and at worst made them ill.

Even harder to bear than these physical discomforts was the mental and emotional cruelty exercised by those in charge. The methods included a rule of absolute silence, the absence or severe limitation of reading and writing materials, and the ceaseless watchfulness of warders whose prospects of promotion appeared to depend on their skill in detecting and reporting violations of the rules. As George Lansbury put it after his release: 'They are set to administer a system which would make a bully and a sneak out of a St Francis or a Tolstoy.'[13]

The councillors were put into what was called the 'second division'. Most ordinary prisoners went into the 'third division'; those in the second were permitted a few 'privileges' denied to those in the third, but their basic routine differed little and their physical conditions hardly at all. Very different was the treatment of 'first division' prisoners who could have books, newspapers, frequent visits and their own food sent in; they did not have to do prison work and could be allowed, if practicable, to follow their trade or profession.

Both Lansbury and his legal adviser, Thompson, had had previous experience of prison, the one for a speech in support of the suffragettes in 1913, the other as a conscientious objector during the war. Knowing better than some of the others what to expect, Lansbury had tried during the court hearing to find out whether they could be put in the first division. The judge had replied that he did not know. The fact was that people jailed for contempt before the war had gone into the first division, but in 1914 the law had been altered without attracting very much notice, so that henceforth those imprisoned for contempt were no longer entitled to first division privileges. The councillors' stay in Brixton was, however, characterised by a prolonged struggle by themselves and friends on their behalf against the harsh conditions imposed upon them.

At the outset the behaviour of the prison staff in Brixton seemed designed to degrade and insult them. Williams had arrived wearing his war medal ribbons; they were rudely stripped off. 'I felt that more than anything else,' he said later.[14] Money, pencils, pens and pipes were all taken from them; they could receive and send one letter a week, otherwise they were deprived of writing materials. They were forbidden to have newspapers; they could have two visitors a week who could be interviewed from behind a heavy wire grating for not more than fifteen minutes in the presence of a warder. They were locked into their cells from 7 p.m. until 6.40 a.m.

The worst thing was the food. Much of it they could not touch and when they did it made them ill. To begin with the bread was sour; towards the end of their stay in prison it became so stale that one councillor asked for a chopper to break it up. The food was brought to the cells in dirty pots and served in tin mugs and on tin plates. The porridge was made of undercooked oatmeal; the cocoa was a disgusting concoction variously described by the councillors as 'slimy' and 'bilious'; the tea appeared to have been cooked in the cocoa boiler, the meat dinner – so-called pork and beans – consisted of a single slice of fat put on a bean mash with dirt in it. It was alleged that the fish served up for dinner on the first Friday after the arrests began had gone bad. The councillors found that they were not the only prisoners who could not eat the food. After every meal large quantities of it were taken out of the cells and sold to pig merchants. Yet they knew that in Brixton with them was a group of Sinn Fein prisoners who were in the first division and could have their food sent in.

Before all the arrests had been completed the news about the treatment of the prisoners in Brixton and particularly about their diet was receiving much publicity. Minnie Lansbury had begun it by her statements to the press and her telegram to the Home Office after her own visit to George and Edgar. Though she was now herself in jail, the *Daily Herald* was following it up with a blow by blow account of the prisoners' sufferings. Since each prisoner was allowed two visits a week, it was not too hard to gather the information. The result was that their conditions became the subject of indignant resolutions and protests to the Government.

By this time government ministers were in a rather embarrassing position. They had received many deputations from Poplar before the councillors had taken their illegal action. Though they had made a show of sympathy with Poplar's impoverished condition and of concern about the level of unemployment on such occasions, subsequent events had invariably revealed their indifference. Much later they had been obliged to receive a deputation from the Poplar councillors' opponents, the London County Council, asking for the introduction of special legislation to enable them to collect the rate over the heads of the Poplar council. They had shrunk from any such proposal and no move had been made. In short, they had tried all along to behave as though the Poplar affair did not exist. Occasionally they had been forced to look in its direction, but had always looked away again as quickly as possible. They had played no part whatever in getting the councillors jailed; that had been done by the LCC, the MAB and the courts. Their only action, if it could be called such, was a discreet decision behind the scenes not to do anything to *prevent* the councillors going to jail, a decision to let matters take their course, not to interfere in any way but to hold aloof. Nevertheless everyone now seemed to be blaming them; the Government had become the chief target of protest and indignation concerning not only the prisoners' treatment, but the fact that they were imprisoned at all.

It was normal for Whitehall to express satisfaction with prison conditions whenever these were criticised, and on this occasion the reaction was according to habit. A Home Office statement was issued to the press:

> The Poplar councillors in Brixton have no cause to complain of their treatment. Their diet is that prescribed by medical authority and is adequate and wholesome. They are allowed to take exercise twice daily, and can associate together. A library of many thousands of books and magazines is at their disposal. Communication with friends is allowed within reasonable limits and they are not obliged to perform any duties beyond keeping themselves and their sleeping quarters tidy. Hospital treatment is available for those who need it, and their only hardship is their loss of liberty. Any suggestion that they are subject to harsh treatment or that they are underfed is an insult to the meanest intelligence.[15]

But the protests were not confined to those of 'mean intelligence'; they came also from people thought to be richly endowed with brains. Thus eight well-known writers petitioned for the prisoners' release, asked that until this took place they should have first division treatment and in particular begged for a

change of diet for George Lansbury in view of his reported illness.[16] Even some of the councillors' bitterest opponents now
rushed forward to complain of the way in which they were
treated. Thus Sir Alfred Warren MP, secretary of the Poplar
Municipal Alliance (he who had suggested that Poplar's action
would reduce local government to Bedlam) now felt obliged to
write personally to the Home Secretary, Edward Shortt, saying
that it was 'altogether unwarrantable' that the councillors
should be placed in the second division; they should have been
put in the first.[17] Meanwhile Councillor Kitcat, the churchman
who had voted against the action, went to Brixton to interview
Joe Banks, and then mobilised the help of other clergymen
in preparing a petition complaining of the treatment of the
prisoners and urging their release.

The protests about the prisoners' treatment went rumbling
angrily on long after their conditions had been appreciably
altered. Indeed some of the assertions in the original Home
Office statement which initially had no basis in fact became
true. Within a few days it was arranged that milk should be
served to prisoners in place of the undrinkable cocoa and tea. A
number of prisoners were put on 'medical diet' including
George Lansbury who had been permitted a visit from his own
doctor, and Albert Baker, who had thrown his food out of the
window and thereafter refused to eat. 'We had our first really
good dinner today,' Councillor Sloman told a visitor on 9
September. 'We are now allowed pencil and paper and to have
our own books sent in,' said Edgar Lansbury on the same day.
'But we are going on asking for newspapers, letters and other
rights of political prisoners.' And indeed on 16 September a
request to the Home Office that they should be allowed to have
newspapers was granted. Instead of being locked up alone in
their cells, they were allowed to associate freely with one
another for certain periods in the day and even to stay out of
doors. It was beautiful weather and after a fortnight the
prisoners were permitted to receive two footballs and some
football boots; these helped to pass the time. As happens when
people are closely confined, they began to discern qualities in
one another of which they had been previously unaware. A
prisoner who made everyone feel better was Councillor Partridge who combined a rock-like determination with unfailing
good humour and whatever happened managed to see the

funny side. 'He can always be relied upon in time of trouble to come up with a smiling face.' said a colleague.[18]

The warders were forced to mend their manners after a number of incidents, the first of which was recounted by Lansbury in his memoirs where he tells how, feeling ill in the night, he rang the bell for the warder who threatened him with personal violence. However, such a noise was made by the other prisoners that the chief warder came to the scene accompanied by the doctor and then the governor. The upshot was that the warder was disciplined. The warders found indeed that petty persecution was less easy when confronted with a group of prisoners acting in solidarity with one another. Moreover, so many important people – JPs, magistrates and such – were making it their business to inquire after the prisoners that it became necessary to avoid doing anything about which a complaint could be made. Thus the Mayor of Stepney, who went to visit the prisoners in Brixton and considered that his treatment by a warder had been derogatory to his dignity, complained to a visiting justice. The official who had insulted him was suspended.[19] The statement from the Home Office that the prisoners had no duties to perform was true, but that was because they had refused from the outset to do any work, and there was no real attempt to make them.

The practice of interviewing visitors behind wire-netting was discarded in favour of receiving visitors normally. As editor of the *Daily Herald*, George Lansbury was allowed a visit a day on business, and continued to write regular articles for the paper all through his imprisonment. At the same time the mayor, Sam March, had almost daily visits from his secretary and from the Town Clerk.

The most important breakthrough came on 11 September when permission was given to the Brixton prisoners to meet together as a group. Their first meeting was held under difficulties in George Lansbury's cell; it was decided that Joe Banks should keep minutes of all meetings in his capacity as Labour group secretary; a request that he be given a special table and chair in his cell for clerical purposes was granted. From then on they met nearly every night and from 17 September, as a result of petitioning the Home Secretary, they were allowed to gather in the boardroom of the prison which was put at their disposal once or twice a day. After it was all over, Joe Banks's minutes were printed and incorporated into the minutes of the Poplar Borough Council, to form a permanent record of an event unique in local government history.[20]

Sam March chaired all the thirty-two meetings. Many began with the reading of letters and resolutions of support from outside organisations. Items about their own treatment in prison came up often and were the subject of continuous interviews with the governor and petitions to the Home Office. Thus a minute recorded on 14 September reads: 'The Mayor reported interview with the Governor on question of baths twice a week for those desiring it. The Governor was arranging for the second bath on Fridays.' On the same day it was 'moved by Councillor C. E. Sumner, seconded, and *resolved* that the Mayor, Councillors G. Lansbury and J. H. Banks interview the Governor on the subject of the food, and replies to our Petitions to the Home Office'. The food had already begun to improve greatly; nevertheless an item on 27 September reads: 'A question was raised as to the quantity of butter supplied. Moved by Councillor H. Sloman and *Agreed* that all Members ask to see the Doctor in the morning with reference to the supply of butter. Councillor D. Adams raised the question of dinners being served up cold. Moved by Councillor D. Adams, seconded by Councillor E. I. Lansbury and *resolved* that complaint be made to the Doctor that dinners are cold when served; that he be urged to remedy this; and also to arrange for eggs to be served with the bacon.'

Another group of items concerned normal borough council business some of which continued to be transacted throughout the period of imprisonment. The maintenance of local work schemes for the unemployed was discussed on 20 September arising from a report received from the borough surveyor. An entry on this day reads: 'Estimates for various paving works sent by the Borough Surveyor were considered. Moved by Councillor W. Green, seconded by Councillor J. J. Heales and *resolved* that the Borough Surveyor be asked for an analysis of his estimate showing the amounts for labour and materials respectively.' And, a little lower down on the same day: 'Moved by Councillor C. E. Sumner, seconded by Councillor Russell and *resolved* that complaints of rats in Ellerthorpe Street be sent to the Medical Officer and Borough Surveyor with suggestions that trial holes be made to trace and exterminate the rats.'

Towards the end a growing proportion of meeting time was devoted to the problem of winning their release.

After they had been in Brixton for three weeks, George Cressall reminded them that Sunday 25 September was the day set aside by the Independent Labour Party to commemorate Keir Hardie. So they started the day by singing 'No Master' and 'The Red Flag' through the bars, and later, on parade, they sang 'England Arise' and Morris's 'March of the Workers'. That afternoon when they assembled in the prison boardroom, John Scurr gave a lecture on Keir Hardie's life and work. They continued to be cheered by the songs and demonstrations which took place almost nightly outside the prison. Various bands came to play and a high spot was the visit of a Welsh choir which 'came and sang as only the Porth choir can sing'.[21]

Meanwhile to those who were demanding the release of the prisoners, the Home Secretary, Edward Shortt, had made the somewhat plaintive reply that 'as he did not order their imprisonment, he cannot order their release'.[22] Elaborating on this in his answer to the writers' petition, Shortt said:

> The power to release prisoners rests upon the exercise by His Majesty of the prerogative of Mercy, and if the Poplar councillors had been convicted of criminal offences and were undergoing punishment for such offences, it would be open to me to recommend the remission or reduction of their sentences. This, however, is not the position. As you know they have been committed by the High Court for their refusal to comply with the Court's directions. In these circumstances the exercise of the prerogative of mercy has no application and I have no power to interfere with the Orders made by the Court for their detention.[23]

But once again events seemed to be proving that the people in charge were liars. For on the very day that the Home Secretary's statement appeared, one of the prisoners actually was released. This was Mrs Nellie Cressall who, at the age of thirty-eight was expecting her sixth child.

The women prisoners in Holloway had not had an easy time. Since there were only five of them, they did not have the advantage of numbers, and two had been put in the sick ward. The men in Brixton had been able to win concession after concession because of their numbers and were, in any case, buoyed up by the sense of solidarity which combined action can foster. But the women remained locked alone in their cells and suffered from a terrible isolation relieved only by the sounds of songs and cheers which came on most evenings from demonstrators outside. They also incurred much discomfort from the prison diet; when a friend visiting Julia Scurr on the day after her arrest inquired about it the wardress stopped the interview. In one respect their experience was different from that of the men in Brixton – the prison officers treated them with reasonable courtesy. Susan Lawrence said afterwards that for her the worst thing was not being allowed to smoke.

Nellie Cressall, however, had had a particularly gruelling experience. In view of her condition – the baby was expected at the end of October – she was immediately put into a cell in the hospital wing. But she was then, apparently, forgotten for twenty-four hours. When others were let out for exercise, she was ignored and remained locked up. She heard the persistent sound of screaming, and while she was there a woman in a nearby cell committed suicide. She found she could not touch the food delivered to her cell and subsisted only on dry bread. The first three nights seemed endless. She was eventually roused from a condition of dazed apathy by the sound of her name being called. It was Minnie Lansbury, who had also been transferred to the hospital wing, and had since been trying to make contact with Nellie. Soon after, Minnie complained to the authorities about the way Nellie was treated and Nellie was then brought some hot milk which she managed to drink. She lived on hot milk for many days after this.

Unknown to Nellie, a tremendous fuss was being made on her behalf outside prison. For even those determined to force Poplar to its knees could see that by imprisoning a woman in late pregnancy, an idiotic blunder had been committed. Following the custom of the time the newspapers had been reticent about Nellie's condition. Nevertheless it was something that everyone knew about, and protests and petitions, including that organised by the clergy, made special mention of her. Since a number of Poplar councillors had been left at liberty, it seemed incomprehensible that Nellie should not have been among them.

Once it dawned on the Home Office that her presence in Holloway was a growing embarrassment, the services of the Official Solicitor were invoked to apply to the court for an order for her release on health grounds. The order was granted and on 21 September, sixteen days after she had arrived at Holloway,

Nellie was informed by the prison authorities that she was to go home.

But then came a hitch. Nellie refused to go until her fellow prisoners were liberated also. Moreover, when she found that she was expected to sign a document, she was afraid she was being tricked into letting down her colleagues. It was only with much difficulty and after the intervention of Harry Gosling, the leader of the Labour group on the London County Council, that she was made to understand that she had no choice but to leave; she was at last driven home accompanied by a nurse.

'I made it quite clear to the Governor that I would not come out if any conditions were to be imposed,' she told a reporter on arriving home. 'I carefully read over the paper I had to sign before receiving my property to make sure I was not signing anything to which I could not agree. The Governor read out the order for my release and said it had come from the highest authority and that he could not keep me there for so long as another meal. He said: 'I have no option but to open the prison-gates and put you into a taxi outside.' I replied: 'You mean, it's like an eviction?' and he said 'Yes.' I was not allowed to go back and say goodbye to my comrades, but the matron, the governor and the wardresses and even the warder at the front gate all came to say goodbye to me and to wish me luck. All I can think about now is getting the others out.'[24] When the men in Brixton heard of her stand they sent her a letter of congratulations. The new baby was born about six weeks later on 31 October.

Although the order for Nellie's release was endorsed by the Home Office, the latter denied any knowledge of how it had come about, a fact made much of by the *Daily Herald* which, on 23 September, published a short description of the functions of the Official Solicitor of whom most people had never heard before,[25] and introduced the subject with the words: 'In view of the statement of the Home Secretary that he had no power to release prisoners for contempt of court, public interest has been aroused as to how it was possible for Mrs Cressall to be virtually "ejected" from Holloway.'

Even before Nellie's release another of the women prisoners had been let out for a few hours on parole. This was Mrs Jennie Mackay who had received news that her father, who was over eighty, was in hospital and not expected to live. She was allowed out of Holloway to visit him; her imprisonment had been kept from him and he could not understand why a strange woman (the wardress) came with her to sit in the room while she was with him. When he died a few weeks later, Jennie was allowed out for the funeral, again on parole. Before returning to prison she went on to attend a town hall meeting which had been called to demand the release of the thirty and was given a tremendous reception. Jennie, who was nearly fifty, had a reputation as a courageous woman. She had been involved with the SDF in early days, was the first woman in the area to join what later became the National Union of General and Municipal Workers, and with Sylvia Pankhurst had been arrested for suffragette activities before the war. But now, circumstances combined to unnerve her; called on to speak she mentioned her father's death and broke down in tears. Sympathetic applause went on for some minutes. She had been prohibited from talking about her experiences in prison, but other speakers made good the deficiency. Councillor Jack Wooster asserted that the Dogs' Home in Battersea was a mansion compared with that 'hell-hole of Holloway'.[26]

All this time, Poplar's critics among the top trade union leaders had kept quiet. Though many of them felt as Morrison did about Poplar's action, they refrained from making their ideas public even when the matter came up at the annual gathering of the Trades Union Congress. This began on 5 September, after the first groups of councillors had already been jailed. Earlier the councillors had arranged to send 1,000 copies of a letter, which had been circulated to Poplar's ratepayers explaining the council's action, to the secretary of the TUC for the information of the delegates. They had also arranged that two of those councillors left at liberty, Wooster and Blacketer, should do what they could to see that Poplar's point of view was understood at the TUC. Both Susan Lawrence and Charlie Sumner had been able to spend some days there as well.

The upshot was that a composite resolution calling for work schemes for the unemployed included the following:

> The Congress also is of opinion that the Poplar Councillors in the stand which they believed to be the best to take under exceptional circumstances to call public attention to the distressful conditions of the unemployed, have rendered a real national service.[27]

The resolution was carried unanimously. In the debate there was nothing but praise for the Poplar councillors, while several speakers, some of whom claimed to be 'constitutionalists' went out of their way to argue that in this instance unconstitutional action was justified. Thus Harry Gosling, who was secretary of the Watermen's Society and soon to become president of the Transport and General Workers Union, admitted that his words were 'entirely against my own creed', but added:

> I believe you cannot get anything done until you rebel, otherwise they do not believe you are in earnest . . . in other words, if you want to amend the law it almost seems as if you must break it.

His words had an added significance insofar as he was leader of the small group of Labour councillors on the London County Council, the very body which had put the councillors in jail.

The president of the TUC, E. L. Poulton of the Boot and Shoe Union, also supported the Poplar councillors saying:

> It is a remarkable thing that Governments and the powers-that-be . . . attempt, and successfully attempt at times, to take advantage of us trying to act in a constitutional manner, and until something is done outside the ordinary methods, ignore the resolutions and the position that we have taken up.

He added that their Poplar friends had exhausted all legal means at their disposal and 'not having been listened to by the Government, felt they were bound to take the action they have'.

Jack Jones, MP for West Ham, said the same:

> We have exhausted the possibilities of constitutionalism. We have done everything the law says we ought to do. We have elected representatives who have carried out the law. Where do we find ourselves? The law leaves us in the lurch and tells us that the poor must keep the poor.

In the week following the TUC, J. R. Clynes, a prominent member of the General Council and also leader of the Parliamentary Labour Party, visited the councillors in jail bringing with him a resolution of support from his union, the National Union of General Workers, and a donation of £25 to the maintenance fund for the councillors' dependents.

However, it is one thing to pass resolutions in support of those taking action; it is quite another to join in the action. The

Poplar councillors had always hoped for solidarity actions by other London boroughs, realising that this might prove decisive. There were eleven Labour controlled boroughs and right from the start, Sumner had declared that if they would take the same course as Poplar the authorities would 'soon be brought to their senses'.[28] However, such solidarity action was not at all easy to achieve because even where a majority in a given Labour group were in favour of following Poplar's lead and refusing to levy rates, any minority against would be supported by councillors from the opposition parties. Moreover, many Labour councillors who admired Poplar's action had doubts about whether it would have a happy ending. Others may have been in wholehearted support in theory, but in practice shrank from the personal sacrifice involved in getting themselves sent to prison.

In Hackney, where Morrison was mayor, a motion to follow Poplar and refuse to levy the rate was, not surprisingly, heavily defeated. The nine Labour councillors who supported Poplar's example were outvoted by about twenty others who joined with their Conservative and Liberal opponents to reject the proposal by forty-five votes to nine. In Shoreditch, on the other hand, a motion to withhold the LCC and MAB rate until the Poplar councillors were released was defeated by only one vote.[29] In Battersea the same thing happened; a resolution instructing the finance committee to omit the precepts of the LCC, the MAB, Water Board and the Police was defeated by twenty-six votes to twenty-five.[30]

However, what is remarkable is not that most councils refused to follow Poplar's lead, but that two did so. They were Poplar's closest neighbours in London's East End: Bethnal Green and Stepney.

The decision at Bethnal Green was taken on 22 September following a recommendation of the finance committee that the council should decline to include the precepts for the four central London bodies in the rate for the coming half year. The mover of the recommendation read a letter from Bethnal Green's mayor, J. J. Vaughan, stating that he supported the recommendation; he was unable to be present at this historic meeting since he had gone to Scotland with the other Labour mayors to try and interview Lloyd George. The recommendation was carried by sixteen votes to ten, a result which was received with great cheering from the public gallery and from a crowd outside. Thereafter, a group of councillors from Bethnal Green were in constant consultation with the prisoners in Brixton and it was jointly agreed that neither council would recognise any negotiations unless conducted by a special joint committee of the two councils.

Moves by the Stepney Borough Council began with a unanimous reolution on 13 September demanding the release of the prisoners and warning the Home Secretary that if this were not done the council would 'give instructions that the rate for the period to 31 March next shall not be collected'. At the same time the Stepney Trades and Labour Council had called a special conference in central London to protest against the circular from the London Labour Party Executive advising Labour bodies not to take action similar to that of Poplar. Twenty-seven London Labour parties were represented at this meeting which was held on 24 September and the resolution of protest was carried unanimously; so also was another urging that all metropolitan borough councils should follow Poplar's example and refuse to levy rates on behalf of the central London bodies. The meeting was presided over by Clement Attlee, then a Stepney alderman. Unlike Vaughan, the Bethnal Green mayor (who was well-known as a Communist) Attlee was not normally regarded as a left-winger. But he did not share Morrison's view of the Poplar action. 'I have always been a constitutionalist,' he told the meeting, 'but the time has come when it is necessary to kick.'[31]

It was Attlee who moved the crucial resolution at the next meeting of the Stepney Borough Council. For the Stepney councillors, having received an unfavourable response to their resolution to the Home Secretary, decided to implement their threat to withhold the rates. So at a specially convened meeting on 5 October a resolution was tabled instructing the finance committee to disregard the precepts of the central London authorities in making the rate for the ensuing half year. In moving the resolution Attlee said that it was unfair that the poor people in Stepney should be asked to keep those even poorer than themselves, and absurd that local authorities should be asked to shoulder the cost of unemployment which was brought about by world wide conditions. The resolution was carried by twenty-nine votes to twenty-one.

NOTES

1. In later life the Cressalls liked to recall that one day a young man had come to their house to see about joining the ILP. He was Clement Attlee, the future Prime Minister.
2. This and farewell messages from other councillors were all printed in the *Daily Herald*, 1 September 1921, except where otherwise indicated.
3. DH, 3 September 1921.
4. ibid.
5. EEN, 6 September 1921.
6. *The Times*, 5 September 1921.
7. *The Times*, 6 September 1921.
8. DH, 7 September 1921.
9. ibid., 9 September 1921.
10. ibid., 13 October 1921.
11. ibid., 16 September 1921.
12. ibid., 30 September 1921.
13. ibid., 14 October 1921.
14. ibid., 5 September 1921.
15. ELA, 10 September 1921.
16. The writers were Robert Donald, A. G. Gardiner, Philip Gibbs, J. L. Hammond, J. A. Hobson, John Masefield, Henry W. Nevison, H. G. Wells.
17. ELA, 17 September 1921.
18. DH, 9 September 1921.
19. ELA, 17 September 1921.
20. The Record of Proceedings in Brixton Prison is to be found under the date 27 October 1921, Poplar Borough Council minutes.
21. DH, 17 September 1921.
22. EEN, 16 September 1921.
23. *The Times*, 21 September 1921.
24. DH, 22 September 1921.
25. Most people had never heard of him fifty years later either, when he suddenly appeared in 1972 and arranged the release of some dockers jailed for contempt in connection with the 1971 Industrial Relations Act.
26. DH, 10 October 1921.
27. Trades Union Congress report of the Fifty-third Annual Gathering. See for this and subsequent extracts from the debate 6 September 1921.
28. ELA, 26 March 1921.
29. *The Times*, 14 September 1921; ELA, 24 September 1921.
30. *South Western Star*, 30 September 1921.
31. DH, 26 September 1921.

6

Release

The councillors had known from the start that there would be great pressure on them to compromise. Since they had shown themselves undeterred by the prospect of prison, and obdurate once inside, they knew that the pressure would begin to take a subtler form. Negotiations would be suggested in which they would be urged to participate; if they did so a few concessions might be offered relative to Poplar's financial future, in return for which they would be expected to agree to levy the rate and so 'purge their contempt' and secure their release.

The councillors were determined to guard against such a development. For one thing, their solidarity which was based on collective decisions and mutual trust, might well be undermined if some among them were to be let out to negotiate while others remained in prison. But in any case their trump card was to make clear that so long as they were in prison there was no chance of the London County Council collecting its money. If, as they believed possible, the Government brought in a law to levy the rate over their heads, they had contingency plans prepared for a rent strike which, since landlords collected rent and rates together, would mean that the LCC would still fail to get its money. Above all, they saw themselves as the vanguard of a movement which was gathering strength outside Poplar. Any sign of hesitation or compromise would discourage this movement.

So it was that 'Release first, negotiations afterwards' was their demand and, as it turned out, it won the day in the end. In maintaining this approach they exasperated their critics within the labour movement and indeed caused certain misgivings among their friends, some of whom were by no means certain that the stand taken was a wise one.

All this was the background to a decision on 12 September[1] at only their second meeting in Brixton when it was reported that the parliamentary committee of the TUC was to visit them.[2] After discussion it was agreed that if the parliamentary committee asked what their terms were, they would be told that these could not be discussed until they were all released.

It was also the background to a decision on 14 September that if Sam March were let out on parole to participate in a planned deputation of Labour mayors to the Government he 'be instructed not to discuss Poplar with the Prime Minister or any other person'. This was not a sign that they distrusted Sam March, who indeed was presiding over the meeting when the decision was taken and who, together with Lansbury and Banks, regularly interviewed the Governor on the prisoners' behalf. But they believed that if Sam March maintained that Poplar could not be discussed until he and his colleagues were once more at liberty, this would strengthen their hand and hasten their release.

They took this line with Harry Gosling, the first visitor to attend one of their meetings. Gosling was an East London man himself, a member of the parliamentary committee of the TUC, as well as chairman of the Labour group on the LCC. Early on, Susan Lawrence had written from Holloway to her colleagues in Brixton suggesting that Gosling be invited to visit the prisoners in Brixton for a discussion. The Brixton prisoners agreed to this suggestion, but then there was a hitch because the prison Governor told Gosling that the regulations would only allow him to see the prisoners one by one.[3] However, Sir Alfred Mond, the Minister of Health was by this time anxious that the meeting should take place and he intervened with the Governor. Following this the regulation was suspended and, on the morning of 20 September, Gosling attended a special meeting of the group in the boardroom.

At this meeting he began by telling them that the Labour group on the LCC (numbering seventeen, of whom three were in prison) was holding a party meeting that evening. He wondered whether they should try to convene a special LCC meeting (which required twenty signatories) to consider the whole question of Poplar and the imprisoned councillors. He asked for suggestions and congratulated the councillors on their stand.

The first to speak was Albert Baker who said 'the councillors had made up their minds that there could be no discussion on the question of compromise whilst they were in prison. Nothing would be discussed until they were together outside.' He was supported by Sloman. Gosling said in reply that he had not come to ask them to compromise which, he agreed, could not be

entertained. George Lansbury then emphasised that the important point was to see what could be done to get them out. They
were at a deadlock, he said. They were in prison and the LCC
was not getting their money. The only thing to do was to
emphasise the futility of the LCC's position. After Williams,
Edgar Lansbury, Ben Fleming and O'Callaghan had all spoken
in support of this stand, Gosling said they could rely on him and
his colleagues to do everything possible to secure their release.

In taking this stand the councillors rapidly found that their
most formidable opponent was Herbert Morrison. All along
they had been obliged to answer his political objections to their
action, but they now had to ward off his attempts to involve
them in negotiations, to act as 'mediator' between them and the
Government and indeed to take the conduct of their campaign
out of their hands.

After the councillors had gone to jail, Morrison had continued to be muzzled by the agreement of the London Labour
Executive on 4 August that there should be no public criticism
of them. Yet they were getting enormous publicity. The *Daily
Herald* was listing organisations that had passed resolutions in
support of the Poplar action. Simultaneously, marches by the
unemployed demanding 'work or maintenance', deputations to
boards of guardians, and clashes with the police were reported
from many areas. Despite the circular which had gone out from
the London Labour Party advising other Labour controlled
councils not to follow Poplar's lead, moves were on foot to get
them to do precisely that. It seemed as though Labour's
responsible image had been submerged in a sea of direct action.

In what looked like an attempt to rescue it, Morrison led a
much publicised deputation of Labour mayors to Scotland to
see the Prime Minister. The move had been preceded by a letter
from Morrison to the Government urging that either Parliament should be recalled to deal with the unemployment
situation or that the Government should provide the necessary
finance for the local poor law authorities to do so. Receiving no
satisfactory response, Morrison announced that a deputation
was to be assembled. The London Labour mayors took the
train to Inverness from where, after a journey through the
Highlands, they eventually tracked down Lloyd George who
was resting in Gairloch, and interviewed him on 22 September.
On hearing of their arrival Charles Key, left in charge as

Poplar's deputy mayor, sent a telegram to Alderman Gentry, the Mayor of Fulham and secretary of the Labour mayors' group, urging that he demand the release of the thirty councillors.

Gentry, like Morrison, was anxious that the mayors' deputation should be in no way identified with the Poplar affair. This had been underlined by an episode just before they left London. J. B. Skeggs, the Town Clerk of Poplar, hearing that the deputation was being formed, had consulted the Town Clerk of Bethnal Green for details and had then telephoned Gentry with the suggestion that permission of the Home Office should be sought for Poplar's mayor, Sam March, now in Brixton, to accompany his fellow mayors. Gentry, however, declined to approach the Home Office. He suggested instead that Skeggs himself should do so. This Skeggs did and permission was of course refused.

The situation was a challenge to Morrison. He had to do something to deflect the glare of publicity away from Poplar. He had to prove that orthodox and constitutional methods of political campaigning could succeed where 'direct action' had failed. He had to prove himself in the eyes of Labour's rank and file. It was therefore crucial for him that his deputation should win some concessions and that some sort of financial relief for the poorer London boroughs be obtained either from the Government or the richer boroughs. At the same time he hoped that the Poplar situation could be disposed of quickly and quietly. He believed this could be achieved as a by-product of the adjustment of London's municipal finances for which he aimed.

So the issue of Poplar only came up at the very end of the interview with Lloyd George after most of Morrison's suggestions for handling unemployment had been rejected or side-tracked. Thus, Morrison stressed the need for big work schemes, such as the construction of arterial roads on which thousands of men could be employed, but Lloyd George was very vague about such possibilities. When Morrison pointed out that as a result of unemployment the financial burden on the poorer boroughs was becoming intolerable, yet well-to-do boroughs escaped, Lloyd George said that any further equalisation of the rates would only arouse the fierce opposition of the majority of London boroughs.

Morrison did not hesitate to express his fears at the direction
in which the movement among the unemployed was heading.
He said:

> There is a bitter feeling and a sheer lack of faith in the whole of
> the institutions of the State which is growing among those bands
> of hungry desperate men. As time goes on the leadership of
> unemployed organisations will tend to be rather distinct from the
> organised Labour movement and the leadership may get into
> hands which cannot be looked upon with ease having regard to
> the possibilities of the situation.
> THE PRIME MINISTER: You mean into irresponsible hands?
> MORRISON: Yes, Sir. I say there is a distinct tendency in that
> direction which is dangerous to National Government and to
> Local Government, and to talk violence in such circumstances is
> exceedingly popular, while to talk law and order is a subject of
> laughter. [4]

But he got no promises at all from Lloyd George; indeed, as
far as anyone could tell the mayors would go back empty-
handed. Finally, almost as an afterthought, Morrison broached
the subject of Poplar and in doing so revealed a certain discomfort at being made to appear the champion of a movement
of which he so greatly disapproved:

> May I Sir, before we separate, raise the question of the situation
> in the borough of Poplar. I express no opinion with regard to it.
> At any rate it is a situation which has arisen in consequence of the
> grave poverty in that Borough, and the result is that the coun-
> cillors for contempt of Court, are in prison now.
>   I am wondering whether anything can be done by which some
> negotiations should take place for the settlement of the problem
> which is very bad for local government and for the control of
> London services and we want to raise the question whether it is
> not possible for some discussion to be raised for the purpose of
> securing that this deadlock shall be ended. [5]

To which Lloyd George replied: 'I have no objection to your
having a discussion with Sir Alfred Mond on the subject.'

Sir Alfred Mond, the Minister of Health, was head of the
firm of Brunner Mond and soon to be chairman of Imperial
Chemical Industries; as such he was one of the country's most
powerful industrialists. He was also one who preferred negotiation to confrontation. Elected to Parliament before the war as a
Liberal, he was now one of the minority of Liberals in the Lloyd

George Cabinet and had succeeded to the post of Minister of Health a few days after the Poplar councillors had launched their action on the rates. He was at Gairloch with the rest of the Cabinet and Morrison and his colleagues interviewed him immediately after seeing Lloyd George. At this interview Morrison suggested that the continued imprisonment of the councillors could be avoided by some amicable settlement. So he proposed that the minister should call a conference of London local government bodies and that representatives from Poplar should be invited to participate. He offered his own services in this connection, though he said that this offer was subject to consultation with the Poplar councillors.

Mond fell in with the suggestion and said he would call a conference the following week, provided the Poplar councillors would agree to participate. But at the same time he made clear that he was determined to resist Poplar's demands. He said he had decided to bring in an Act enabling the LCC to levy the rates direct if Poplar continued to refuse to do so and, moreover, that the equalisation of rates could not be considered until after the Report of the Royal Commission on Greater London whose labours had not even begun. He emphasized that he had no power to release the prisoners; 'They can only be released by a judge of the High Court when they obey the order of the Court'.[6]

On the evening of 23 September, Charles Key visited the group meeting in Brixton for the first time. It was quite an occasion. With him came four other councillors who had been left at liberty (Blacketer, Wooster, C. J. Kelly and Rawlings) and the newly released Nellie Cressall. Key reported on Mond's inflexible attitude. The response of the meeting was to compose a message to their supporters which in somewhat exalted language conveyed their unyielding attitude: 'Comrades, stand fast! We will stand out to the bitter end. We believe we are fighting the fight of the poor and heavy-laden not only in East London and Poplar but throughout the world.'[7]

Key also told them that Morrison had proposed to Mond that they should participate in a conference. Their reaction was predictable. They immediately reaffirmed 'their determination not to enter into any negotiation or discussion as to future action until Poplar Borough Council was able to meet as a corporate body as free men and women in their own council chamber.'

Their distrust of Morrison's endeavours was referred to obliquely in the *Daily Herald*:

> The men and women in prison have learned who their friends are. They understand quite well the underhand intrigues which have been carried on against them, and they are not willing to hand over their future to any but friends who are trusted, tried and true.[8]

Mond, however, was anxious to follow up Morrison's suggestion. Accordingly, J. B. Skeggs, Poplar's Town Clerk, was invited to the ministry where he was asked to convey to the prisoners a proposal that they appoint a deputation to attend a conference. This the Town Clerk did, suggesting that Susan Lawrence, John Scurr, George Lansbury and Sam March should form the deputation. It was also reported that Herbert Morrison had inferred at Gairloch that he had been asked to act as intermediary on their behalf. On hearing this, the prisoners sent a telegram to the Prime Minister: 'We are prepared to enter into a conference of all parties concerned outside prison as free men and women. No one has had or has authority to suggest any other course.' They thus made clear that Morrison's proposals had been made without their agreement. And Lansbury in a special article devoted space to explaining their refusal to negotiate:

> The Poplar councillors and Aldermen have served over three weeks in prison, during which time the Government, the LCC and the MAB have preserved a discreet silence. . . . Now we are informed a conference is to be held, and the Mayor of Hackney has offered his services as an intermediary between Poplar Council and the Government and other authorities. Now, it needs first of all to be put on record that until this moment Sir A. Mond and his friends on the LCC have treated Poplar councillors with studied insolence and contempt. Up till last week no word of a conference or consultation, either before we came to prison or since our incarceration, has been forthcoming.
> The Poplar Council has always been willing to meet and discuss . . . Consequently no neutral person, no good offices are needed to ensure the attendance of the Poplar councillors at a conference such as is suggested by the government. . . . All that is needed is freedom for the Councillors and Aldermen to attend. . . . It is also necessary to remind friends and enemies that Poplar is governed by democrats, and that as such we do not intend handing our future over either to a few selected delegates or friends.[9]

Morrison felt obliged to defend himself against the implication of this article. He wrote to the *Daily Herald* saying that he had asked the Prime Minister for a conference in his capacity as spokesman for the Labour mayors; he had made the request on their behalf, and it would be wrong to give the impression that his action had been personal rather than representative.[10] But by this time, conscious that their actions had not been well received, the Labour mayors decided it was time for a visit to Brixton for a meeting with the imprisoned councillors.

This meeting with eleven London Labour mayors took place on 27 September. It was notable for the fact that for the first time the four women prisoners, Susan Lawrence, Julia Scurr, Jenny Mackay and Minnie Lansbury, were brought from Holloway to attend it. Evidently the authorities did not want the absence of the women to be used as a pretext for refusing to participate in the conference. 'We were more glad than any of us could express to see our women comrades,' wrote Lansbury next day. But he could not resist pointing out that it demonstrated once more 'what liars Governments and their officials can be,' since John Scurr and Edgar Lansbury had been told by the Home Office that there was no power whatever which could allow them to visit their wives in Holloway; 'Yet on Tuesday the women came here. We are all asking what authority brought them here.'[11]

Sam March, who presided over the meeting with the London mayors, began by inviting them to state their case. Their spokesmen then gave somewhat contradictory explanations of their actions. Councillor Girling, Mayor of Shoreditch, said that before going to Gairloch it had been decided to raise the question of Poplar with Mond who had promised a conference of representatives from the LCC, the MAB, the London mayors and Poplar Borough Council. Alderman Gentry, Mayor of Fulham and secretary of the group, said they had acted as they did on receiving Key's telegram urging them to demand the prisoners' release. He also stated that the Government was considering a Bill giving power to the LCC to collect rates from defaulting councils.

In reply to this Sam March from the chair explained that they were not prepared to enter discussions until they were released unconditionally. Any idea that the women who had been isolated in Holloway might have a different attitude was quickly dispelled as Susan Lawrence backed him up, saying that before they were sent to prison she had repeatedly urged the LCC to arrange a conference with Poplar, but nothing had been done. Things being as they were, their only possible position was to insist on release, after which they would be fully prepared to join in a conference.

When the Mayor of Woolwich expressed his disagreement with this George Lansbury counter-attacked. He said that the proposal that they should appoint delegates to attend the conference and then return to prison was 'outrageous'. 'Their deliberate conclusion was that they would not attend or be represented at any conference unless they were outside the prison as free men and women.'

It appeared that Herbert Morrison (who was present in his capacity as Mayor of Hackney) had difficulty in accepting this statement as final. And, indeed, it meant that everything for which he had planned was being blocked. He once more put the question, asking the Poplar councillors point blank whether they would consider the appointment of delegates to attend Mond's conference and then return to prison. He was told definitely that they would not.

After this the mayors retired to another room while the Poplar councillors discussed what to do next. They decided to press the mayors to urge the LCC to make application to the High Court for their release and to confer with their lawyer, W. H. Thompson, over the possible legal steps. And they drew up a statement explaining their attitude:

> We are specially anxious to make it clear that our demand for unconditional release is not made in order to render a settlement more difficult to attain. We are willing to confer as we always have been, although other authorities have ignored us, on solutions of the rating problems, both temporary and permanent, but as some members of our council are in Holloway prison, some in Brixton prison, and some free, we are not in a position to choose representatives to a conference, to consult with our permanent officials, neither have we access to official documents. For this reason (and because we are not criminals and appear to be imprisoned because of the unreasonableness of our opponents) we can only enter into a conference when we are all free.[12]

When the Labour mayors returned they were handed a copy of this statement, after which they withdrew to Lambeth Town

Hall where they held a prolonged discussion on their next moves. In the end they drew up a statement addressed to Mond urging the release of the prisoners and suggesting that it was likely that the matter could be settled by means of a conference, but explaining that the Poplar councillors would not participate unless freed. They also visited the Clerk to the London County Council and delivered a letter on the need for the prisoners' release.

Shortly after this came the first sign that the Government was preparing the way for some concessions. Mond's secretary approached Gentry and asked him for a scheme for the equalisation of London's rates, hinting at a temporary Bill to cover the critical winter months. Since until then Mond had insisted that equalisation of rates must be first considered by the forthcoming Royal Commission, this revealed an important shift in attitude. It looked as though Poplar's stand might after all produce the desired result. Gentry instantly consulted some of the other mayors and they agreed to hold a meeting the following day, 30 September, to draw up a scheme to submit to Mond.

However, once again Poplar was to frustrate the attempts of the London mayors to open negotiations. For when Gentry went to Brixton to report on the new development to Lansbury, Scurr and Banks, he was met for a second time with indignant protests. He was told by Lansbury that to draw up a scheme for rates equalisation without the participation of Poplar or Bethnal Green would not be accepted.[13]

In the end the mayors found themselves obliged to accede to Poplar's demands. At their meeting on 30 September they decided to send a message to Mond saying that although anxious to give him their view on the equalisation of rates there were 'grave difficulties' in the way owing to the absence of Poplar representatives at their deliberations.

Sir Alfred Mond, despite his emphatic public statements, was by this time convinced that something must be done to bring financial relief to the poorer London Boroughs. At the same time he wanted the Poplar business settled. Vaughan, Mayor of Bethnal Green, who was present at an interview with him after Poplar had turned down the suggestion for a conference, reported that he was 'in a frame of mind in which he wished the whole business over. He looked extremely fed up.'[14]

Mond's situation was not indeed a very happy one. Among

Conservative MPs there was a growing impatience with the Coalition Government which, with Lloyd George at its head, had now been in office three years. As one of the few Coalition Liberals in the Cabinet, Mond was vulnerable to attack. For months past both Conservative and Liberal MPs had been demanding that he take the Poplar affair in hand and, in particular, that he bring in a law to enable some central body to step in and collect the rates over the heads of the Poplar council. He had at last publicly committed himself to do this. But he was aware that getting such a Bill through Parliament might be a time consuming business and that, once through, it might lead to new and worse troubles. It is one thing to have power on paper, it is another to exercise it. The Home Office already had power to collect the police rate, but had shrunk from using it on grounds that it would be 'unwise' and that 'resistance was not unlikely' (see above, p. 58).

But if resistance had been likely before the councillors went to prison, what would it be now? The councillors had issued a call to all tenants to declare a rent strike should any outside body attempt to collect the rates. A rent strike would automatically involve withholding rates as well as rent. It was reported that thousands of people had already enrolled in a Tenants' Defence League set up to organise this strike, with active committees in every ward. Innumerable window cards had appeared in the borough with the words: 'We support our Borough Councillors.' The prospect of trying to collect rates in such circumstances was not inviting.

Moreover, another difficulty had arisen. Mond's original idea was that power to levy rates in default should be vested in the London County Council. It was after all their rates that needed to be collected; it was they who had taken legal action. But it turned out that the LCC strongly objected to the proposal that they should be responsible for collecting the rate and was insisting that the responsibility should be taken by the Minister of Health. Mond, not unnaturally, did not relish such a prospect. And now on top of everything else, Bethnal Green had decided to follow Poplar's lead and Stepney looked like doing the same.

Mond had therefore become convinced that the most sensible thing to do was to make some concession to Poplar which would induce it to call off its action. If this happened default powers need not be used. He had hopes that such a settlement would result from the activities of Morrison and the Labour mayors after the Gairloch meeting. But when it became clear that Morrison had failed, Mond once more got in touch with Gosling to see what could be done. He explained his action in a special memo submitted to the Cabinet later on 7 October:

> The London mayors having failed to arrive at any settlement after their return from Gairloch, Mr Harry Gosling was requested by the Minister of Health to see whether any action was possible, tending towards the release of the Poplar councillors, as part of a temporary settlement of the difficulties which have arisen . . . Such a settlement is extremely desirable in view of the fact that the Councils of other poor boroughs are threatening to follow the example of Poplar and in one case have determined to do so.[15]

It seemed that the councillors' release was now an urgent matter for all concerned. Indeed, their continued imprisonment had become not only a political embarrassment, but a positive hindrance to the solution of the very problem which had inspired their action. However, obtaining their release was easier said than done. Weeks had been spent getting them into jail; it now looked as though weeks might equally be spent getting them out again.

The councillors had long been aware that, legally speaking, the problem was not a simple one. As early as 17 September they had decided at a group meeting 'that the question of who is responsible for our being here and who is responsible for releasing us be referred to Mr Thompson, Solicitor, on Tuesday'. The legal system is not, after all, designed to react instantly to matters of political expediency. At times of political urgency it can display a certain rigidity and even governments have to tread carefully if these rigidities are to be overcome. Judging by the resolutions pouring in to demand that the councillors be freed, there was a widespread conviction that the Home Secretary could release them with the stroke of a pen. And though the Home Secretary had denied this and had explained that the prerogative of a free pardon could not be used to let out people imprisoned for contempt in a civil action, the intervention of the Official Solicitor in the case of Nellie Cressall had reinforced the belief that the Government could get them out if it chose. But the fact was that even if the use of the Official Solicitor to liberate all thirty had been technically feasible it would have been politically impossible. Governments are always reluctant to let it be thought that they are overriding the decisions of the courts.

The Times at this juncture appeared bent on making things difficult. It published a legal note explaining that it was quite impossible for the Government to intervene, since the prisoners had been committed on grounds of contempt of court and in particular for failing to obey an order of the court. In such cases only the High Court itself could release the prisoners, and this could be done only upon the application of the persons imprisoned who must provide evidence that they had 'purged their contempt' by agreeing to obey the order of the court. Therefore 'it would appear that no action is possible either by the Government or any Minister to bring about the solution of the difficulties in Poplar until the imprisoned people themselves take the necessary steps'. Under the circumstances, observed *The Times* correspondent, 'it would appear useless to expect an early issue out of the impasse.'[16]

And, indeed, if their release depended solely on their agreement to levy the rate it seemed that the affair would go on for months and months. However, a few days later there appeared a letter from another legal expert which in effect explained that the obstacles to setting them free were not quite as formidable as had been suggested. 'The parties in contempt can offer an apology to the Court and apply for their discharge and if the plaintiffs [i.e. the LCC and MAB] state that they no longer desire to enforce their rights the Court will, no doubt, grant the discharge.'[17]

This, of course, was the plan followed by W. H. Thompson, their solicitor, who had been in close consultation with Harry Gosling and with C. J. Mathew, another member of the Labour group on the LCC, who was also a KC.

Even so the process leading up to release was not carried through without difficulty. In the first place it was necessary to persuade the plaintiffs – the Metropolitan Asylums Board and the London County Council – to tell the court that they no longer desired the continued imprisonment of the councillors. To get the former to cooperate turned out to be easy, but the latter, it soon transpired was determined to be awkward. The reasons for the difference were connected with their composition. The LCC was a politically motivated body; the MAB much less so. The majority of the MAB's members – fifty-five out of seventy-three – were appointed by various London boards of guardians. In practice they included people who were genuinely 'independent' in politics and were primarily concerned with the hospitals for the sick poor under their care. At the same time eighteen of the seventy-three were directly appointed by the Minister of Health, and over these people at least, he might be presumed to have a certain influence.

In negotiating for steps towards their release Poplar had the help of members of the Battersea Borough Council which had so nearly followed Poplar's example. The first results of all the behind-the-scenes manoeuvring was a meeting of the Metropolitan Asylums' Board on Saturday 1 October, specially convened to consider the Board's attitude to the continued imprisonment of the councillors. The meeting took place at the Board's offices on the Victoria Embankment; a deputation from councillors not in prison, headed by Key, was in attendance, while outside were detachments of unemployed with bands and banners.

A member of the Board, the Rev. A. G. Pritchard, a councillor from Battersea, opened by moving a resolution declaring that in the event of the Ministry of Health being satisfied that there was substantial hope of the dispute being settled, the Board would offer no opposition to any application for the councillors' release. Pritchard said he thought they would all deplore the long continuance of the quarrel between the Board and an important local authority. The steps that had been taken in the court were within the legal right of the Board and might have been necessary at one stage, but events had moved since. 'Whatever our view of the matter we are all agreed that this action was coercive,' said Pritchard. 'I hold that the time for coercion is ended and the time for conciliation is come. The result of the action of the Poplar Council has been that they have established the essential justice of their cause.' Another Board member who was also the mayor of Battersea, Councillor Winfield, seconded this resolution, after which the chairman, Canon Sprankling, said somewhat surprisingly that the Board had no quarrel at all with Poplar and he hoped there would be a speedy settlement. He appealed to the Board to pass the resolution unanimously and indeed it was then carried without dissent.[18] Thus the first step was taken with unexpected ease.

This was not to be the case with the London County Council whose members were still indignant at the way the whole business had developed. From their point of view the Poplar councillors had broken the law in order to cheat the LCC out of its money, and the LCC had quite correctly taken the only legal steps open to it to recover the money and assert the rule of law. Yet as a result the LCC was worse off than it would have been had it done nothing, since it had actually had to spend money to get the councillors sent to jail, with so far no result whatever. Moreover, it now looked as though the minister's new Bill would put the onus of collecting the rates upon the LCC itself; those who knew anything of Poplar could hardly relish that prospect. Indeed it seemed that if matters continued in their present direction the LCC could say goodbye to its money. In this situation the only thing which could break the deadlock was to get the councillors out of jail and so open the door to some settlement. The LCC leaders knew that this would be a sensible course to pursue and, indeed, were under official pressure to smooth the way. Nevertheless they were reluctant to make any move which could be interpreted as a climb-down. On 30 September a special subcommittee set up to watch the Poplar position discussed the matter without coming to any conclusion though they had before them both the memorandum from the Labour mayors and a communication from Mond.

The Labour group on the council had in the meantime also discussed the question and had tabled a motion for the regular fortnightly meeting of the full council due on 4 October. This motion simply said: 'That the Council would welcome the release from imprisonment of the members of the Poplar Borough Council.' It was moved by an old friend of Lansbury's, Alfred Watts. A compositor by trade, Watts was now a Communist ('He had learnt Marx's *Das Kapital* backwards and forwards. He could explain the theory of value so that a child could understand' recalled Lansbury after Watts's death.)[19] He was a member of the Poplar Board of Guardians but had been chosen by the left-wing North Battersea labour movement to stand as their candidate in the LCC elections and had been elected councillor in 1919. Now he urged the LCC members to agree to the Poplar councillors' release. 'Nothing will be gained,' he said 'by keeping them a day longer in prison. The spirit of these men and women is unbreakable.' Bryan, Labour member for Limehouse, seconded the motion. But George Hume, the leader of the dominant Municipal Reform group (Conservatives) then intervened. Saying that they would all like to see their Poplar friends back among them, he appealed to the mover and seconder to withdraw the motion, and adjourn the matter for consultation. The councillors then withdrew from the council chamber and on their return another resolution was submitted in place of the original. It said:

> That this Council would welcome a conference between the Ministry of Health and the Poplar Borough Council with the object of overcoming the existing difficulties, and would further welcome any action by the Poplar Borough Council which would enable them freely to participate in such a conference.

This half hearted resolution which put the ball back into Poplar's court was supported by the Labour members present, presumably on the grounds that their own resolution would not be passed and that half a loaf is better than no bread. It was carried unanimously accompanied by cries from the gallery of 'Release them' and 'You put them there.'[20]

There was just as much difficulty to be overcome when it came to formulating the application for discharge which the Poplar councillors had to make to the court if it was to be persuaded to release them. For there were two things the councillors were determined not to do; one was to 'purge their contempt' by collecting the rate and the other was to apologise for their action in refusing to levy it. On 3 October, the night before the LCC meeting, Harry Gosling accompanied by Alderman C. J. Mathew and W. H. Thompson went to Brixton for a further gathering of all the prisoners including those from Holloway. Representatives from Bethnal Green also attended.

At this meeting, Mathew and Thompson gave advice on the difficult question of how to draw up an affidavit which would satisfy the court yet safeguard their principles. The two men were asked to prepare a draft; this they did; it was discussed; subsequently at a further meeting on 7 October it was amended and the final draft agreed. It ran as follows:

> We desire to express our profound regret that our action has involved us in disobedience to the order of the Court, and further to disclaim any wish to treat the Court otherwise than with the

respect due to it. We are very sensible of the consideration already shown to us both by this Honourable Court, and by the Court of Appeal, and we are anxious to disavow any intention whatsoever of contumacy. We are informed and believe that a conference of all parties interested is being called by the Minister of Health to consider the admitted financial difficulties of the present financial situation with a view to arriving at a satisfactory solution of them.

We earnestly desire to be present at this conference, and to assist to the very best of our ability in putting an end to the unhappy position in which our constituents are placed through economic causes beyond their control. We are hopeful that such a conference will have a successful issue, and no efforts of ours will be spared towards that end.

We therefore most earnestly ask that this Honourable Court will be pleased to release us from our present imprisonment and to grant us an indulgence which we desire emphatically to assure the Court will neither be misplaced nor abused.[21]

It was hoped that the court would accept this form of words even though it made no offer to obey the court, and contained no apology for disobeying the court, but apologised for something subtly different. Meanwhile the councillors had had explained to them that additional grounds for release which the court might consider would be proof that the situation had changed. In fact, legally speaking, the situation had not changed at all. But a further affidavit was prepared and sworn by Sam March on 8 October which began: 'Since the initiation of these proceedings in June last the conditions prevailing in the district of Poplar have become worse and the number of destitute persons has largely increased.' The affidavit then gave detailed figures of the rise in the numbers on poor law relief.

Armed with these two affidavits, the councillors' barrister, Disturnal, applied for their discharge from prison on 12 October. The Lord Chief Justice presided, together with Mr Justice Bray and Mr Justice Sankey. Macmorran again appeared for the LCC. It immediately became clear that he was going to do nothing to help the Poplar councillors out of jail. Thus when the Lord Chief Justice asked him whether the LCC supported the Poplar application he replied in the negative, though he said that the LCC would agree to anything the court directed. But he said with reference to Poplar's affidavits, 'I should hardly have thought they were in the nature of apologies such as are usually put forward in cases of this kind.'[22]

After which the following exchanges took place:

BRAY: What is to happen about levying this rate?

MACMORRAN: My Lord, I do not know.

BRAY: The London County Council, I suppose, want the money?

MACMORRAN: No doubt, my Lord.

BRAY: They cannot get it without a rate being levied?

MACMORRAN: No.

BRAY: Is there any machinery by which a rate can be levied without a resolution of the Borough Council?

MACMORRAN: No, my Lord.

BRAY: There is nobody else deputed in default who can do it?

MACMORRAN: No, my Lord.

BRAY: Then what do the London Council want? Do they no longer want the money or what?

MACMORRAN: I feel a little difficulty myself in defining what my position is (*laughter*).

After some discussion about the proposed conference, Sankey pressed him on the question of whether the LCC would welcome the councillors' release, to which Macmorran said again 'I do not know, my Lord' and the Lord Chief Justice said, 'Really they ought to make up their minds, you know, one way or the other', and there was more laughter.

Bray then asked Disturnal whether there was any precedent for release of the councillors without their obedience and Disturnal was obliged to say: 'I do not know that there is. Of course the circumstances are very peculiar in this case.'

Their Lordships retired to consider their decision and, returning after half an hour, the Lord Chief Justice said that the Court had found considerable difficulty in dealing with the matter because nothing had been said in the affidavits about carrying out the order of the Court. 'Now it is said they ask to be released, and they certainly make a very – I do not like to say plausible – but rather an attractive affidavit in asking for it. They say they are desirous of doing what they can at this conference to relieve their community of the difficulty in which it is at present placed. That is a very laudable position to take up.' Moreover, the judge went on, the LCC had said it would welcome 'any action on the part of the Borough Council which would enable them to freely participate in such a conference'.

'That is an ingeniously framed sentence,' said the Lord Chief Justice, 'and exactly what it means I do not know', but the court thought it might treat it as consent on the part of the prosecutors to their discharge. 'Under these circumstances and having regard to the change in the circumstances of Poplar which are set out in this second Affidavit . . . we have with considerable difficulty come to the conclusion that we can discharge the prisoners from custody.'

Thus after six weeks in jail the councillors came out undefeated and with the prospect of some concessions which would help the poorer areas. As soon as he had obtained release orders, Thompson drove with Charles Key and Harry Gosling to Holloway prison. They picked up the women prisoners who were presented with bouquets and drove with them on to Brixton where, at ten minutes past six, the twenty-five men stepped through the prison gate singing, laughing and shouting. They were all driven to Sam March's house and from there the Irish band marched them home one by one. As they passed through the streets with pipes and drums playing, men took off their caps and waved them in the air, and everyone was smiling.

NOTES

1. This and other decisions referred to in this chapter are taken from the Record of Proceedings in Brixton Prison reprinted in the Poplar Borough Council minutes of 27 October 1921.
2. The parliamentary committee of the TUC was the predecessor of the General Council.
3. Harry Gosling, *Up and Down Stream*, p. 97.
4. DH, 28 September 1921.
5. London Labour Party, Folios 2839–48.
6. DH, 24 September 1921.
7. Record of Proceedings in Brixton Prison, 23 September 1921.
8. DH, 24 September 1921.
9. ibid., 26 September 1921.
10. ibid., 27 September 1921.
11. ibid., 29 September 1921.
12. Record of Proceedings in Brixton Prison, 27 September 1921.
13. ibid., 29 September 1921.
14. DH, 29 September 1921.
15. PRO Cab 24/128, CP 3379.
16. *The Times*, 30 September 1921.
17. ibid., 4 October 1921.

18. ibid., 3 October 1921.
19. George Lansbury, *Looking Backwards – and Forwards*, 1935.
20. DH, 5 October 1921.
21. DH, 13 October 1921.
22. This and the ensuing account is taken from the record of Court proceedings reprinted in the Poplar Borough Council minutes of 20 October 1921. See also pamphlet by John Scurr, *The Rate Protest of Poplar*, 1922.

7

Victory

Inevitably the day after the release 2,000 enthusiastic supporters crowded into Bow Baths to cheer their councillors, while an overflow meeting of another 2,000 had to be held outside in Roman Road. That weekend there was a 'monster demonstration' in Victoria Park to welcome them home. But, thankful as they were to regain their liberty, the councillors faced the future with some anxiety. They had been promised a conference, but whether anything substantial would emerge from it was uncertain. Prison had undermined the health of some. Lansbury later suggested that it had shortened the life of five among them: Sumner, Rugless, O'Callaghan, Julia Scurr and Minnie Lansbury. George Lansbury's own doctor advised him to take a rest, but this he declined to do, going on 14 October, with Sam March, Sumner and John Scurr to an interview with Mond to discuss Poplar's demands. The following Monday afternoon, 17 October, the conference opened with representatives from the London County Council, the City of London and the metropolitan borough councils.

The conference met at a time when, as a confidential Cabinet document put it, 'profound unrest and bitter feelings' were growing among the unemployed.[1] By this time Mond was persuaded that the poorer London boroughs must get help without delay. As we have seen the decision of other boroughs to follow Poplar's lead had helped to bring about this change of view. Yet to grant extra money from central funds would conflict with the drastic reduction in state expenditure already announced as government policy. For the Geddes Committee had been set up only a few months previously to advise the Cabinet on economies. Thus it appeared that the only way in which boroughs such as Poplar could obtain financial help was by some redistribution of resources in London. Mond knew that this would be resisted by the richer boroughs and might well arouse anger among the Conservative supporters of the coalition who were in any case beginning to be restive under the Lloyd George administration. But after the Poplar councillors had been some weeks in jail, Mond had come to the conclusion that it was the only way out.

In his memorandum to the Cabinet of 7 October he suggested that terms for a settlement should include an increase from 6d to 1s under the Equalisation of Rates Act and an increase from 5d to 10d in the daily amount allowed for inmates of Poor Law institutions under the Metropolitan Common Poor Fund. (This was a fund set up for the purpose of pooling workhouse costs between the London local authorities.) He suggested that these two measures would be 'reasonable on their merits' and represented a 'temporary compromise between the claims of the poorer boroughs and the richer boroughs.'[2] A few days later he had a draft Bill in preparation.

The first of these measures would mean that the eight richest authorities would pay into the equalisation fund £800,000 a year instead of £400,000. The extra money would be distributed among the other twenty-one London boroughs. Because the formula for its distribution was based on a combination of rateable value and population, its impact was somewhat uneven; those faced with the most acute poverty problems would not necessarily get the most out of it. It would give Poplar an additional £21,000 a year. Such an increase, though of course welcome, was not going to make a major contribution to solving the borough's problems; already the Board of Guardians was spending £7,000 a *week* on out-relief caused mainly by unemployment. The Poplar councillors had of course told Mond that they would like an equalisation rate of 2s in the £; this would have given them an extra £61,000. However, in addition they had urged that either the cost of supporting the unemployed should be borne by the Government, or some arrangement for pooling the costs of maintaining them on a London basis should be made. For this reason they had suggested to Mond a central Board of Guardians for the whole London area. But Mond refused to consider this.

On the morning of 17 October just before the conference was due to begin, the draft Bill and the issues involved were discussed at the Home Affairs committee of the Cabinet. Mond told the committee that the financial position of some of the East London boroughs was one of serious embarrassment. He said that, with the exception of the City of London, the richer boroughs would probably assent to an increase in the equalisation rate from 6d to 9d. He then described the financial advantages to the poorer boroughs if this rate should be raised from 6d to 1s. During the subsequent discussion it was suggested that this proposal would not get Poplar out of its financial difficulties which were attributed to the high scale of outdoor relief given by the Poplar Guardians and the 'reckless' way it was distributed. But against this it was argued that 'even if the Bill did not wholly meet the Poplar situation, it would have a very beneficial effect in restraining other boroughs which were at present thinking of imitating the defaulting procedure of Poplar'.[3] It was also emphasized that Poplar would get considerable relief out of the proposal to increase the MCPF capitation grant.

Mond told the committee he wanted to be in a position to override the conference if no agreement was reached and to tell those present that the Government had definitely decided to increase the equalisation rate from 6d to 1s. In the end the committee agreed to this.

With this decision up his sleeve, Mond went on to make the opening speech at the conference. Quoting figures which showed the inequalities of resources among the London boroughs, he said that pending the findings of a Royal Commission, some temporary steps should be taken to relieve the more hard-pressed among them. He then made the proposals agreed to by the Cabinet that the capitation grant from the MCPF be increased from 5d to 10d for each adult in an institution and that there should be an increase from 6d to 1s under the Equalisation Act.

The London Labour councillors had previously decided on the policy they would put before the conference. The most important demands were: (1) an increase in the MCPF capitation grant from 5d to 1s 8d; (2) the whole cost of the unemployed to be transferred to the Government; (3) if this was not accepted, then Guardians expenditure on outdoor relief to be pooled and equalised over the whole of London; (4) that the equalisation rate be raised from 6d to 2s in the £. For Poplar, by far the most important of these demands were numbers two and three. But Mond had hitherto refused outright to consider number two and had shown little interest in the possibilities of number three.

As spokesman for the Labour boroughs, Herbert Morrison

laid stress on the importance of their second demand, that the cost of the unemployed should be borne by the central government. But Mond from the chair refused to allow this question to be discussed.

The wealthy boroughs on the other hand made clear their great aversion to any increase in the equalisation rate and were prepared to agree that it be raised only to 9d or at most 10d. Their objections were based much less on the cash involved than on the political implications. To them equalisation of rates meant equalisation of wealth. *The Times*, in a leader about the Poplar case, had attacked Lansbury and his friends for identifying themselves with 'a revolutionary movement for the equalisation of wealth or, as London generally sees it, for the equalisation of poverty.'[4] Earlier, another leader had asserted that 'the Socialists of the East End turn hungry eyes upon such boroughs as that of Westminster. They desire that while the richer or more efficiently managed districts should provide the money, the socialist prodigals of the poorer ones should have the spending of it.'[5]

This was a crucial point. Equalisation of rates meant allocating money from richer to poorer with no control over how it should be spent. The thought of this stirred up age-old prejudices. The representatives of the wealthy boroughs knew that if they agreed to anything more than a token increase in the equalisation rate, their fellow councillors and supporters would be outraged. So instead they proposed that Mond's suggested increase in the MCPF capitation grant should be trebled; it should go up from 5d to 1s 3d. Unlike the equalisation rate, transferring money from rich to poor for this purpose could be defended on rational grounds.

Labour speakers now declared that the proposals of the wealthy boroughs were inadequate. But their protests appeared to make no impression. Mond suggested the appointment of a sub-committee to negotiate a detailed settlement. Morrison on behalf of the Labour boroughs objected. He said that in view of the attitude of Westminster and the City, he could not see that such a sub-committee would achieve anything. The Minister could see, he said, that the wealthy boroughs were taking up an utterly impossible attitude and it was for the Minister to decide between the 'self-interested opposition to elemental justice' of a few boroughs against the grave needs of the majority.[6]

It looked like deadlock. But at that stage the Town Clerk of Westminster submitted a new proposal. He suggested that as the real difficulty in the poorer boroughs arose from the cost of outdoor relief to the unemployed, the proper way to meet the emergency was to equalise the charge for such relief. He therefore proposed that the Labour demand for an increase in the equalisation rate should be withdrawn, and that instead the cost of outdoor relief, up to a scale approved by the Minister of Health, should be pooled all over London through the Metropolitan Common Poor Fund.

Now this proposal came near to fulfilment of the third demand of the Labour boroughs. For Poplar and some other east London boroughs it was much more important from a financial point of view than any increase in the equalisation rate. Poplar would gain greatly from such a move and so would other areas with disproportionately high unemployment. On the other hand, some Labour boroughs which happened to have fewer out of work, might not gain much from it. However after rapid consultation, Morrison said that while the Labour boroughs could not agree to withdraw the demand for an increase in the equalisation rate, the proposal to pool outdoor relief costs was substantial enough for them to agree to the appointment of a sub-committee for further negotiation. This sub-committee met next day and reached agreement on the new measure.

The Westminster Town Clerk was John Hunt, an eminent local government expert. His suggestion was a shrewd one. He knew that something had to be done if serious unrest in the poorer boroughs was to be averted. But the problem was to find a method of transferring money from the rich authorities to the poor ones which would not arouse the furious antagonism of his own borough councillors.

His proposal was highly orthodox in origin, since the idea that poor law expenditure in London should be pooled was among the recommendations of the Royal Commission on the Poor Law. The difficulty had always been that it implied a centralised administration, whereas at the moment twenty-eight different boards of guardians were implementing widely differing standards of relief. In such a situation pooling costs would enable the poorer areas to indulge their 'extravagant' leanings. Hunt's proposal seemed to offer a temporary way of overcoming this difficulty, since it provided for the pooling of costs only up to a level or on scales laid down by the Minister of Health; any undue 'extravagance' would therefore still fall on the local rates. Finally although the eight richest boroughs would be contributing the lion's share of money transferred – far more, as it turned out, than they would have done under Mond's rate equalisation proposal – some other boroughs with few unemployed would also make a certain contribution.

As soon as agreement had been reached over the Hunt proposal, Mond rapidly amended his original Bill from which the proposal to increase the equalisation rate was dropped, and the arrangements for pooling the costs of out-relief incorporated instead.

However, among the Labour boroughs the settlement provoked some dissension. According to the official White Paper issued with the Bill the new pooling arrangements would mean an increase in rates in thirteen areas and a decrease in fifteen, as shown overleaf.

The boroughs which would do best out of the new proposals on first calculation were precisely those with the highest unemployment; they included nearly all the dockland areas so greatly afflicted by casual labour: not only Poplar, but Bermondsey, Southwark, Greenwich and parts of Stepney. Woolwich was a special case since in addition to being a riverside area it accommodated Woolwich Arsenal, a government establishment in process of being run down; it was discharging workers at the rate of three hundred a week.

Poplar was to get a much bigger share of the money made available than any other borough; indeed about four or five times as much as it would have got under Labour's proposal for a 2s equalisation rate. It was believed initially under the Hunt proposals that it stood to gain an additional £250,000 a year – equivalent to a rate of 5s 6d in the £. Actually in the ensuing year it was nearer £350,000. No other borough did as well as this, but Bermondsey, Shoreditch, Southwark and Camberwell all did much better than they would have done under the equalisation rate demand.

One or two Labour boroughs, however, lost by the Hunt settlement. Ironically enough they included Hackney and Fulham, represented respectively by Morrison himself and by Gentry, secretary of the group of Labour mayors. The proposals

EFFECT ON THE RATES FOR HALF A YEAR IN AREAS OF
POOR LAW UNIONS*

Increases in Rates		*Decreases in Rates*	
	d		d
City of London	7·5	Hammersmith	1·3
Westminster	6·8	Wandsworth (including †Battersea)	2·9
Hampstead	6·7	Lewisham (including part of	
St Marylebone	5·7	†Woolwich)	3·4
Kensington	5·5	St George in the East (part of	
Chelsea	5·4	†Stepney)	4·7
Whitechapel (part		Mile End Old Town (part of	
of †Stepney)	4·6	†Stepney)	4·8
†Fulham	4·3	†Islington	4·8
Holborn	3·7	†Camberwell	8·3
Paddington	2·1	†Greenwich (including †Deptford)	9·0
St Pancras	1·5	†Southwark	10·2
†Hackney	0·7	†Shoreditch	12·0
†Lambeth	0·5	†Bermondsey	18·5
		Limehouse (part of †Stepney)	19·3
		†Bethnal Green	19·8
		†Woolwich (including part of	
		†Greenwich)	28·4
		†Poplar	33·2

* The areas of Boards of Guardians were not exactly the same as those of the borough councils. The table shows in which borough the area of the various boards fell.

† Indicates borough councils which were either Labour controlled or in which Labour was the biggest party.

In practice the estimates made in the White Paper were not very accurate and Lambeth, which was estimated to lose on the new arrangement, gained considerably.

meant that Hackney would get a little less out of the Common Poor Fund than before. Fulham, which had hitherto received a small amount out of the fund, would be turned into a contributing instead of a receiving borough. The reason was not difficult to seek. Though Fulham Borough Council had a Labour majority, its Board of Guardians had not, and indeed was dominated by people who resisted the dispensation of outdoor relief to the able-bodied unemployed, offering to send them instead to an institution named Belmont which became notorious. At the time when Poplar was supporting 4,000 unemployed on out-relief, Fulham was supporting only 455, one of the lowest numbers in any London borough. Since Fulham's expenses on out-relief were so limited, it followed that it would in future be paying more into the pool than it got out of it.

It was for these reasons that, while the conference was still in session, but after Hunt's proposal had been agreed to, Morrison and Gentry both pressed for an increase in the equalisation rate in addition. However, Hunt stressed that the richer boroughs had only put forward the new arrangements under the Common Poor Fund on the understanding that there would be no alteration in the equalisation rate. The latter, he said, could await the Royal Commission; relief for the unemployed could not. At this point, to Morrison's anger, Lansbury spoke up, saying that although he was never satisfied, he took the new agreement as a very decent instalment; it was more than he had expected. It is possible that Lansbury feared that continued pressure for Morrison's demand might jeopardise the Hunt settlement, but he said afterwards that as the richer boroughs were adamant on the rates equalisation issue there was no point in going on arguing. In the end Morrison's proposal that the two sides should once more meet separately for further consultation was turned down; the richer boroughs remained obdurate and there the matter rested.

Gentry of Fulham was very indignant. In a letter to the *Daily Herald* he put the blame on Lansbury for the situation in which his borough was placed. He accused both Lansbury and the representative from Bermondsey of 'breaking solidarity'. 'They seemed more concerned with scrambling to get the most for their respective boroughs, not troubling who else was hit, whereas if they had acted more in unison with the rest of us, they would probably have secured more for their boroughs and some of us who are to be penalised because of their parochial greed would also have gained.'[7]

Meanwhile Morrison got into trouble with the Hackney Borough Council of which he was mayor. Here Brown, the chairman of the finance committee, complained that the Town Clerk had taken Mond's invitation to the conference direct to Morrison, whereas it should have been brought first before the committee, or at least before its chairman, for consultation. The finance committee failed to support Brown in his protest, so he resigned his chairmanship and at the next meeting of the full council moved the rejection of the finance committee report. He obtained a majority in support of this motion, which was tantamount to a vote of censure on Morrison. The debate was acrimonious. It was said that there had been 'too much Morrison' and too little cooperation.[8]

The settlement seemed to underline what was for Morrison and those who thought like him a very disturbing fact; the supporters of 'direct action', whether in Poplar or elsewhere, had won an overwhelming victory after the supporters of 'constitutionalism' had for years failed to make headway. True, Morrison had played his part in persuading Lloyd George and Mond to hold a conference at which he had then acted as Labour's spokesman. But nobody could be in doubt; it was not Morrison's visit to Gairloch, but Poplar's illegal rate strike which had won the day. From Morrison's point of view, the negotiations he had led had not gone at all according to plan. Indeed he had emerged from the conference with his own borough in a worsened position and nothing but trouble on his hands.

When the new Bill[9] to pool the costs of out-relief was debated in Parliament, MPs from all parties went out of their way to stress that this was a victory for 'direct action', and heaped blame on Mond's head for not acting sooner to redress the grievances of poor boroughs, instead of waiting until Poplar forced his hand. Thus the Liberal MP Sir Donald Maclean, who had headed the government enquiry into London local government, thought it a sorry comment on the administration that reforms recommended for years by experienced observers and embodied in Blue Books should have been put on one side until Poplar's *mandamus*; Jack Jones, Labour MP for West Ham, congratulated 'Poplar and those who believe in direct action on the results of their efforts'; J. D. Kiley, Liberal MP for Whitechapel, said that Poplar could 'boast that they have achieved something that other members that have been busy with this problem for many long years have not been able to achieve.' T. Thomson, Coalition Liberal MP for Middlesbrough, said there never was a time when it was more necessary that appeals to force and direct action should not succeed, yet Poplar could achieve what local authorities in the provinces had failed to secure. Ormsby-Gore, Conservative MP for Stafford, said of the clause for pooling the costs of outdoor relief 'This clause, I understand, is popularly known as "Lansbury's victory".'[10] J. H. Thomas, Labour MP for Derby and general secretary of the National Union of Railwaymen, asserted that they would not have had the Bill had it not been for Poplar's action and 'that is a bad thing for the constitution'.[11] Sir Reginald Blair, Conservative MP for a Poplar division felt obliged to say: 'I am sorry to think that this Bill owes its inception to the policy of direct action carried out by the Poplar Borough Council, an example likely to be followed by other poor districts in London. This is a great discouragement to those who believe in constitutional action and a great encouragement to those who believe in revolutionary methods.'[12]

In vain Mond insisted that the new Bill would have been introduced in any case; nobody believed him.

In Poplar, of course, there had never been any doubt about whose action had brought victory. But its extent in financial terms only became clear some weeks later. The prophets of gloom had repeatedly forecast that the sums of money withheld from the central bodies would have to be paid in the end. In one sense these prophecies were fulfilled but the matter was so arranged that the operation was painless. The unpaid precepts amounted to £300,000, but by special arrangement Poplar was allowed by the Minister of Health to borrow this money and pay it over forthwith to the LCC, the MAB, the police and the Metropolitan Water Board. After which Poplar was to be allowed five years to pay back the loan with interest at 6½ per cent. Since the extra income from the Common Poor Fund would be far more than enough to compensate for these repayments Poplar would be very much in pocket. As Charles Key suggested, by the time the £300,000 was paid back with interest, they would have gained over a million pounds. 'In other words,' he said with some exaggeration, 'you put down your bob and draw back a quid.'[13]

The ultimate financial gain could be gauged from the rates in the £ levied in Poplar which turned out to be lower in 1922–3 than they had been in 1920–1 before the great rise in unemployment:

RATES IN THE POUND IN POPLAR

		s	d
1919–20		15	6
1920–21		22	10
1921–22	(if the precepts had been levied)	27	3
1921–22	(actual)	18	3
1922–23		22	8

At the borough council meeting after their release the mayor thanked all those who had stood by them. A deputation of women presented flowers to the women who had gone to prison 'as a token of the love and gratitude of the givers'. George Lansbury said they had taken action to prevent the poor being compelled to keep the poor and though they had not got all they wanted, he thought they had made a good bargain.

NOTES

1. PRO, Cab 24/128, CP 3371.
2. ibid., CP 3379.
3. ibid., Cab 23/27, Cab. Committee on Home Affairs 98, 17 October 1921.
4. *The Times*, 3 September 1921.
5. ibid., 1 September 1921.
6. *London Labour Chronicle*, November 1921.
7. DH, 21 October 1921.
8. Bernard Donoughue and G. W. Jones, *Herbert Morrison: Portrait of a Politician*, 1973, p. 50.
9. The Local Authorities (Financial Provisions) Act, 1921.
10. House of Commons, *Hansard*, 28 October 1921.
11. ibid., 2 November 1921.
12. ibid., 3 November 1921.
13. ELA., 18 February 1922.

The Unemployed and the Poor Law

As the numbers out of work in Poplar mounted, the signs of poverty multiplied. Sometimes it led to disturbances of an unusual kind. For example, one night in October 1921, 24,000 wooden road blocks were torn up by a crowd in Upper North Street and taken away for firewood. Children began it, then men and women joined in, so that in a short time nearly a thousand people were hurriedly prising up blocks with hammers and chisels, putting them in sacks and dragging them home. They ran away when the police came, but half a dozen were caught. When they came before the magistrate the borough engineer told the court that the council had no wish to prosecute.

At the November meeting of the borough council, Charlie Sumner was elected mayor for the ensuing year. He happened also to be chairman of the Poplar Board of Guardians and had been one of Lansbury's closest colleagues in the fight to reform the Poor Law in Poplar before the turn of the century. It was over the Poor Law that Poplar's next battle with the central Government was to be fought out. Now, to the speeches nominating him as mayor, Sumner responded with characteristic simplicity, saying that he was very pleased, because he regarded himself as a worker and he had been all the way through; it was very nice after thirty years to come along to a position of this sort and to know you held the confidence of your people.[1] Sumner was a great favourite among the local rank and file and his appointment was greeted with loud applause, the singing of 'For he's a jolly good fellow', and three cheers.

But at the turn of the year the high spirits engendered by their victory were lowered by the illness and unexpected death of one of them: Minnie Lansbury. She caught influenza just before Christmas; it turned to pneumonia and she died on New Year's Day at the age of thirty-two. Minnie had been a popular figure and thousands of women assembled in the street near her home and walked in procession to her funeral. It was widely alleged that her experiences in Holloway had undermined her health.

Her death occurred on the eve of a further confrontation between Poplar and the Government. This time it concerned the attitude of society to the unemployed and the controversial question of how people for whom there is no work should be treated. In the course of the next months, Poplar was to challenge all the accepted principles derived from the 1834 Poor Law.

The arrangements then in existence for relief of the unemployed had not been designed for a slump of the magnitude now seen. The insurance Poor Law framework rested on the assumption that for those who wanted work, unemployment need be only short term. The unemployment insurance scheme financed by contributions from workers, employers and the state, was intended to help workmen laid off only temporarily for seasonal reasons or during short recessions. Unemployment benefit was in any case not meant to be enough to live on by itself; if it were, it was argued, it might act as an inducement to idleness. It was merely intended to supplement the unemployed person's own resources and was payable for a limited period only.

But by 1921 the assumptions on which the whole framework had been built had collapsed. For unemployment was proving to be long term rather than temporary; for many it had begun to run into months and would soon stretch into years.

In response to this situation, the Government introduced a series of hasty modifications of the unemployment insurance scheme. The number of weeks for which benefit could be drawn was increased, and something called 'uncovenanted benefit' was provided, subject to periods of interruption known as 'gaps'. Despite these expedients, hundreds of thousands of unemployed men and women found themselves without any benefit, some because they had exhausted their rights, others because, for one reason or another, they failed to qualify.

Those in such a position had a last resort: they could apply to the local Poor Law Guardians for relief. In theory the boards of guardians were still expected to enforce the principles of 'less eligibility' laid down in 1834. 'Less eligibility' meant that in no circumstances should the situation of a person on relief be as good as that of the lowest paid independent labourer. Moreover, no able-bodied person should be given relief without being compelled to work for it, such work to be as hard as that of the independent labourer, but less well paid. This was considered crucial to the health of the economy which, it was believed, depended on a labour market open to the free play of supply and demand. The aim was to foster sturdy independence, hard work and habits of thrift among workers. 'Every penny bestowed that tends to render the condition of the pauper more eligible than that of the independent labourer is a bounty on indolence and vice' had been the argument of 1834.

'Less eligibilty' had meant in practice a harshly deterrent system, which offered relief under conditions so degrading that few would go near it unless starving, and sometimes not even then. In working-class minds it was associated with disgrace. Orthodox opinion encouraged such an attitude; it was assumed that those who could fall so low must suffer from some personal flaw. This in turn had led to the growth of charitable organisations through which the compassionate could direct funds to those whose misfortunes had not been of their own making. In collaboration with the Poor Law authorities, the Charity Organisation Society was busy sorting out the 'deserving' from the 'undeserving'.

In normal times the doctrine of 'less eligibility' was quite irrelevant to the situation of the majority who came to the Poor Law Guardians for help, since they consisted mainly of the sick and disabled, the aged and infirm, widows or deserted wives with small children. But even for these groups, reformers were up against the assumption that so far as possible people must be deterred from applying for relief.

George Lansbury had been an early rebel against the cruelties of the system. As a Guardian he had helped to reform Poplar's workhouse, and had later served on the Royal Commission on the Poor Law; he had been a joint signatory, together with Beatrice Webb and others, to the famous minority report, and a leader in the campaign which followed it. At a conference held in London in 1910 he had made a withering attack on the attitude of Poor Law administrators to the sick people who came to them for relief. The ordinary doctor, he alleged, was trained to believe that a person who came within the Poor Law was something just a little less than a criminal, and that he must be made to feel that. The object of the Relieving Officer 'was always to find reasons why he should not administer relief, not why he should'. Indeed 'the sole business in life of a Relieving Officer was only to relieve distress where it was quite impossible to him to find out any reasons why he should not'. Moreover, 'the Board of Guardians which the Local Government Board looked on with most favour was the Board which had the fewest number of people on its roll and in fact relieved nobody'.[2]

Since that time the Local Government Board had been replaced by the Ministry of Health as the government department responsible for supervising the Poor Law and the local boards of guardians which administered it. But the inauguration of a Ministry of Health, long demanded by the reformers, had not resulted in any marked change of approach towards the Poor Law.

In 1921 the growth in unemployment and the consequent flood of applicants for relief from among the able-bodied workless subjected the system to quite unprecedented strains. Under the pre-war rules, no able-bodied worker could get out-relief without working for it.[3] This had originally meant – and still meant in some places – that he must be offered the workhouse; the more up-to-date approach, however, was to force him to undergo a 'labour test' which usually meant spending many hours on very heavy work, such as stone-breaking, for roughly half the prevailing rate of wages. According to the rules, out-relief without a labour test could only be given in cases of 'sudden or urgent necessity'. But the Guardians could depart from these rules 'upon consideration of the special circumstances of any particular case' provided it was individually reported to the Ministry of Health.

By 1921 such a procedure, ostensibly designed to test a workman's willingness to take a job, had become glaringly inappropriate. For now there were no jobs to be had. Moreover, so great was the flood of applicants asking for relief that any kind of test was out of the question in many areas; the Guardians and their staffs found it difficult to get through the paper-work involved in issuing vouchers for cash and kind to those who daily besieged their premises. More and more Guardians took refuge in a new procedure: that of granting unconditional outdoor relief, but automatically reporting 'special circumstances' to the Minister in each individual case. The Ministry continued to urge on the Guardians the desirability of enforcing either the workhouse or the labour test, but when, during the summer, vast numbers of those drawing unemployment benefit came to a 'gap' and turned to the Poor Law, Sir Alfred Mond was obliged to accept the inevitable. In September 1921, while the

Poplar councillors were in jail, he sent out a circular to boards of guardians acquiescing in the grant of out-relief to the able-bodied unemployed *without* either a workhouse or labour test. This impelled Edgar Lansbury to declare that Poplar's victory could not be measured only by the amount of money which had been saved to the borough. 'The real victory,' he said, 'was that the Government had at last admitted that outdoor relief was a suitable method of relieving unemployment.'[4]

The right of the Poor Law Guardians to support the unemployed was thus for the time being no longer in doubt. The battle to come was to be over the level of allowances permitted.

On 5 January 1922, the day after Minnie's funeral, Sir Alfred Mond sent out the regulations governing the pooling of out-relief costs under the new Act which had been passed as a result of Poplar's protest.[5] As anticipated, it was laid down that the cost of relief up to a standard scale would be borne by the Metropolitan Common Poor Fund; relief in excess of this scale would continue to be paid for out of the local rates. The standard scale adopted was not ungenerous in comparison with that of most London boards of guardians, only three of whom had Labour majorities, of which Poplar was one. Indeed Mond appeared to be trying to steer an uneasy middle course between those who believed that high rates of poor relief demoralised the working man and those who thought that if society could not offer a man a job, he was entitled to adequate maintenance. Of the twenty-seven London Poor Law boards, fifteen operated a lower scale than the new Mond scale (as it began to be called) eight revised their scales so as to be in line with it, and four, including Poplar, operated a higher scale.

The Mond scale offered in cash or kind up to 25s for a man and wife, 6s for the first child, 5s for the second or third child, 4s for the fourth or subsequent child, and an additional 3s a week in winter and 1s 6d in summer for fuel. But it allocated no rent allowance, so that these amounts were expected to cover rent as well as the cost of food and clothing.

The allowances were subject to two rules which were of overriding importance to the upholders of traditional Poor Law practice and were indeed to emerge as major issues in Poplar's struggle against the Ministry. The first was that the relief for a family, whatever its size, must not exceed a figure 10s *below* the standard rate of wages for a labourer.[6] Soon after Mond's circular went out the standard rate under this formula became £3 4s; it followed that the maximum chargeable to the Common Poor Fund for any family, whatever its size, would be £2 14s a week.

This rule touched on the most sensitive and controversial question of all: the relationship between unemployment allowances and wages, and the maintenance of the principle of 'less eligibility'. Even in normal times the employers were fearful that payments to an unemployed man might approach the level of the lowest wage. But now these fears were reinforced by the conviction of both employers and, indeed, the establishment as a whole, that the country's economic salvation depended on the degree to which wages could be reduced since, it was argued, it was only thus that prices could become competitive. So bit by bit wages were being forced down. Since it was obvious that relief standards which approached the level of a normal wage would inhibit this process, Mond had underlined in his Circular 240, sent out the previous September, that the amount of relief given to the able-bodied unemployed 'must of necessity be calculated on a lower scale than the earnings of the independent workman who is maintaining himself by his labour. This is a fundamental principle any departure from which must in the end prove disastrous to the recipient of relief as well as to the community at large.'

But those who tried to operate this 'fundamental principle' were up against the indisputable fact that the wages of the average independent workman, though they might be regarded as sufficient to keep a wife and baby, were not enough to keep a wife and seven or eight children from hunger. Families of this size or larger were in a minority, yet they were not uncommon, and they usually suffered great privation, even when the father was in steady work, until the eldest children were old enough to start earning. If the breadwinner lost his job and the family turned to the Guardians the likelihood was that out-relief on a scale to enable the children to be adequately fed would cost more than the breadwinner normally earned when in work.

After World War Two this problem was to be partially overcome by the introduction of family allowances paid for every child after the first, whether the breadwinner was in work or not. But in 1922 there were no family allowances, and this meant that in the case of every large family on relief there was bound to be a conflict between those who wanted to make sure that no child went hungry or barefoot, and those who were determined to uphold the principle of 'less eligibility'.

The second guiding rule concerned the treatment of resources. Mond's regulations laid down that in fixing allowances 'income or means from every source, whether in money or kind, received by or available to the applicant or by any other members of the household shall be taken into account'. What this meant was that if the eldest boy or girl in a family was working, the whole of their earnings could be counted as part of the family's income in assessing relief for the parents and younger brothers and sisters. Or again if young unemployed men and women living with parents applied for relief, they could not get it unless the parents could prove that they were unable to support them.

Any means test is a disagreeable process, since the applicant is required to lay bare personal and private matters to a stranger. But a personal means test cannot be compared with a household means test, which is not only a violation of privacy for the individual, but extends to the whole family and ensures that the latter shares in the poverty of the former. Indeed, hatred of the household means test was to dominate the struggles of the unemployed in the inter-war period and to become an emotive issue second to none in areas of high unemployment. Among other things it highlighted the contradictions in the system. For it undermined the 'less eligibility' principle itself. If every time a son or daughter earned a few shillings extra the family's relief was reduced by an equivalent amount, there was no incentive to young people to get work; the family got as much if they stayed at home. Such was the inter-war version of what later became known as the 'poverty trap'.

The two guiding rules described above meant that in practice the scale on which costs could be charged by the London Guardians to the Common Poor Fund was reduced below the Mond scale as set out. Moreover, having fixed a scale which was relatively generous compared with prevailing standards, Mond appeared anxious to dissociate himself from some in the labour movement who instantly began to demand that all Guardians who gave relief on a lower scale should bring their allowances *up* to the Mond level. In Circular 276 which was sent to Guardians at the same time as the new regulations, he made clear that

Guardians should not interpret the new scale as an encouragement to raise allowances. 'The Minister desires to state definitely that the scale prescribed fixes the maximum which may be
charged on the Fund and that it is not lawful for the Guardians
in any case, the needs of which can be met by a smaller amount
of relief than the scale would admit, to give more than the
amount necessary to relieve destitution.' What was meant by
'destitution' was never precisely defined, but such an instruction enabled the parsimonious to argue satisfactorily against
anyone who wanted to level up allowances. At the same time
the circular suggested that Guardians might exceed the scale at
their own expense, but apparently they were not expected to do
this as a general rule judging by one rather ambiguous sentence
in the circular 'It is equally within the competence of the
Guardians (though not at the cost of the Fund) to exceed the
scale to meet exceptional needs.'

How did Poplar's practices compare with those laid down in
the new regulations? Since the spring of 1919 when a Labour
majority of fifteen seats out of twenty-four had been won on the
Board of Guardians, considerable improvements in the treatment of those on relief had been initiated. Poplar now had a
scale of allowances of 20s for man and wife, 6s 6d for the first
child, 5s for each subsequent child, but added to this a rent
allowance which was equal to the actual rent paid up to 10s a
week. One of the objects of a separate rent allowance was to discourage rent arrears and evictions; another was to discourage
overcrowding, since, if faced with a financial crisis, a family
living in two rooms might well reduce its accommodation to one
and let the other to a lodger. In addition to the rent, Poplar was
in the habit of granting a good many extras such as boots,
clothing and bedding. These were given at the discretion of the
relief committees.

The combined effect of the scale of allowances plus rent
allowance meant that the amount given to Poplar families on
relief was above that laid down in the Mond regulation as
chargeable to the fund (see Appendix A). But the gap between
the two was further enlarged by Poplar's approach to the two
guiding rules described earlier. In the first place Poplar operated no maximum; the larger the family, the larger the relief
which, in the case of families with many children, could come
well above the wages of the lowest paid labourer. In the second

place, Poplar refrained from treating the resources of the rest of the family as wholly available for the support of the applicant. The Poplar Board took into account all the resources of the applicant and his wife, but if there were children in work they disregarded the first 15s earned and made only small deductions from earnings above this level. Thus if there were wages of 30s, 6s only would be calculated as income for the family. The Guardians were in fact opposed to taking account of any earnings other than those of the applicant and his wife and were to pass a resolution to this effect on 25 January 1922. Meanwhile they operated a household means test, but in a very much modified form in comparison with the usual practice. In any case the Poplar Board considered its own relief scales to be inadequate; they were all that it could afford when relief had been paid for entirely out of the local rates.

The newly published Mond scale was considered on Saturday 14 January 1922 at a municipal conference convened by the London Labour Party. At this conference Poplar was represented by A. A. Watts who, as described earlier, had played some part in securing their release from jail in his capacity as an LCC councillor for North Battersea. But Watts was a Poplar man and a member of the Poplar Board of Guardians on which he had served for some years. Now at this London conference he moved that a deputation should ask for an interview with the Minister of Health concerning the new scale. Watts criticised this scale as 'inadequate' and secured the agreement of those present that it should be increased by 'an amount to cover the rent'.[7] As secretary of the London Labour Party, Herbert Morrison accordingly wrote to Mond saying that the scale was 'gravely inadequate'. In characteristic fashion he embellished the demand made at the conference with provisos intended to make clear the statesmanlike approach of Labour. 'The London Labour Party has never associated itself with demands for scales of relief which it could not regard as practicable in existing circumstances.' This looked like an oblique reference to the kind of relief scales for which unemployed organisations were busy agitating in various parts of London. The letter, dated 19 January, asked Mond to receive a deputation to discuss a separate rent allowance, a request which Mond instantly turned down.[8]

However, the Poplar Guardians, including Watts himself,

had a very different attitude to the agitations of the unemployed from that of Herbert Morrison; so far as possible they encouraged them. So when, on 18 January, a deputation of unemployed came to see the Poplar Guardians they were made welcome. In support of the deputation several hundred people squeezed into the waiting hall. They came to ask that the Mond scale should not be operated. Declaring that the unemployed were starving, the spokesman for the deputation urged that the allowance for a man and wife should be raised to 27s 6d a week with higher allowances for children and rent, etc., in addition.

The chairman of the Poplar Board, Charlie Sumner, presided at this meeting. Also serving on the Board were eight of the councillors who had been in prison with him a few months earlier – George and Edgar Lansbury, Julia Scurr, David Adams, Alfred Partridge, Albert Baker, Ben Fleming and Joe Banks – together with A. A. Watts, Helen McKay and Councillors Chris Kelly and Peter Hubbart. On this occasion the members of the Board were sympathetic to the deputation and suggested that they should come again the following week, promising to invite Sir Alfred Mond to attend and meet them. Both Sumner and George Lansbury emphasised that Poplar could not stand alone and that other districts must be 'wakened up'. They believed that only combined efforts of workers all over the country would win justice.

After the deputation had retired the Board passed a resolution to inform Sir Alfred Mond that 'it is impossible for this Board to administer the scale laid down by him as the present scale of relief administered by this Board is totally inadequate', and to invite him to attend the following Wednesday or to send one of his principal officers to meet the unemployed in person. This invitation was conveyed in a letter to Mond from Charlie Sumner dated 19 January. The letter protested at the limit in total relief to be allowed to large families, and also at the instruction to take into account the resources of the whole household. 'To pretend that the larger families of 10, 11 or 12 persons have adequate means of support if one of the elder sons living in the house is earning £3 1s od or that this can in any case be available as income of the household is, in my opinion and that of the Board, ridiculous,' wrote Sumner. He then set out the scale of allowances which had been asked for by the deputation.[9]

Mond replied to this letter, pointing out that his scale was higher than that of a number of the London boards of guardians; moreover 'it would be unfair and entirely contrary to public policy to adopt a scale such as that suggested in your letter which would have the effect of placing many recipients of relief in a better position than many independent workmen who are supporting themselves by their own wages'. He stressed that 'if the Guardians . . . elect to give relief in excess of the scale, the excess must necessarily be a charge upon the funds of their own Union'. And he declined the invitation to attend the next meeting of the Poplar Board.[10]

On the Wednesday named, 25 January 1922, the Poplar Board of Guardians met at the appointed time. Perhaps because they did not know until the last moment that no Ministry representative was coming, Summer and his colleagues had not thrashed out the policy they intended to pursue in advance of the meeting. Unlike the action on the rates which had been worked out in previous discussion, not only in the Labour group on the council but also with the local trade union movement, they came to this meeting with no concerted policy. This turned out to be unfortunate; it meant that members were pushed into a decision which they later realised had been a mistake.

About a thousand young unemployed men and women, most of them in their twenties, had marched to the Guardians' office in the hopes of meeting a Ministry official. Two deputations went into the boardroom where the Guardians were meeting. The first consisted of women who merely stated that it was impossible to live on the Mond scale. The second put before the Board a list of demands considerably in excess of those presented the previous week. They were, indeed, the demands which had first been laid down at a national conference of unemployed held in April 1921. This event had laid the basis for the formation of the National Unemployed Workers' Committee Movement and its main platform was 'work or full maintenance for the unemployed at trade union rates of wages'. It also formulated the following demands to be put to all local Guardians: 36s for a man and wife, 5s for each child, rent in addition. These demands, already the subject of agitation in other parts of the country, were now put to the Poplar Guardians.

George Lansbury was aware that the Poplar Board did not have enough money to pay relief on the scale requested. He warned those present that if their demands were agreed to, there was a danger that the men would 'cut their own throats'. He moved a resolution that the Board's present scale, which was already higher than the Mond scale and which, Lansbury claimed, was the highest in the country, should continue in operation. But it became clear that the rest of the Board were not happy about this proposal; their scales might be the highest in the country but they believed them to be inadequate. A. A. Watts therefore moved that the national demands of the unemployed (36s for a man and wife, etc.) be granted. He was seconded by David Adams, the dockers' leader. Realising that the majority of the Board would be in favour of Watts' proposal, Lansbury withdrew his own motion, despite misgivings.

It was then that Charlie Sumner from the chair made a quite unexpected move. Declaring that the demands of the unemployed were too modest, he moved that the rate for man and wife should be 40s, the rate for every child 6s and the other items such as rent allowance should be provided in addition. Taken by surprise, most of Sumner's colleagues felt disinclined to argue with him. His motion was seconded by Joe Banks. David Adams withdrew his support of Watts's motion and backed Sumner's amendment; however Watts stuck to the 36s demand and Hubbart supported him. In the end Sumner's amendment was carried by eight votes to seven, those in favour being Adams, Banks, Fleming, Kelly, both Lansburys, Partridge and Sumner himself. Those against were Watts, Baker, Hubbart, Helen McKay, Julia Scurr and two non-Labour guardians. Sumner's motion was finally carried as a substantive motion by twelve votes to one with Julia Scurr and Helen McKay abstaining.

Sumner's move reflected his whole approach to the political scene. As a trade union official he was struggling against unprecedented pressure from employers to force down wages. He knew the strong temptations to undercut which faced the unemployed. He said later that all his days were spent fighting against wage reductions and that these would be even larger were it not for the fact that the unemployed were getting some sort of decent treatment. He believed that 'workmen had been pushed into the unemployed market to bring wages down as low as possible and he and others had decided from that moment that in default of work those out of work should be properly maintained'.[11] Edgar Lansbury also defended the decision; he said he voted for the £2 for a man and wife because he believed that once the Government and the nation realised that it cost more money to keep people unemployed than at work, they would very soon find useful work for them.[11] The truth was that faced with having to take a public attitude the majority of the Guardians had not wanted to appear as though they thought £2 was too much for a man and wife.

However, in his eagerness Sumner had broken two guiding rules normally followed by the Poplar Labour group. One was never to give a promise which could not be carried out. The other was to be careful to consult with members before giving a lead.

The decision was, of course, the signal for furious attacks on Poplar in the newspapers, which were all the more virulent because Poplar had never been forgiven for emerging as the victor from its previous struggle. *The Times* devoted a leading article to the issue on 28 January. How is it to be expected, it said, that the unemployed will look for work and accept it if it comes their way, when a man and his wife can get £2 a week besides extra allowances for rent and coal, etc., for nothing? 'They must be good men indeed to stand such a test.' A few days later there was another leading article: 'The average human being who can get something for nothing will not in any class go out of his way to search for work.' It accused the Poplar Guardians of creating 'an army of wastrels'.[12]

The Poplar Municipal Alliance was immediately on the war-path. George Armstrong & Co., a firm in the Isle of Dogs, wrote a hostile letter to the Board of Guardians:

Dear Sir,
    Our employees who live in Poplar have pointed out to us that they can get more money by being unemployed than working for us and as we have no wish to prevent them from getting as much as possible we propose to dismiss them so that they can take advantage of your relief.[13]

George Lansbury, who had personally regarded the Poplar decision as a tactical mistake, did not hesitate to defend it. In a letter to *The Times* he argued that the real danger the nation had to fear was the wholesale demoralisation caused by unemployment itself.[14]

Sumner wrote to Mond on 30 January telling him of the new

scale which Poplar had adopted and making it clear that the prime consideration was the relationship between relief and wages:

> It is not in the power of the Guardians to alter the fact that independent workmen are receiving inadequate wages . . . this is no reason for giving less relief than will properly maintain the families on public assistance . . . the Guardians' opinion is that the working people are entitled to work or maintenance.[15]

The reply from the Ministry reflected the prevailing sense of outrage:

> The Minister understands that this scale is in excess of even the revised scale submitted at the Guardians meeting by the deputation to which you refer. It is in excess of any scale in force either in the Metropolis or in the Provinces. And it appears to be admitted by the Guardians themselves that it is in excess of what is required for the relief of destitution.

The last sentence in the letter contained a threat:

> Inasmuch as the legal powers and duties of the Guardians are limited to the relief of destitution, the grant of allowances in accordance with the scale proposed will be unlawful.[16]

Whether or not the new scales were 'unlawful' was a matter which the Guardians might have been tempted to dispute. But the fact was that within a week other circumstances had forced them to abandon their new scale. Their difficulty was that the Board had not got enough money to operate it and there seemed no way of raising it speedily.

The funds at their disposal on the face of it consisted of an allocation from the Common Poor Fund together with the proceeds of the rate levied on their behalf by the borough council. Now, it was true that the new arrangement made as a result of their action the previous year enabled the Guardians to be paid back out of the Common Poor Fund any money spent on outrelief up to the level of the Mond scale. But this had turned out to be less simple than it sounded. The claims for repayment had to be made after the end of the financial half year. In anticipation of refunds which would be due to them at the end of March, the Guardians were allowed to borrow, provided they got the permission of the Ministry of Health. Thus they had got permission in December to borrow £146,000 due to be refunded later; in addition to this they had received £61,000 from the rate levied on their behalf. But they discovered that even if their scales remained as they were this money would not take them to the end of March; they would require a further overdraft which could only be obtained if the Ministry sanctioned it. They could expect no additional help out of the rates until the next quarter's rate was due to be levied. In normal circumstances the Minister could be expected to give loan sanction for a sum which would one day be refunded from the Common Poor Fund. But if by any chance the Minister hesitated they would face a financial crisis. And since they were in the middle of a row with him, it was obvious that he would not easily grant them the necessary borrowing power.

It was at this stage that the Clerk to the Board told Sumner that if the new scale were operated their funds would be exhausted by the first week in March and there would be no money left to give any relief to anybody, nor would they be able to pay the staff's wages. Here then were the difficulties foreseen by George Lansbury. With great reluctance Sumner summoned a special meeting of the Board for 31 January at which Mond's letter was read and the Clerk's figures examined. Chris Kelly moved that the scale adopted the previous week be rescinded since it was 'impracticable and unfair'. This was seconded by Partridge. George Lansbury, anxious to put the best face possible on retreat, moved an amendment that the new scale should not operate at present. That would give time to consider the position, he said. They knew they were up against both the bank and the Ministry, but he was not going to be jumped into rescinding the scale until he knew there was no other way. The Government had them in a corner now, he said, but they could have the Government in a corner on another day. The amendment was carried, after which it was agreed that the Ministry be asked for permission to raise a further loan of £56,000.

Representatives of the national press had attended the meeting and next day reported the proceedings under triumphant headlines such as POPLAR'S CLIMB DOWN. One week later the papers had an even more enjoyable time. Some hundreds of young employed, angry at the Guardians' decision to withdraw their new scales, arrived at a Board meeting, occupied the building and laid siege to the Guardians, refusing to let them leave. Since the Guardians would not send for the police there was deadlock for several hours. Mrs Melvina Walker, a well known local activist,[17] denounced the Guardians saying: 'You appear to be hopeless and are merely the bulwark between us and the capitalist class to keep us in subjection.'[18] At this Julia Scurr lost patience and said that the members of the deputation were cowards who would not turn out to fight the real enemy but would threaten their best friends. George Lansbury, adept at defusing quarrels, said: 'If we are going to sit here all night we're not going to have speeches. Let's have a song.' Thereafter, as well as argument there was singing and dancing. In the end the Guardians were allowed to leave at 4.30 a.m. *The Times* reported the affair with relish: 'It is the fate of extremists to find their actions challenged by others more extreme than themselves.'[19]

Despite its retreat to its former scales of relief, the press appeared reluctant to abandon Poplar as a target; it was continually held up as an example of frenzied finance, with liberal use of such words as 'spendthrift', 'feckless', 'lax', and 'lavish'. Shortly afterwards the word 'Poplarism' began to be used as a term of contempt, and even found its way into the *Oxford New English Dictionary* where it was defined as 'the policy of giving out-relief on a generous or extravagant scale . . . and later any similar policy which lays a heavy burden on ratepayers.' The term was adopted by the Poplar Guardians with pride.

Sir Alfred Mond, the Minister of Health, did not feel he could let the matter of Poplar's behaviour drop. The affair had blown up at a time when Conservative impatience with the Lloyd George Coalition was beginning to erupt. Mond's method of settling the previous Poplar rebellion had not redounded to his credit in the eyes of either Conservatives or Liberals. Ironically he had then taken power to deal with any similar rebellion in the future with a firm hand; if a borough council ever again refused to collect the rates he was now empowered to install a Commissioner to do the job.[20] But as it turned out, this reserve power was no help in his present predicament. For the new quarrel was not with a borough council but a board of guardians which he had no authority to unseat. The traditional means of coercing awkward boards of guardians did not appear to be either suitable or effective in this case.

Now that Poplar had reverted to its original scale, Mond could have ignored the whole affair. But he chose not to; on

8 February he drafted a memorandum to put before the Home Affairs committee of the Cabinet.

Mond had been convinced that when the Guardians adopted their high scale on 25 January they were acting illegally, since he argued, their powers were limited to the 'relief of destitution' and anything given in excess of this was thought to be unlawful. But the term 'destitution' was not precisely defined, certainly not in terms of pounds, shillings and pence. And what was left unclear in Mond's new memorandum was whether he and his advisers thought that the original Poplar scale to which the Guardians had now reverted was also illegal. Since he repeatedly insisted that his own scale was sufficient to relieve destitution in all normal cases, it must be inferred that he regarded anything above it as an infringement of the law unless exceptional circumstances could be proved. But he hesitated to say so, and his hesitation was understandable. For the Poplar Guardians had been operating this same scale for a long time, all through the period when they were compelled by the Minister to report individually on each case in which out-relief had been granted to unemployed. The scale on which this out-relief had been administered had never been challenged by the Ministry and it was therefore possible for the Guardians to argue that it had been condoned.

Mond, in his memorandum to the Cabinet, now summed up the situation rather ambiguously:

> The position therefore is, first that the Poplar Guardians will be unable to charge on the Common Poor Fund any expenditure in excess of the prescribed scale, and secondly, that insofar as the relief given by them exceeds their legal powers, the expenditure will not be a lawful charge even on their local rates.[21]

But he failed to define these alleged legal powers which must not be exceeded.

He did, however, describe the powers available to him to deal with Poplar, and in so doing made clear that he did not believe they would be very effective. First he pointed out that if the Guardians persisted in granting relief in excess of their legal powers, the expenditure could be disallowed by the District Auditor and they could then be surcharged. But, 'in view of the sums involved and the financial status of the Guardians in question this remedy would not be very effective'.

He then considered another possible course of action: 'it would be open to any ratepayer to apply to the Courts for an injunction to restrain the Guardians.' But 'in the not improbable event of the Guardians disobeying the order from the Court we should merely have a repetition of the imprisonment of Mr Lansbury and his colleagues last year'.

He had come to the conclusion that the most effective weapon was finance, since the Guardians could only carry on by means of borrowed money and could not borrow without his (Mond's) sanction. And he would clearly not be justified in sanctioning a further loan except on condition that the Guardians adhered to a reasonable scale of relief. He felt bound, however, to recognise the possibility that the Guardians might refuse to accept his condition and that there might be 'a consequent deadlock in administration'.

He therefore made two proposals. One was to conduct an inquiry into the Poplar Guardians' expenditure. The other was to give himself much stronger legal powers. He advocated a Bill enabling him to suspend boards of guardians and appoint an administrator in their place.

The Cabinet Committee agreed that Mond should prepare such a Bill, which he did. It came before the committee on 14 February and they authorised him to introduce it in the House of Commons. But they patently had doubts concerning the wisdom of such a course. For it was also agreed that Mond should avoid introducing the Bill if it were 'reasonably possible.'[22] Indeed, Mond himself by this time clearly regarded the Bill as a last resort; he said that it might not be necessary to introduce it and he would not do so if it could be avoided.

Meanwhile Mond began to apply pressure through his control of the Guardians' borrowing powers. As mentioned earlier, Poplar had applied for permission to raise a further overdraft of £56,000 to see it through to the end of March. But Mond replied that he was prepared to authorise a further overdraft of not more than £25,000 *if* the Guardians would undertake not to increase their scale of outdoor relief. He also told them that he intended to hold a special inquiry into their expenditure.

Although £25,000 was less than half the money the Guardians required, they wrote back to Mond saying that they were 'willing and anxious to give every facility to anyone appointed by the Minister to inquire into their financial position.' They adroitly expressed their pleasure at the continued sanction of their Board's present scale of relief, declaring that they had 'no intention of departing from their present practice in administering this scale.'[23] Mond, of course, felt compelled to reply that he could not accept the suggestion that he had ever approved Poplar's present scale. To this Sumner instantly wrote back accusing the Minister of 'down-right moral cowardice', and pointing out that all individual cases reported by Poplar in the past on the basis of this scale had been approved by the Minister.[24]

At the beginning of March the Poplar Board was told that a Mr H. I. Cooper, Clerk to the Bolton Board of Guardians, had been appointed to hold the promised inquiry into Poplar's administration. This news was received with some indignation. It was a period when the standards and attitudes of boards of guardians were beginning to change. Some boards were frantically clinging to the old deterrent practices enjoined on them since 1834, and were doing their best to adhere to the doctrine of 'less eligibility'. But such an approach was being increasingly challenged and discarded, and some Guardians were moving slowly, if not in Poplar's revolutionary direction, at least in a much more compassionate one.

However, the Bolton Board of Guardians was renowned for its adherence to the narrow viewpoints of 1834, and the Clerk to the Board was likely to be of the same mind. 'When we agreed to give facilities for an inquiry we never for a moment contemplated that you intended putting an employee of another Board of Guardians to investigate the work of this Board,' wrote Sumner to Mond. 'I desire to put on record the most emphatic protest possible against so insulting a proposal as that which you have levelled against us as a Board.'[25]

It looked as though Mond's brush with Poplar and the appointment of Cooper had been timed to have some influence on the local elections. Those for the London County Council were due in March; those for the boards of guardians in the first week in April. In both elections the Municipal Reformers (Conservatives) concentrated on three main lines of attack. One was to link the London Labour Party with 'Bolshevism'.[26] The second line of attack concerned the indifference of the Labour Party to economical administration. The third target was Poplarism.

Once more Herbert Morrison and his colleagues were put in the embarrassing position of being identified with Poplar policies of which they strongly disapproved. For, as with the rates protest, the London Labour Party had been divided in its attitude to Poplar's stand on relief scales for the unemployed. But as compared with the rates revolt, there was a good deal less sympathy for Poplar, and there was no doubt that a large number of members had been critical of Sumner's original resolution for £2 for man and wife. At a conference of the London Labour Party called to discuss policy for the LCC elections some hard things were said against Poplar. One delegate was alleged to have stated that he did not mind a man committing suicide, but he objected to him murdering other people first, and this was the position in which Poplar had placed the party in London.[27] At the same time a letter from the secretary of the Bermondsey and Rotherhithe Trades Council had appeared in the *Daily Herald* on 1 February declaring that Poplar's new scale would give more to the unemployed than to the average family in work and that the Poplar Guardians had been irresponsible and played into the hands of the Northcliffe press. As we have seen, the high scale so criticised had been abandoned within a week, but the accusations continued.

Morrison's response to the attacks on Poplarism was to devote the bulk of his propaganda for the LCC elections to proving that Labour did not raise the rates and that, thanks to the efficiency of Labour control, the ratepayers' interests were better looked after in Labour boroughs than elsewhere. This defensive line of propaganda did not appear to inspire his supporters, judging by the results. For the Labour Party which had hoped to make progress in this election, merely increased the number of its LCC seats by one to sixteen. J. H. Thomas, general secretary of the National Union of Railwaymen and leading Labour figure, put the blame on Poplar for this failure to advance:

> Many of our political opponents will construe the election as a rebellion on the part of the people against Labour policy . . . I do not interpret the result as a determination on the part of the people not to trust Labour, but I do frankly admit that it is a revolt against the kind of Poplar methods of administration which certainly alarmed people.[28]

John Scurr wrote an indignant reply to Thomas in the *Daily Herald*: 'I notice that J. H. Thomas has joined the capitalist and landlord chorus which exists to denounce the methods of Poplar Labour men and women . . . Mr Thomas must try again. . . . Out of sixteen elected, Poplar can claim six as their very own.'[29] The six were the four sitting councillors for the two Poplar constituencies (Charles Sumner, Edward Cruse, Sam March and Susan Lawrence) all of whom achieved big increases in their former majorities; A. A. Watts, who did the same in North Battersea, and Chris Kelly who stood for Whitechapel and won it for Labour for the first time. It was indeed arguable that the exponents of 'Poplarism' did better than most Labour candidates.

The press campaign against Poplarism intensified in preparation for the elections to the Boards of Guardians at the beginning of April. *The Times*, for example, published a special article on 'Spendthrift Boards of Guardians' which referred to 'fantastic and extravagant schemes of relief of which Poplar has given a recent and striking example,' saying that the demand that those out of work should get as much as those in work would 'lead to the collapse of industry and national bankruptcy'.[30] By the end of March *The Times* was linking Poplar with sinister Communist plots:

> The Communists' approval of the policy recently pursued by the Poplar Guardians clearly shows that they desire extravagant expenditure not because of their sympathy for the poor and unemployed, but because they believe that ruinous finance will produce a state of chaos which would lead to the destruction of the present social organisation of this country.[31]

No doubt in the hope of countering such propaganda the London Labour Party executive on 9 March decided to circulate to local parties a draft election address for Labour Guardians compiled by Dr Salter of Bermondsey which, instead of following the previous resolution and attacking the Mond scale as 'inadequate', promised on the contrary to use it as a basis. The draft began by saying that Labour looked forward to the abolition of the Poor Law and the establishment of schemes on a national basis.

> Till that day arises we would administer the existing poor law system generously and humanely while at the same time exercising

proper discretion and economy . . . The Ministry of Health has laid down a fixed scale of Out-Relief and, if this is adopted by Boards of Guardians the relief given will be chargeable to a Fund common to the whole Metropolis. We shall utilise this official scale as a basis and shall adhere to it as a general rule, but shall exercise discretion in exceeding it according to the human needs and necessities of each particular case. In determining the amount to be paid to an applicant however we shall always ensure that it bears a proper relation to the whole family income from all sources, and that the sum total does not exceed the average rate of wages paid in the district to workmen in work.[32]

This attempt to prove to ratepayers that Labour Guardians combined a humane approach with a keen sense of responsibility did not appear to have much effect. There was a more than usually vigorous campaign by the Municipal Reformers (Conservatives) and Progressives (Liberals) in London as a whole and in Poplar itself by the Municipal Alliance. Perhaps because of this campaign the poll rose in Guardians' elections from about 7 per cent in April 1919 to nearly 23 per cent in 1922 over London as a whole. The results confirmed Morrison's worst fears that the trends shown in the LCC elections would be repeated. Taking all the London boards of guardians together Labour had a net loss of eighteen seats, winning 125 as compared with 143 in 1919. Moreover Labour emerged with a majority on two boards only instead of the previous three.

But in Poplar, which was of course one of the two (the other was Shoreditch) the percentage going to the poll was the highest in London: 43·2 per cent. And here Labour increased its representation on the Board of Guardians from sixteen to twenty-one. The Municipal Alliance members were reduced to three. Most of the Labour candidates got over 1,000 votes in place of the hundreds they had received three years earlier, and Julia Scurr and David Adams each got over 2,000.

George Lansbury underlined the irony of these results in a special article in the *Daily Herald*:

The Guardians' elections have once more proved the power of the Gramophone press. With one single voice during the past six months this press has, morning, noon and night, proclaimed to the world that Poplar Labour men and women were either fools or knaves, that the ratepayers were ruined, and any district electing Labour members would be in an equally sad plight. In most places this malignant lying has done its deadly work; in Poplar itself, where people are supposed to be groaning under the iron heel of ruthless Bolshevism, the electors by a record vote, return 21 Labour men and women out of a total of 24.

It is only outside Poplar that Poplar's woes appear to be realised. Poplar Labour people won their tremendous triumph at the LCC and Guardians elections because the ratepayers knew by their rent-books and rate receipts that the morning and evening stunt Press were simply lying. In other places, the damnable iteration about 'Poplar's bankruptcy and frenzied finance' deceived thousands of people, some of the 'very elect' even being carried away by the mere repetition.[33]

NOTES

1. ELA, 12 November 1921.
2. *The Abolition of Destitution and Unemployment*, Report of a London Conference published by the National Labour Press, 1910.
3. 'Out-relief' was relief given in cash or kind to people living in their own homes. 'Indoor relief' was that given in an institution.
4. ELA, 29 October 1921.
5. Metropolitan Common Poor Fund (Outdoor Relief) Regulations 1922; Ministry of Health Circular 276, S.R. and O. 1922, No. 3.
6. Defined in the Order as the rate for workpeople in Grade 'A' under the agreement of the London District Industrial Council for Non-trading Services (Manual labour).
7. London Labour Party, folios 874, 875.
8. *Poor Law Officers Journal*, 3 February 1922.
9. BGM, 25 January 1922.
10. ibid.
11. DH, 1 and 2 February 1922.
12. *The Times*, 1 February 1922.
13. Letter quoted in the Cooper Report, see Chapter 9.
14. *The Times*, 30 January 1922.
15. BGM, 31 January 1922.
16. ibid.
17. Mrs Melvina Walker was a colleague of Sylvia Pankhurst. The latter had participated in the formation of the Communist Party in 1920, but had since parted company with it.
18. DH, 8 February 1922.
19. *The Times*, 8 February 1922.
20. Under the Local Government Financial Provisions Act, 1921.
21. PRO, Cab 24/132. CP 3694.
22. PRO Cab 23/29 Committee of Home Affairs 104, 14 February 1922.
23. *Poor Law Officers Journal*, 24 February 1922.
24. ibid.
25. ibid.

26. A link emphasised by Lord Peel at an eve-of-poll meeting and the subject of a leader in *The Times* which quoted him as saying that the Labour programme for the LCC had a 'foreign flavour about it and seems to have emanated from the desolate regions of Russia, which have been wrecked by communist fury. . . . Today the electors are free to choose between potential Bolshevists in Labour Socialist clothing and the tried supporters of our British system of representative democratic government' (*The Times*, 2 March 1922).
27. *The Times*, 30 January 1922.
28. Speech at Bromley, *The Times*, 6 March 1922.
29. DH, 7 March 1922.
30. *The Times*, 10 March 1922.
31. ibid., 23 March 1922.
32. LLP, Folios 993 and 986.
33. DH, 8 April 1922.

9

'Guilty and Proud of It'

H. I. Cooper, Clerk to the Bolton Guardians, had arrived in Poplar on 13 March to begin his special inquiry into the Guardians' expenditure on behalf of the Ministry of Health. Aware that the Guardians had denounced his appointment as 'insulting', he found the hostile relations between himself and those he was supposed to investigate confirmed on the day after his arrival. He had invited Sumner, as chairman of the Guardians and Mayor of the Borough, to meet him, but according to his account of the interview, given some time afterwards, George Lansbury, though uninvited, accompanied Sumner and was 'most abusive. He entirely lost control of himself and threatened I would not be allowed to do what he termed the dirty work of a dirty government. He then instructed the clerk to see that two guardians were present during any interviews I had with others. . . . After the first afternoon, no guardians attended.'[1]

According to Sumner's version of the interview, he protested to Cooper at the way the inquiry was to be conducted and told him it should have been undertaken by an inspector from the Ministry. To which Cooper replied that the Ministry 'had not got an official capable of it'.[2]

According to Lansbury, they asked Cooper how he was going to conduct the inquiry: 'He did not want to know anything from us. We were the people he was investigating, and all he wanted was access to our books. He never attended a single relief committee, never attended any committee of the Board, never went anywhere where the Guardians were doing their work.'[3]

That Cooper never consulted any member of the Board he was supposed to be investigating seems indisputable; indeed he carefully kept away from the Guardians, confining his inquiries to the books and records to which he was given access. To a later generation, such behaviour would have seemed rather odd. But at the time Labour majorities were new, and neither civil servants nor administrators had quite accustomed themselves to the idea that some pretence of impartiality was required when dealing with Labour members of elected bodies.

Cooper's attitude towards the Municipal Alliance was in marked contrast to his treatment of the Labour Guardians. As soon as he arrived in Poplar he contacted the Alliance's secretary, Sir Alfred Warren. He had two interviews with Warren, for one of which he went to the Municipal Alliance's headquarters at 52 Bow Road (owned by Bryant and May but rented by them to the Municipal Alliance) and on both occasions showed himself anxious to fall in with Warren's wishes.

Warren had indeed been actively engaged in organising a movement of protest against the Guardians among Poplar employers. He had begun with a letter to Mond on 27 January in which 'on behalf of a very large body of the largest ratepayers in this Borough' he had urged Mond to refuse Poplar's request for an overdraft.[4] In contrast to his treatment of the London Labour Party's request for a discussion, Mond had been most accommodating. He had sent Warren copies of his correspondence with the Guardians and suggested that he might like to come to the Ministry to discuss the matter. The upshot had been a deputation representing Poplar firms on 20 February when a petition was placed before Mond voicing complaints and calling for a 'very exhaustive enquiry by your Department' into the proceedings of the Guardians.[5] Shortly afterwards they had been told that their request was granted and an inquiry would be held.

Since Warren had originally asked for the inquiry to be in public, one of the first things Cooper wanted to know on his arrival in Poplar was whether he still wished for this. Warren put off his decision until after the Guardians' elections in which, despite his efforts, the Municipal Alliance seats were reduced to three out of twenty-four. By this time Warren had realised that a public inquiry would be unwise. He and the chairman of the Municipal Alliance explained to Cooper that 'in view of the difficulty of obtaining persons to give evidence owing to the disturbed conditions existing in the Parish at the time, they did not feel justified in proceeding with the application which they had made for such an inquiry.'[6] Cooper instantly concurred.

The decision to avoid a public inquiry was no doubt a

prudent one, since the Guardians could have made a great occasion of it to the enjoyment of the populace. However the Cooper report makes clear that this decision was taken, not by the Ministry of Health or even by Cooper himself, but by the Poplar Municipal Alliance. Cooper, indeed, left himself wide open to the charge, made later by the Guardians, that 'he made a private and one-sided inquiry, and apparently his reason for doing so was to satisfy a discredited political organisation which has been repudiated repeatedly by the overwhelming majority of the people of Poplar'.[7]

The report was completed on 10 May, but, in line with Cooper's practice throughout, was not shown to the Board members who, had they seen it, could have corrected some of the factual errors and distortions it contained.[8] Instead it was printed and released to the press on the evening of Thursday 18 May so that long summaries of it appeared in the newspapers on Friday 19 May, though the Clerk to the Poplar Guardians did did not receive a copy until Monday 22 May, when it arrived through the post. One newspaper, the *Pall Mall Gazette*, appeared to have received a copy even before 18 May. Some time later the Guardians had the chance to complain personally to Mond about the way his Ministry had made the report public. Albert Baker said to him: 'Do you think this is fair treatment? I have to work in a large yard with a large body of men and sit there at meals with a newspaper on the table. I could not answer the thing because I had not had it.'[9] Mond's somewhat lame reply was that he had given instructions that the report was to be sent to them at the same time as it was given to the press and that it was a 'slight accident' that the press got it on the Thursday night. When he was asked how it was that its contents had been leaked to the *Pall Mall Gazette* even before the Thursday he said: 'The press get hold of a good deal of information – information for which I am not responsible.'

It had been repeatedly hinted that the report, when it appeared, would uncover some horrific scandal. Once before, in 1906, allegations about drinking orgies and jobbery over contracts had accompanied an inquiry into the Guardians' affairs. But so far as this report was concerned, such evidence was conspicuous by its absence. Indeed the Board's members appeared to be nothing if not high-minded. Cooper was not only unable to accuse them of corrupt practices; he was unable to charge them with any clear breach of the law. What he could and did say was that the policy adopted by the Poplar Board of Guardians was 'in many instances foreign to the spirit and intention of the Poor Law Statutes'. What he meant by this he illustrated in some detail.

He alleged that the relief scale in operation in Poplar was 'too generous' and, moreover, was not regarded as a maximum but was granted in full to all cases. So far as the able-bodied unemployed were concerned, he complained that before awarding relief no attempt had been made to put into force any labour test. And there had been no attempt, either, to discriminate between 'those of the unemployed who were deserving and those who were undeserving.'

In applying the scale to families of more than seven persons, the Guardians had failed to comply with the principle that 'the amount of Relief under the Poor Law should, of necessity, be calculated on a lower scale than the earnings of an independent workman who maintains himself by his labour'. As we have seen, the interpretation of this rule under the Mond scale was that no family should get more than £2 14s a week whatever its size. But, as an example of Poplar's disregard of this rule, Cooper cited the case of an unemployed stevedore with a wife and nine dependent children. The relief granted for this family of eleven was £4 7s, yet when the man was working he earned no more than £4 4s 6d – less than the relief granted. Therefore he was better off on relief than while working.

Much of the report concerned the Guardians' treatment of resources of parents and/or children. They had made 'insufficient deductions of childrens' earnings in calculating the allowance' so that relief had been granted 'in cases in which no real destitution exists'. An example was that of an unemployed dock labourer with a wife and seven dependent children, and another two elder children earning respectively 15s and 14s a week. The husband was drawing unemployment benefit of £1 7s, making an income of £2 16s for this family of eleven persons. The Guardians granted relief of £2 1s 0d in addition, making the total for this family £4 17s.

Another case quoted by Cooper was that of an unemployed man and his wife with no dependent children, but one son earning £3 5s a week. Here again 'no real destitution' existed, yet the Guardians had given the parents 11s a week out-relief.

What appeared to be the most flagrant case of this kind was that of an unemployed man and his wife with four adult single daughters, each earning 30s a week, thus bringing £6 a week into the household. Relief of £1 5s was accorded to the man and his wife.

Not only were parents failing to live on their children, but children were not being obliged to live on their parents. 'There are many cases on the Guardians' books of boys and girls as young as sixteen years living with their parents being granted relief of 10s od per week, although the total income of the household exceeds £2 14s od per week.'

When it came to widows with children 'only one half of any earnings of the woman are deducted from the amount due under the scale'. Thus a widow with five dependent children who earned £1 16s was given £1 10s relief.

Apart from the weekly allowances, boots and clothing could be provided at the discretion of the relief committes and over a twelve month period, 13,255 pairs of boots had been granted and clothing and bedding to the value of £529 5s 2d. 'The clothing is not marked and could be pawned or sold without a chance of detection.' The Guardians had refrained from prosecuting various people who had concealed the fact that they were earning while drawing relief. Such people had been merely cautioned and their relief cancelled.

The Guardians had spent £3,000 at Christmas time on extra Christmas allowances of 5s per adult and 2s per child, given to everyone on relief. They had sent 140 children of families on relief for a fortnight's holiday to their Poor Law school at Shenfield during the summer. In addition to maintaining them they had spent £18 in conveying them there and back. The children had been nominated by the district Medical Officer who had been asked to select those in need of a holiday. Cooper said:

> The sending away of children of outdoor relief recipients for a summer holiday at the expense of the rates is, I think, a new departure in the Poor Law. I have little doubt that there are in the Poplar District many children whose parents are not in receipt of relief, who cannot afford to send their children away for a holiday, and I think that the ratepayers should not be called upon to bear this extra expenditure in respect of outdoor relief children.

On outdoor relief in general, Cooper summed up:

> The lavish allowances of outdoor relief encourage persons to apply who would not otherwise do so and it is made altogether too easy for persons to obtain assistance from the Guardians. The Guardians' policy has a tendency to demoralise the recipients and is calculated to destroy incentive to thrift, self-reliance and industry.

Cooper also criticised the treatment of the 800 inmates of the Poplar workhouse. The diet was 'too liberal'[10] – among other things the Guardians had substituted butter for margarine at an extra annual cost of £600. Those inmates who were able to work were employed in serving meals, making beds, laundry work, window cleaning on the ground floor and as messengers, 'but the amount of work required from them is slight'. On the other hand, those unable to work were allowed to be absent from the workhouse after breakfast until 9 p.m. daily:

> All the inmates who go out are allowed to return to the Institution for their meals if they so desire, and I am informed that practically the whole of them do so. The Institution is regarded more as an almshouse than a workhouse.

Another main criticism of Poplar's indoor relief arrangements was that the establishments were overstaffed. Cooper found that eighteen paid scrubbers were employed at the Institution, but he had been told that if this number were reduced by six, the work they were doing could be done by inmates. He said that the Guardians had taken the view that if they dispensed with the services of these scrubbers they would have to give them outdoor relief. Cooper commented:

> If this did happen it is doubtful whether the relief would amount to as much as the wages (£2 1s per week each) the women are receiving, and the women would, if placed on the Outdoor Relief List, have more time to attend to their children and their homes.

Cooper emphasised the fact that nearly two-thirds of the rates in Poplar were paid by non-residential occupiers, i.e. railways, canals, and docks, factories, wharves, warehouses, shops and pubs. These occupiers 'pay rates but are practically not represented on the Electorate'. This point, which had no bearing on the matters into which he was inquiring, was seized on by Warren and the Municipal Alliance and was to be stressed in public statements thereafter. Finally Cooper thought that with 'careful administration' a saving of at least £100,000 per annum would result.

It was clear from this report that Cooper was a firm supporter of the old Poor Law methods, many of which had in fact been criticised by the members of both the majority and minority of the Royal Commission on the Poor Law in 1909, a Commission of which George Lansbury had himself been a member. Sir Alfred Mond, however, received the Report with much satisfaction. Before it was published he put in a memorandum to the Cabinet saying that, in view of what it contained, 'I have little doubt that public opinion will support any action which the Government may think proper to take.' He thought he should do what lay in his power to reform Poplar's administration and, since the Poplar Board was among those to whom he was obliged to advance loans to meet current expenditure, he proposed to refuse any further loans until he had some assurance that 'the Guardians are prepared to mend their ways'. If the Guardians declined to give such an assurance it would be necessary, he thought, to introduce the Bill, for which he had already received provisional approval, empowering him to suspend the Board of Guardians and appoint others to take their place.[11]

In a letter to the Guardians enclosing the Cooper Report dated 19 May, Mond asserted that the grant of relief in cases where there was no destitution was unlawful. On the other hand by adherence to recognised principles 'the guardians could check the progressive demoralisation of the poor of the parish and could afford a much needed encouragement to those who have persisted in reliance upon their own thrift and industry'. Therefore, he trusted the Guardians would set on foot the reforms advocated by Cooper and he looked to 'receive from them within a month a statement of the action they proposed to take'. He also said that it would not be possible for him to make further advances of public money unless they brought their policy into conformity with the principles and procedures accepted by other boards of guardians. In response to a question in the House, Sir Alfred caused the whole of this very long letter to be reproduced in *Hansard*.[12]

The Poplar Guardians were thus faced with a declaration from the Minister that much of the relief they were dispensing was illegal, a demand from him that they 'mend their ways' and a threat that unless they did so he would cut off their funds.

The Guardians considered this letter at their meeting on 24 May. Since their election in April, Edgar Lansbury had succeeded Sumner as chairman of the Board. Now at this first meeting after publication of the Cooper Report, Edgar announced that they would go on with their present scale of relief as long as they could; it remained to be seen, he said, whether those above them would be able to stop them.[13]

They appointed a sub-committee to draft a reply to Cooper; this was ready within a week and was published as a 2d pamphlet entitled *Guilty and Proud of It: Poplar's Answer*. In this pamphlet they challenged the whole philosophy on which the Poor Law had been based for nearly a hundred years. They attacked all the 'recognised principles' which the Ministry, with Mond at its head, had sought to preserve.

They opened with a new concept of Guardians' responsibilities:

> The people of Poplar have steadily supported the view that the duty of members of the Board of Guardians is to be Guardians of the POOR and not the Guardians of the interests of property. In Poplar there is no cringing or whining on the part of those who apply for public assistance . . . Relief is accepted without shame or regret – in fact, in exactly the same spirit as that in which ex-Cabinet ministers, Royalties, and others accept their pensions and allowances from the Government. In Poplar it is well understood that the poor are poor because they are robbed, and are robbed because they are poor.

Of Cooper himself they said:

> He belongs to the old school of Poor Law administrators who believe that poverty is a crime and that no relief should be given except under degrading and severely deterrent conditions. . . . That is the charge against Poplar – that it refuses to treat poverty as a crime and paupers as criminals. Worse, it has succeeded in its campaign to compel the richer Boroughs to take up a portion of their fair share in the work of relief. *To that double charge and all that it involves, Poplar, we repeat, is proud to plead guilty.*

The inquiry, they alleged, was undertaken purely for political propaganda, because the Poplar labour movement was a 'growing danger to continued capitalist government' not merely because of what it had done but because of the example it set and the encouragement it gave to militant Labour everywhere.

To the charge that they failed to discriminate between deserving and undeserving they replied that their duty was 'to care for the poor, to relieve the destitute, but not to act as a judge of moral character or social desirability of particular individuals'. To accuse them, they said, of granting relief strictly in accordance with their scale, was to accuse them of doing their duty as fairly and justly as possible. Defending their habit of giving more to the larger families, they characterised the Mond scale as 'illogical and indefensible', since it allowed £2 12s to relieve a man, wife and five children, but only £2 14s to relieve man, wife and ten children. 'Not even the great business ability of a Sir Alfred Mond could accomplish the task of feeding and clothing the extra 5 children on a total extra income of 2s a week.'

They declared their opposition to the theory that the amount of relief should always be on a lower scale than the earnings of an independent labourer:

> Poplar has fought strenuously against the damnable doctrine that because a sweated worker and his family starve slowly in the employ of a greedy profit-monger, they should as a matter of course be made to starve more quickly under the care of the Guardians of the Poor.

They denounced the practice of taking children's earnings wholly into account when assessing the relief to be given to father, mother and younger brothers and sisters, arguing that such a policy would, in Cooper's own words, be 'calculated to destroy the incentive to thrift, self-reliance and industry'. In support of their practice of issuing boots they said that their relief scales were inadequate to buy them.

They had fun over Cooper's charge that they had sent 140 children of families on relief for a summer holiday: 'Did ever Board of Guardians commit so heinous an offence! . . . We cannot defend ourselves against this charge. We are guilty.' They scored over the case of the stevedore with nine children, held up by Cooper as a man who was getting more on relief than he could earn. Did this man become 'demoralised'? On the contrary he was only on relief for one week, and went back to work the week after. 'The only possible explanation of Mr Cooper's omission to state the full facts of the case is that they would have destroyed his argument that the workers of Poplar will not seek work while they can get out-door relief.'

On the charge that the Poplar Institution was regarded more as an almshouse than a workhouse, they said they were 'very glad indeed'.

It is hard indeed that men and women who have spent their lives grinding out profits for other people should have to end their days in an institution of any sort; but what must be the misery of those unfortunate ones who are driven by starvation or sickness in their old age to seek the prison-like shelter of workhouses organised according to the ideas of Sir Alfred Mond?

Describing how efforts had been made to set workers against one another, 'the employed against the unemployed, the deserving against the undeserving, and the healthy against the sick,' they ended with an appeal to the workers all over the country to help them in their fight:

The day for a deterrent Poor Law policy is past. . . . Our work in Poplar will not be finished until we have compelled the Government itself to face the problem of unemployment by providing full and adequate maintenance for those for whom there is no work.

The issue of this pamphlet was not a very encouraging sign to Mond who was expecting a reply to his letter of 19 May; while still waiting he continued his attempt to coerce Poplar by means of a financial squeeze. At the beginning of June, Poplar asked for sanction to borrow a further £100,000 for which they could anticipate a refund from the MCPF after 30 September, but Mond withheld permission. Sir Reginald Blair, Conservative MP for the Bow and Bromley Division of Poplar, began to harass Mond with hostile questions in the House. He pointed out that 14,000 of Poplar's voters were on outdoor relief, and when Mond said that he had no power to prevent people on outdoor relief from voting, Blair said rudely: 'Is the right hon baronet's policy to do nothing until some unconstitutional action takes place and then bring in panicky legislation?'[14]

The Municipal Alliance was meanwhile writing to Mond urging him to bring in a Bill enabling him to take over control of the Poor Law in Poplar.[15] This was, indeed, what Mond had intended to do; he had earlier received provisional approval for just such a Bill. But he now ran up against an unexpected difficulty. Parliamentary business had become so congested that on 13 June the Home Affairs Committee of the Cabinet found itself obliged to rethink its timetable. It appeared that unless some Bills were dropped it would be necessary to sit well into the middle of August. The committee agreed that no further legislation of a controversial kind should be authorised unless it was a matter of urgency.[16]

The Bill to suspend boards of guardians was highly controversial and it is not surprising that Mond in this situation failed to press for it. Discussing the Poplar situation with the full Cabinet on 16 June at a moment when it was already clear that Poplar would resist any reduction in their scales of relief, Mond said that 'it was not improbable certain difficult and troublesome questions might come up for decision'.[17] The Cabinet merely decided that he should have discretion to deal with the Poplar case.

The Poplar Guardians were meanwhile still considering their next move. They believed that their administration of the Poor Law had the support of their electors. Should Mond obtain definite legal powers to enforce his lower scale and rigorous rules they would not be afraid to break the letter of the law. On the other hand, if he succeeded in depriving them of the funds to carry on, their cause would be in jeopardy.

On 14 June they approved a 'reasoned answer' to Mond. In this they denied that lower allowances would bring adequate relief. The suggestion that they were 'manufacturing paupers' was, they said, 'ridiculous' as there were large numbers of unemployed people in the area who had not asked for relief. They denied that Mond's powers gave him the right to enforce his scale as a maximum; if he claimed this right he should do so by a definite Order and take the responsibility instead of adopting the 'illegal course' of depriving them of loans to which they were entitled. They therefore asked once more for an advance of £100,000, said that if the money was not made available they would not have the means to go on with the Poor Law service, and proposed a meeting between the Minister and the Board to try to avoid an impasse.[18]

The Guardians were of course actively explaining their case throughout the East End of London. On 15 June they addressed a rally at the Mile End Assembly Hall attended by 10,000 people, several thousand of whom had marched in procession from Poplar with bands and banners. Edgar Lansbury made a lengthy statement explaining the position. The expression 'Poplarism', he said, was used as a bogey to frighten people. Poplar was poor but honest. Its public men were trying to do what was right for the destitute in their midst. He raised a laugh when he described Poplar as a place where 'people who could afford to live out of it would not be found dead in it'. When boards of guardians neglected the poor and the sick there was no inquiry, but when it was alleged that there was a lavish scale of relief the higher authorities came on the scene with objections. He explained that the Minister of Health was refusing to sanction loans to which the Guardians were entitled and said that if Mond persisted in this, Poplar would take care that the money collected in the borough should be used locally. At the end of the meeting a resolution was carried pledging support for the Poplar Board of Guardians in any action they might take.[19]

The Guardians and councillors were indeed discussing what to do if Mond continued to refuse them the money. One course they considered was to hand over to the Guardians the proceeds of rates levied for the LCC and the other outside bodies. This would be a variation on their previous tactic. In 1921 they had refused to levy the rates for the outside bodies at all and the rates had gone down. In 1922 they were contemplating levying the rate as usual but using it for another purpose.

However, Poplar's suggestion of a meeting between the Minister and the Guardians was accepted by Mond and on 20 June a delegation of eight consisting of Edgar and George Lansbury, the two Scurrs, Charlie Sumner, A. A. Watts, Albert Baker and a newcomer to the Board, the Rev. C. G. Langdon, met Mond and his parliamentary secretary, the Earl of Onslow, together with two officials of the Ministry of Health.

Edgar acted as chief spokesman for the delegation. After briefly making a complaint concerning the way the Ministry of Health officials had been 'working in company' with the Poplar Municipal Alliance to produce 'political propaganda' which, he suggested was 'contrary to all traditions of the English Civil Service' he explained that under the Local Government Financial Provisions Act some £380,000 would be due to Poplar out of the Metropolitan Common Poor Fund for the year ending 30 September next; of this, the Minister had so far sanctioned some £221,800 in loans; they now wished to borrow the remaining £158,000. Edgar explained that they wished to borrow, because they had no right to raise from the rates money which would later be refunded to them through the MCPF. 'The Act passed last year gave us the right to borrow,' he said. 'We consider the Act did not give you power to withhold these loans arbitrarily, nor do we consider that the Act gave you power to enforce a policy upon Boards of Guardians by the withholding of sanction to borrowing. Remember, we are not asking the loan of a penny which is not covered by the Metropolitan Common Poor Fund.' After dealing with charges of 'lavish relief' in individual cases he said:

> We are not here to threaten, but we ask you to understand quite clearly that if you drive us into a corner by refusing to grant us loans which we are legally entitled to receive, and which we require before the end of the present month, we shall be obliged in conjunction with our colleagues on the Borough Council to raise a rate for the future sufficient only to cover the needs of the Boards of Guardians, leaving you, the County Council, the Metropolitan Asylums Board, the Water Board and the Police to collect your own. We are under no illusion as to the effect of this. We know that it will cause great confusion and loss of money and that it may entail some suffering on ourselves, especially if, as is very likely, a rent strike should follow. But we have no option. . . . Therefore we once again make formal request that you will grant these loans."[20]

In the discussion which followed, Mond took on an aggrieved air. When George Lansbury charged him with being prejudiced by the figures thrown at him by the press, he said: 'Remember last year the effort I made in the establishment of the Common Poor Law Fund. It is not fair to go and charge me with being biased against Poplar; it is not true . . . I made a great effort.'

The detailed discussion ranged around two matters: whether parents should get relief if their children were earning, and how much should be given to large families.

On the first question Mond asked 'whether a person who has a number of children in his house earning considerable wages is destitute or not; and if he is destitute to what extent he is destitute'? The Guardians explained that they regarded what they considered to be a fair percentage of a child's earnings as family income, to which Mond said: 'Quite so. It is really a

question of degree. I do not think anybody has contended that
the whole of the wages of an adult child living in a house with
his parents should be looked upon as reasonable payment.'
When Edgar pointed out that his rules did just this, Mond said
nothing. Later he suggested, however, that the man and wife
with four daughters earning £6 between them had 'a considerable amount of money. It does seem to my mind that that ought
to be enough to keep them going.' Baker tried to explain to
Mond why four working daughters, each earning 30s, would
have difficulty in keeping their parents. 'You take the price of a
pair of boots. One will want boots one week and clothing
another week. You try to keep the daughter for what is left out
of the 30s a week. Surely you want the working-class girl to go
to work respectable?'

As for the large families with many children, the maximum
under the Mond scale had by this time been reduced from £2
14s to £2 10s 6d, owing to a cut in the weekly wages of Grade A
local authority workers. The Guardians tried to explain that a
family of more than seven children would starve on this sum. At
one stage the dialogue went like this:

> MOND: You pay a man more when he is on relief than when he is
> at his ordinary job.
> GEORGE LANSBURY: If people starve on wages, there is no reason
> why they should starve on relief.
> MOND: Evidently they do not starve on wages. . . . The difficulty
> you get into is that you pay people more for doing nothing.
> EDGAR LANSBURY: They should be paid more for doing things.
> MOND: You finally land yourself in keeping everybody in the
> country.
> GEORGE LANSBURY: The whole country as a last resort has to
> keep everybody in the country. The question is only how keep
> is distributed.

A. A. Watts emphasised the inadequacy of the average wage
when there were many children, saying that such people
became half starved:

> The wife looks after the breadwinner getting enough to eat, and
> they go short at home – the wife goes short and the children go
> short. There is many a woman who cannot go out on Sunday
> because she is not respectable enough. They look after the men
> because they have to go out and work.

Julia Scurr explained how low their relief scales were:

> I have been chairman of one of the relief committees for three or four years . . . I often feel ashamed to offer the people the amount we offer, taking into consideration the other few shillings that are coming in. I feel that the women cannot do what they ought to do for the children and the home. I can assure you that the people are careful people. We live among them and go among them and there is not a shilling too much given in the scale of relief that we give.

'What I cannot understand' said Mond at one point, 'is why Poplar has to operate on the basis of splendid isolation rather than on the line that the other people find they can run their relief on'. He said he was not anxious to adopt a rigid scale: 'The only thing is whether or not we can arrive at some basis in which your scale would come down more towards what other people are doing and bring your administration more into conformity with other areas.'

In practice this meant reducing the relief for large families and adopting strict rules about the treatment of resources. In the end Mond suggested they should appoint two or three members to have a discussion with the Ministry of Health officials present 'and see if we cannot arrive at some modus vivendi which would enable me to grant a loan'.

After further argument Edgar said they were prepared to appoint a small committee but, 'in the meantime, Sir, we want some money', to which Mond replied: 'Not until the end of the month.' To that Edgar said 'Yes we do. We have had a lot of this handing us out the last farthing and then giving us a week to go on with.' The Clerk to the Guardians who was present then intervened to say that by the week ending 8 July they would be £22,500 overspent and that did not include cheques owing to tradesmen, the Asylums Board, etc. Also they owed the London County Council for two quarters. £22,500 was needed and £70,000 would be still outstanding.

At this stage Mond left the meeting and one of the Ministry of Health officials suggested that they nominate two or three people to discuss the scale in detail. Edgar Lansbury was doubtful about having any further discussion, but on being assured that nothing agreed would be binding on the Board, he and three others stayed behind.

Realising that what the Minister wanted was some compromise on the issues of large families and the parents of earning children, Edgar tried to get the Ministry officials to make suggestions on what they thought a fair compromise would be. But the officials refused to commit themselves and Edgar and his colleagues finally left after it had been stated that the onus was on the Poplar Board to submit proposals.

The Poplar Guardians did indeed discuss the issue at some length the next day. In the end they decided to tell Mond that they could not agree to cut down the amounts given to large families but would report individually the circumstances of every case to the Minister. As regards parents of earning children, they proposed to keep their present scale of disregards for the first 30s, but would deduct 6d for every shilling earned over that amount. Under such an arrangement the position of the parents with four daughters each earning 30s, which had so scandalised both Cooper and Mond, would have remained unaltered.

Mond believed that there was some chance of persuading the Guardians to compromise, but when he received this letter he realised that he had failed. Indeed, as he put it to Edgar Lansbury when they again met face to face: 'It is very difficult to understand why what is possible for all the other boards of guardians is impossible for Poplar'; he had hoped they would come nearer to what other boards of guardians did 'but really you have not come within a hundred miles of it'.[21]

It had, however, occurred to Mond that the Guardians' suggestion that he should prohibit them by law from granting relief in excess of the Mond scale might be a way out for both parties. The Guardians had repeatedly argued that they had been elected to follow a certain policy. But if that policy was definitely made illegal, might it be easier for them to abandon it?

Mond therefore decided to give up any further attempts at persuasion and a few days later sent down to Poplar a peremptory Order issued under the 1834 Act[22] which declared that any outdoor relief granted in excess of the Mond scale was illegal. Here at last was the Order which the Guardians had suggested to Mond as an alternative to withholding the money. But accompanying it was a letter saying that the Minister was prepared to grant a loan to the Guardians on condition that the Order was strictly complied with. This continued withholding of the loan after the issue of an Order was something which the Guardians had not quite anticipated.

However, the councillors had already taken a decisive step towards bringing the issue to a head. The full council meeting had taken place on Thursday 22 June at which the estimates for the ensuing quarter had been due for debate. But Charles Key, by this time vice-chairman of the finance committee, moved that the estimates be withdrawn, explaining that he did this because of the situation between the Ministry of Health and the Board of Guardians. Edgar Lansbury seconded, explaining that Mond had withheld consent to a loan; if he persisted, the Guardians, with the help of the council, would take steps to see that relief did not come to a standstill.[23]

The councillors were indeed making ready to put into force their plan to take the money raised for outside bodies and use it for poor relief. However, the Guardians decided to make one more attempt to persuade the Ministry to provide the money, and on 28 June a deputation from the Board was once more in conference with Mond. Edgar Lansbury led the delegation which included Charlie Sumner, Julia Scurr and Helen Mc-Kay. Charles Key, though not himself a guardian, went with them.

The interview took place in an atmosphere very different from that of the previous week. Then each side had been trying to get the other to see his point of view; the Guardians had endeavoured to convince Mond of the reasonableness of their approach and to tell him about circumstances in Poplar.

On this occasion the Guardians deliberately left the negotiations in the hands of Edgar; indeed, they did not speak at all until the end of the meeting was in sight. Edgar set out his position simply and never allowed himself to be diverted from the point. 'It was evident very early that Mond had not before realised how strong the Board's case was,' commented Charles Key afterwards. 'The officials looked glum as Edgar went quietly on. I think I have never heard a case stated so well.'[24]

The officials had reason to be glum. Any hope that Poplar was about to give in vanished within the first few minutes as Edgar told them that the Guardians would not obey the Order.

I am to say from the Board that we cannot administer that Order. We want you to believe that we are conscientious guardians and we try to do our duty. . . . We were elected definitely on our scale and inasmuch as excess relief over your scale is paid by the very people who elected us, we say we cannot conscientiously administer another scale.[25]

He went on to describe the financial crisis which Mond's action had precipitated:

At the end of this week we shall have no money unless you send this money, and shall be unable to carry on; the affairs of the Union will come to a standstill. If people are not to starve the Ministry will have to send down someone to carry out the Order. We cannot.

Edgar continued to stress that Poplar was only asking for money sufficient to meet the expense of the Mond scale; anything above it would be met out of their own local rates; the money was due to them out of the Metropolitan Common Poor Fund when the half year expired. Towards the end, Mond went out of his way to confirm that Poplar was not asking for more out of the MCPF than would suffice to meet the Mond scale. This was well known to Mond; indeed he himself had been at pains to emphasise it to the Cabinet. Yet he now behaved as though he were unaware of what had led up to Poplar's financial crisis. He said to Edgar: 'If the CPF were paid week by week instead of every six months you would not have come to us?' Edgar replied: 'All we are asking for is for the money under the scale.' Mond said: 'I see, yes I think we had better consider this. I know now what you have come to see me about'. He then adjourned the meeting in order to have a discussion with his officials.

When they returned it was stated that £31,000 would be advanced on Friday and £8,000 the following week. But the argument then reverted to its previous pattern: Mond saying that the money could only be advanced on condition that the Order was carried out; Edgar saying that the Government had no power to refuse them the money since it was owed to them under the 1921 Act.

Towards the end Helen McKay tried to explain to Mond why his scale was inadequate; in particular why Poplar believed a separate rent allowance essential:

The Minister said he could not understand why we could not carry out the Order. It seems to be absolutely wrong in two regards: in regard to rent and in regard to the larger families of small children. You know Sir, that down in our area we have a great deal of tubercular trouble, also in children physical conditions which will develop into tubercular trouble. Whenever such a family comes under our notice, with housing conditions as they are we cannot say what we should say in a great many cases – you should get a larger house; but we can say – you must rearrange your sleeping arrangements, that will help the situation. What is going to be the result of this scale? Inevitably the result will be that a family who is already overcrowded will take in a lodger or someone to pay the rent and they will do it against their better judgement.[26]

Julia Scurr backed her up:

The majority of cases are already overcrowded which come to us . . . The rent is going up all over the East End of London in every borough. Some women have not got proper clothing on and how they are living on that scale I do not know. . . . We are in one of the areas which is called tubercular and we know that in many cases women stay at home for confinement under conditions which are really wrong and which are going to tend to be more crowded still. As Miss McKay says they will take in lodgers.[27]

In response to these statements from the two women, Mond was instantly conciliatory. 'We cannot of course lay down an Order for every case. You report these cases to us and if you want to pay more we shall take a reasonable and generous view.'

In the end Mond was obliged to agree that the money should be advanced even though there had been no undertaking to operate the Order. It was simply emphasised that the Guardians would be expected to report individually to the Ministry every case relieved at a rate higher than the Mond scale.

Mond knew perfectly well that the Poplar Guardians had defeated him. They had made clear that they were going to operate their own scale, not his. True, any payments above the Mond scale were illegal now, unless subsequently legalised by Ministerial approval because they were exceptional cases. Without this approval the Guardians could eventually be surcharged for all the money they spent in excess of the Mond scale. And surcharge meant that they could be made individually liable to find the money. But, as Mond had already suggested to the Cabinet, surcharging was not a very effective deterrent to people of the financial status of the Poplar Guardians.

But what else could Mond do? His intention to pass a Bill

enabling him to step in and unseat the Guardians had been frustrated by pressure of parliamentary business. His tactic of withholding sanction for loans on which he had pinned his hopes had not proved an effective deterrent and if he held up the money any longer one of two things would happen: either Poor Law relief in Poplar would come to a halt accompanied by a great outcry that he was starving the sick, the widows, the orphans, etc.; or, since it was obvious that in practice the Poplar Guardians were not going to allow this to happen, there would be a repetition of the kind of thing which had happened the previous summer and the Poplar Council would use the money due to other bodies to support those on poor relief. Neither of these prospects was appealing. So he agreed that the money should be advanced to Poplar because he quite simply could see no alternative. It meant however that his enemies sneered, while the *Daily Herald* carried a triumphant headline: 'Mond Climbs Down'.

Predictably, the new Order proved quite ineffective. In the first week after it came into operation the Guardians reported 1,829 cases where out-relief had been awarded in excess of the Mond scale. Except for those where Ministerial approval as an exceptional case was received, the Guardians had acted illegally. But if they were to be brought to book by way of a surcharge or in some other fashion, each case had to be individually investigated by the Ministry. It meant that Mond's officials had to spend many hours scrutinising the cases one by one in order to decide which were exceptional enough to warrant approval and which should be disallowed. Most of the cases were, of course, disapproved; but the process was a highly laborious one which continued week after week apparently stretching into the future without end.

Meanwhile in Poplar the whole affair was being celebrated as another victory. As soon as it was certain that Mond would grant the loan, the emergency plans for transferring money due to other authorities were abandoned.

The following Sunday, 9 July, there was a demonstration of several thousand people in Victoria Park headed by twenty-five trade union banners. Sumner, the mayor, addressed the meeting, saying that although Poplar had to bear the brunt of the fight for a decent scale of relief for the unemployed, the question was really one for all the boards of guardians up and down the country. It was time that Guardians in London and the provinces got a move on, he said, for the fight ought not to be left in the hands of a few men and Poplar. Charles Key told the meeting that Poplar's fight was only part of a great national fight. The conflict with Sir Alfred Mond was really a conflict with the men behind Mond who saw that if adequate relief were given to the unemployed the capitalist would lose his greatest power: that of using the unemployed to reduce wages. Councillor J. H. Jones of the NUR moved a resolution approving the Guardians' scale of relief and pledging support for any action taken to maintain it. The resolution was carried unanimously.[28]

After this the Guardians continued week after week to operate their own scale, defying outright the Mond Order; week after week the cases were reported to the Ministry and there the matter rested. At the same time Mond was the victim of further sarcasm from MPs on the government benches in the House. Sir Reginald Blair in particular would not leave the matter alone, but kept on reminding the House that the Poplar Guardians had, in his words, 'set all the hon. Baronet's Rules and Regulations at defiance'.[29]

Mond's final public pronouncement on the subject of Poplar was on 31 July. Asked by Conservative MP Sir John Leigh whether he would promote legislation 'to avert a continuance of the malpractices disclosed in Mr Cooper's report', he replied: 'I should not hesitate to promote legislation if it is found to be necessary.' But the truth was that he *had* hesitated and now his chance was gone. For in the middle of October the coalition between Conservatives and part of the Liberal Party ended. On 19 October at a meeting of the Carlton Club the Conservatives finally decided to leave the coalition; the Prime Minister Lloyd George resigned, and with him the remaining coalition Liberals in the Cabinet, including Sir Alfred Mond.

In the temporary Cabinet formed by the new Conservative Prime Minister, Bonar Law, the post of Minister of Health was given to Sir Arthur Griffith-Boscawen who, however, promptly lost his seat at the subsequent general election held on 15 November 1922. In this election the Conservatives won a clear majority over all other parties. On the other hand the number of seats won by the Labour Party rose to 142, more than double the number in 1918. Among these were both Poplar constituencies. George Lansbury, who stood for Bow and Bromley, easily defeated his Conservative opponent, while Sam March won South Poplar from Sir Alfred Yeo who had been Liberal MP for the constituency since 1914. Among those who went to the House of Commons at the same time as Lansbury and March was a newcomer who had shown solidarity with them in their struggle the previous year: Clement Attlee was elected MP for Limehouse, Stepney. And a few weeks later Harry Gosling, who had helped to get them out of jail, became MP for Whitechapel.

NOTES

1. EEN, 22 February 1924.
2. Interview with Mond: *Lansbury Papers*, vol. 28, pp. 132–46.
3. House of Commons, *Hansard*, 13 February 1924.
4. Municipal Alliance correspondence: Tower Hamlets Library, Local History Collection, referred to below as THL, Poplar Box 880.
5. Firms whose representatives volunteered to form part of this deputation were: Aberdeen Steam Navigation; Anderson and Son, paint manufacturers; Bringer and Goodwin, engineers; Dux Chemical Solution Co.; Fraser and Fraser, boilermakers; Fraser and Son, boilermakers; E. LeBas, Cyclops Iron Works; Locke Lancaster and Johnson; London Graving Dock Co.; Maconochie Bros.; Mathew Keenan and Co.; Passingham Ltd.; Sir W. A. Rose and Co., paint manufacturers; J. Westwood and Co.
6. Report of Special Inquiry held under the direction of the Ministry of Health into the Expenditure of the Guardians. Parish of Poplar Borough, 1922. Referred to below as the 'Cooper Report'.
7. *Guilty and Proud of It* (pamphlet written by the Poplar Guardians, 1922).
8. For example it asserted that a single unemployed man received £1 5s 6d a week in out-relief from the Guardians, whereas in fact the maximum Poplar scale rate for a single person was 19s (12s 6d plus 1s 6d fuel, plus rent up to 5s).
9. *Lansbury Papers*, vol. 28, pp. 132–46.
10. Breakfast: ¾ pint tea, 3 oz bread, ½ oz butter, ¾ pint porridge, ¼ pint milk.
    Dinner: (for men) 3 oz meat, 12 oz potatoes, etc., 4 oz rice or treacle pudding (this was varied with meat pudding, or cheese, or fish).
    Tea: 6 to 8 oz bread, 1 pint tea, ½ oz butter and either cake or jam or cured fish, or cheese according to the day of the week.
11. PRO, Cab 24/136, CP 3970.
12. House of Commons, *Hansard*, 24 May 1922.
13. *Poor Law Officers Journal*, 26 May 1922.
14. House of Commons, *Hansard*, 29 May 1922.
15. THL Poplar Box 880, letter dated 24 May 1922.
16. PRO, Cab 23/30. Committee on Home Affairs, 114.

17. PRO, Cab 23/30. Cabinet meeting, 16 June 1922.
18. BGM, 14 June 1922.
19. DH, 16 June 1922.
20. *Lansbury Papers*, vol. 28, pp. 132–46.
21. ibid., vol. 28, pp. 147–54.
22. Relief Regulations (Poplar) Order, 1922. S.R. and O., 1922, No. 649.
23. ELA, 1 July 1922.
24. *Lansbury Papers*, vol. 28, pp. 127–31.
25. ibid., pp. 147–54.
26. ibid.
27. ibid.
28. DH, 10 July 1922.
29. House of Commons, *Hansard*, 24 July 1922.

10

Divisions in the Labour Movement

On 1 November 1922, a fortnight before the general election, the borough council elections had taken place. As in both the LCC and the Guardians' elections of that year, Poplar's actions had been used once again by the press to mobilise anti-Labour opinion. Charlie Sumner had seen this coming. At the end of August 1922 he had written a long letter to the *Daily Herald* pointing out that it appeared the Moderates and Progressives (Conservatives and Liberals) were combining to smash Labour at the coming council elections in November under the war cry 'Down with Poplarism'.

> What is the London Labour Party going to do about this attack? Does it intend to allow judgement upon Poplar to go by default? . . . I venture to think that if the London Labour Party would face the Moderates and Progressives on this issue of Poplar we should beat them to a frazzle not only in Poplar but also all over London . . . London Labour has nothing to be ashamed of in connection with Poplar. On the contrary, everything to be proud of.[1]

But there was no response to this plea, for most of the London Labour leaders, if not exactly 'ashamed' of Poplar, certainly looked on that council as an embarrassment. In the event, as Sumner had predicted, the word 'Poplarism' was used by Labour's opponents to denote high rates, extravagance and incompetence, misuse of power and neglect of duty. In answer, London's Labour leaders stressed the achievements of Labour-controlled boroughs other than Poplar. 'Despite the predictions of our opponents that Labour was unfitted for the responsibilities of municipal administration, general efficiency in the Labour boroughs is higher than it has ever been under other control' declared the London Labour manifesto.[2] The *Daily Herald* (from which Lansbury had just resigned as editor) assiduously publicised those Labour councils which were reducing the rates, in particular Morrison's borough, Hackney, which, it was claimed, had fixed the lowest rate of any metropolitan borough. When the November borough elections took place, however, it could be seen that this line of propaganda had not succeeded and, indeed, that the trends apparent in the LCC and Guardians' elections had intensified. Whether or not a bolder and less defensive attitude to 'Poplarism' would have made any difference is questionable. The fact was that the hope and confidence which gripped Labour supporters in 1919 had, for the most part, evaporated with the slump. On this occasion a united fight by Conservatives and Liberals meant that in many cases the Labour candidates who had previously won three-cornered contests, now faced the added disadvantage of a straight fight. Whatever the reasons, Labour lost over 300 seats and, as a result, now controlled only four metropolitan borough councils in place of the eleven won in 1919. The four were Battersea, Bermondsey, Woolwich and, of course, Poplar. In most areas it appeared that the emphasis on Labour's 'efficiency' had failed to draw Labour supporters to the polling booth. In Hackney, Morrison's own borough, every single Labour councillor lost his seat.

In Poplar, too, the Municipal Alliance had made a concentrated attack but succeeded in dislodging only the three Labour councillors who stood for the Bow Central ward. In comparison with the heavy Labour losses in nearly every other borough, this was a minor setback. They had won thirty-six seats out of forty-two instead of their previous thirty-nine, and most of them received considerably more votes than in 1919. There was a 51·5 per cent poll compared with an average of 36·4 per cent throughout London.

Poplar's local triumph failed to convince its critics and, after the election, opinion within the Labour movement continued as divided as before. For the London Labour Party's annual conference soon afterwards, Woolwich had tabled a resolution:

> That this Ninth Annual Conference approves of the action of the Poplar Board of Guardians in attempting to provide the unemployed workers with a reasonable standard of maintenance and deprecates the speeches and statements issued by prominent members of the London Labour Party, which were opposed to the Poplar action.

After an amendment, which would have totally altered the sense of this resolution, had been heavily defeated, someone moved 'next business'. This was carried on a show of hands,[3] from which it would seem that Poplar was admired rather than criticised by the majority who shrank, however, from the prospect of bring the issue to a head.

In March 1923 Charles Key was given the opportunity to write an article in the journal which Morrison edited, *London Labour Chronicle*, explaining Poplar's standpoint. Key wrote: 'The Labour Movement here had to face the question which sooner or later, nationally and locally, the whole Movement will have to answer: "You now have power – what are you going to do with it?"' Over and over again, he said, they had been asked why they could not do as other borough councils and boards of guardians did, and their answer had been: 'We are the advance guard of those who will do far otherwise than has been done of old. *We have come to make a change.*'

Morrison's comment on this statement suggested that making a change was not his prime object. 'After all,' he wrote, 'the ultimate justification for Labour policy is not that it is *different* but that it is *sound* in the interests of the people.'[4]

The behaviour of the Poplar councillors and Guardians had certainly been different. In Poplar nobody said: 'They're all the same when they get in,' a remark frequently made to canvassers in other areas. The impact of their activities had been considerable. Through their out-relief policy they had aimed to abolish absolute want, and to a large extent had succeeded. They had tried to ensure that every family at least got enough to eat, a fire in the grate, shoes for the children, and moreover that those obliged to come to them for help, whether through unemployment, sickness, old age or bereavement, should preserve their self respect. Through their action on the rates they had secured that the major part of the cost had been shouldered by the richer boroughs rather than by their own poor.

This policy, they believed, had paid dividends. Since 1919 there had been a dramatic fall in both the general death rate and the infant mortality rate.[5] And although a significant decline had taken place in other parts of London also, the councillors were convinced that, so far as their own borough was concerned, the lower death rates were in part the result of their own actions. The fall in child deaths was, they believed, linked not only with their attack on basic poverty but also with the expansion of maternity and child welfare services. This had included the appointment of seventeen full-time health visitors and the wide distribution of free and cheap milk to expectant and nursing mothers and children under three.

There were other ways in which, despite heavy unemployment and severe restrictions on public expenditure at the centre, the council was contributing to improved standards of life. Few houses had baths and most families had no running hot water, but the number of those taking baths in the newly-opened council bath houses had risen enormously, while more and more women were regularly making use of the council's new washing machines. The number of books borrowed from Poplar's public libraries had doubled; the borough's electricity undertaking was expanding fast and its current was claimed to be the cheapest in London. The council had suceeded in building 150 new houses and with difficulty had persuaded the Ministry of Health to sanction a level of rents below that prevailing elsewhere.

Many of these activities were eminently respectable and such as Herbert Morrison, J. H. Thomas and other Labour leaders could approve. Where then did the disagreement lie?

First of all, Morrison disagreed with Poplar's tactics. As we have seen, to break the law, as Poplar had openly done, with its rates strike and later with its out-relief, was in his opinion indefensible. In his view the need to prove to the rest of the world that Labour's way forward was to be constitutional was paramount; anything which smacked of lawlessness or anarchy played straight into the hands of Labour's opponents.

Secondly, Morrison also disagreed to some extent not only with Poplar's tactics but with its aims, many of which seemed too far in advance to be acceptable to the average member of the public. The councillors' approval of £2 a week as a relief scale for man and wife the previous January had been a case in point. The fact that such a scale had been adopted without previous discussion illustrated the kind of irresponsibility which prevailed. Later they had abandoned it, not because they disagreed with it in principle but because they had not the money to operate it. To Morrison this was a lamentable episode; he recalled it over a year later, insisting that Poplar's adoption of the scale had 'brought out large numbers of people to vote MR who otherwise would not have voted'.[6] Morrison disagreed with such a scale as a matter of principle and emphasised this whenever he could. Thus a leaflet issued for the borough council elections headed 'STARVING THE POOR' stated that 'unemployment benefit has been reduced and restricted. Public assistance for the unemployed and their families has been ruthlessly cut to a semi-starvation basis'. It went on to assert in bold type **'The London Labour Party does not associate itself with demands for public assistance of a character which cannot be regarded as practicable in existing circumstances.'** The party was thus carefully dissociated from extravagant demands, whether those of Poplar or of the National Unemployed Workers' Committee Movement which was gathering support.[7]

A third question on which Morrison disagreed with Poplar concerned the wages paid to municipal employees. When prices and wages were at their height in 1920, Poplar had introduced a minimum wage of £4 a week for its employees; so had some other London councils, including Hackney. But with the fall in prices and in wages which took place during the slump, some Labour people argued that municipal wages should fluctuate with those paid by private employers; when these fell, as they had been doing, it was right to reduce municipal wages too. This had in fact, been one of the methods whereby certain local councils were suceeding in bringing down the rates. Morrison was one who believed municipal wages should follow the rise or fall of wages outside. In March 1922 he persuaded the Hackney Borough Council to reduce its wages to conform to scales agreed through the Whitley Council system. In a privately-circulated memorandum for the information of other local Labour Parties he explained: 'The £4 minimum was maintained for months after the JIC rate fell below but at last the Party on the Council was compelled out of consideration to other grades of workpeople and the general working class community of the Borough, to reconsider the £4 minimum, with the result that an adjustment is being spread over four months whereby the rate will be the JIC rate . . . plus 2s.'[8]

Poplar however, resisted attempts to bring down the wages paid to its employees and continued to pay the £4 minimum fixed in 1920. 'This of course cost money, but it was money which they had no right not to spend,' Susan Lawrence told a conference called to explain Poplar's policy to others. 'The municipalities ought to hold up wages to a minimum living standard', she said, 'just as Trade Boards had been set up in certain industries to hold them up to such a standard. Certainly no Labour man ought to take objection to such a policy.'[9] Though she could not know it, this issue would shortly be at the centre of Poplar's next conflict with the judges and the civil servants.

On the whole issue of the rates Poplar profoundly disagreed with the line of the London Labour leadership. In a pamphlet entitled *Labour and the Rates*[10] John Scurr criticised those in the labour movement who endeavoured to prove that Labour could reduce the rates. Morrison was of course the most influential of these. The ratepayers, said Scurr, were divided into three: the manufacturers and occupiers of industrial premises, the shop-keeping and professional classes, and the manual workers. The first two groups were normally keen opponents of municipal expenditure and their battle cry was 'Keep down the rates'. But the Labour Party should come out into the open and show clearly to the worker that municipal expenditure was in his interests, because it was a method of distributing wealth more equally. Therefore: 'Labour policy should be directed towards increasing rather than diminishing local expenditure upon those services which add to the real wages of the worker.' Though admitting that rates were an unsatisfactory form of taxation – he would have liked to see a radical reform of the rating system – he nevertheless insisted that 'Labour policy must be concerned with the extension of municipal activities and not with their reduction. I repeat that the greater part of municipal expenditure is a method whereby a more social distribution of income is obtained.'

George Lansbury was highly critical of the tendency among some of the leaders to make demands of the Government without any attempt to implement these demands in whatever ways were open to them. Just after the Cooper inquiry, he had defended Poplar against its critics in the labour movement in an article in *Labour Monthly*. 'The attack on Poplar,' he said, 'is the direct result of Poplar's endeavour to do the things that others only talk about.' 'The issue that is raised by Poplar is larger than an issue of local government,' he added. 'It is the whole question whether the Labour Movement means business. Are we going to attempt to carry out what we say on the platform, or are we to be misled and side-tracked by considerations of "stateman-ship"?'[11] Lansbury was not among those who believed that 'municipal socialism' was the way to bring about the end of capitalism. 'I know that we are not going to end Capitalism by Poplar methods,' he wrote; 'it is for the workers through their national organisations to put an end to the system of wage-slavery and exploitation.' In practice, at the same time, he tried to bring about much greater changes by municipal means than most of the more ardent disciples of municipal socialism. He believed that 'the workers must be given tangible proof that Labour administration means something different from capitalist administration, and in a nutshell this means diverting wealth from the wealthy ratepayers to the poor'.[12]

The victory in the rates dispute had done exactly that. As John Scurr explained, the councillors saw much of their municipal expenditure as doing the same thing: transferring wealth from richer to poorer. They believed they should take any step open to them, no matter how limited, towards removing the injustices created by the capitalist system. Morrison would have explained that this was his aim also, but in practice he gave the impression of trying to prove that his side, if elected, could do rather more efficiently what the last party did. Just as the Webbs devoted much of their writings to showing up the inefficiencies of capitalism and thereby sometimes created the impression that the only reason for wanting to get rid of it was to abolish 'muddle', so Morrison denounced his Conservative opponents for 'muddle' and inefficiency. But his alternative programmes which were concerned above all with responsibility and economy, were not such as to persuade the poor that a new kind of life was possible, or to encourage the downtrodden to stand up.

This in turn highlighted another difference. The Poplar councillors always directed their message to working-class people and in particular to the trade unionists who were the backbone of their organisation. But Morrison believed that Labour's propaganda was too much directed towards the workers. In 1923 he published month after month in the *London Labour Chronicle* a long series of articles on the necessity for Labour to win the middle class to vote Labour.[13]

In marked contrast to some Labour controlled councils, which were torn by inner-party dissensions, a characteristic of the Poplar councillors and Guardians was their solidarity with one another. They were made up of many diverse strands;

among them were socialists of various kinds and Communists; Roman Catholics and Protestants; pacifists and non-pacifists. Some believed in parliamentary socialism and some in the workers' republic; some supported institutions like the monarchy and some looked forward to their destruction. And some were simply active trade unionists, not much concerned with politics outside the bread-and-butter struggle. Yet they had shown themselves a living example of what can be achieved when people of diverse views unite for a common purpose. George Lansbury's influence had much to do with this; he had a unique ability to search out and pursue points of agreement so that matters on which discord could arise receded in importance. 'Wherever Mr Lansbury is, you will find laughter and eagerness and the sense of a need to get something done,' said a contemporary observer.[14] This sense of purpose was to a much greater extent than usual shared by the membership. About a year after the 1922 elections, Herbert Morrison gave it as his opinion that the reason why Labour lost ground was 'the insufficient time devoted to preparation and the lack of scientific constituency organisation'.[15] But in Poplar it was well understood that effective organisation depends more than anything else on the enthusiasm of the participating members.

The other unique characteristic of the Poplar councillors and Guardians was their relationship with their electors. One of the problems of parliamentary democracy is that once an MP is elected, life for him begins to revolve almost exclusively round the House of Commons, and the supporters in the constituency gradually cease to be the first consideration. In the same way, the life of a councillor can revolve round the town hall, his relations with his fellow-councillors and with the administrative staff can become central, his relations with those who elected him peripheral. This situation is less inevitable with councillors than it is with MPs because the former are not full-time; they often spend their working day with people who are not councillors or administrators. Even so, it is noticeable how distant many councillors are from their electors, how little they know them or are known to them.

In Poplar it was not like this. The huge mass meetings, marches and gatherings of supporters which took place so frequently, particularly at moments of crisis or excitement, served as a crucial means of communication. At such meetings the councillors explained their attitude and asked for endorsement of their actions. The numbers who attended such meetings were one sign that the link between elected and elector was unusually strong. Yet such meetings were in one sense only the visible outcrop; beneath the surface was a confused network of communication which hummed with life.

To begin with, there were the trade union branches of which there were over seventy in Poplar; they covered railwaymen, engineers, building workers, shipwrights and boilermakers, tram and bus drivers, dockers and stevedores, seamen, post office workers, gas workers, municipal employees, and general labourers of all descriptions. As we have seen, several of the councillors were secretaries of trade union branches, the majority of which (though not all) were affiliated to the Poplar Trades Council and Borough Labour Party of which Councillor Banks had been for many years the secretary. The decision to embark on the rates strike in 1921 had been arrived at only after a conference of representatives from trade union branches where every aspect of the proposed action had been considered. Apart from these obvious channels of communication, there were among the councillors men who were the acknowledged leaders among their fellow-workers on the job, whether as employees or as trade union officers. These men spent their lives in close contact with the problems of Poplar's workplaces. The women councillors, on the other hand, with the exception of Susan Lawrence, were housewives. The fact that their daytime opportunities for council work were more flexible than those of the men meant that they often took on very special responsibilities. Thus Minnie Lansbury had used her home as a 'surgery' and every morning between nine o'clock and half past ten people flocked to her house to consult her. The work of all the women councillors took them into active contact with other women in the borough, whether through the Maternity and Child Welfare Committee and the rather makeshift clinics and welfare centres which had been opened after the war, or in other ways. The two women Guardians, Julia Scurr and Helen Mc-Kay, put in far more hours than most of the other Guardians could manage, chairing relief committees and interviewing applicants, though the work of all the Guardians took them directly into the front line of poverty.

Finally, the organisation of the Labour Party itself was such as to impress Herbert Morrison despite his disapproval of Poplar's policies. Indeed, Morrison even suggested that other areas should follow Poplar's example in this respect. In South Poplar, where the individual Labour Party membership was 2,800 in 1923, the individual member's subscription was one penny a week. It was well understood that if not collected each week it was unlikely to be saved. So the keenest members were turned into dues collectors, each with the names of twenty people listed on a card, who must be visited every week. This system not only brought in the money; it meant that members were kept in touch with events. One of the results was well attended meetings, both centrally and locally, where the issues facing the movement could be discussed. Indeed one of the matters on which Lansbury and Morrison disagreed was that the former thought the Labour group on a council should be subject to the decisions of the local Party organisation, while the latter was entirely against this, believing that a Labour group should feel itself solely responsible to the electorate.

Curiously enough the mere fact that the Poplar Labour group felt itself subject to the local party itself resulted in an unusually active and participating electorate, rather than one which put a cross on a ballot paper every three years and then forgot about it in between. By the standards of later decades the Poplar electorate was backward and uneducated, with the limited horizons which the never-ending struggle against hardship can impose. Here was no pattern of comfortable firesides with television or radio to keep you informed of events in the outside world. Those who wanted to be in touch had to venture out and participate in political events – and large numbers did so. They came to political meetings of all kinds, were stirred by what they heard, raised their voices, were drawn in and consulted and, from time to time, were filled with excitement and a sense of power.

It was really the mass support of the electorate which had enabled the councillors to win their battle over the rates. And this, in turn, had a very striking further result. Their term in prison and their victory meant that on subsequent issues throughout 1922 and 1923 the Government hesitated to take Poplar on again. Even when the Guardians ostentatiously broke the law, as they did week after week, in paying relief above the scale laid down in the Poplar Order, no steps were taken by the

Ministry to bring the matter to a head. Aware of the possibilities of court injunctions and other devices which would have brought other borough councils meekly to heel, those in charge at the centre knew by now that it was not so simple to deal with Poplar. So they looked at Poplar, and then looked away again and made no move for a long time.

NOTES

1. DH, 31 August 1922.
2. ibid., 1 September 1922.
3. London Labour Party, folio 1234.
4. *London Labour Chronicle*, March 1923.
5. The death rate per 1,000 living in Poplar in 1919 was 14·5; in 1923 it was 11·2. The infant mortality rate per thousand live births was as follows: 1918, 110; 1919, 84; 1920, 82; 1921, 83; 1922, 79; 1923, 59. Most London boroughs had a similarly striking fall in the infant mortality rate. Thus Shoreditch which in 1918 had the top rate of any London borough – 163 – had reduced it to 80 by 1923. Detailed figures for all London boroughs were given in reply to a question from John Scurr in *Hansard*, 15 February 1924.
6. *London Labour Chronicle*, March 1923.
7. London Labour Party, folio 1146.
8. ibid., folio 1045.
9. *Poplar Finance and Poplar Policy*: report of speeches made at a conference called by the Labour Research Department, 23 September 1922, and published as a supplement to the LRD's *Monthly Circular*.
10. Published by the Labour Research Department, 1923.
11. *Labour Monthly*, July 1922.
12. ibid.
13. By 'middle class' Morrison meant clerks, shopkeepers, doctors and lawyers. This was at a time when three-quarters of the population were manual workers and their families. Even in London which had a proportionately larger share of the middle strata than other parts of Britain, manual workers and their families comprised two-thirds of the population.
14. Harold Laski in the *Daily Herald* reprinted in the second edition of George Lansbury's *My Life*.
15. *London Labour Chronicle*, September 1923.

II

Wages: The Auditor Intervenes

It was not until 1923 that the argument about wages for council employees came to a head, though it had been going on for about eighteen months.

Among Poplar employers there was a growing sense of grievance. The Cooper inquiry had revealed that in Poplar over 60 per cent of the rates were paid by ratepayers 'not represented on the Electorate'. In other words, the owners of the railways, gas works, canals, docks, factories, wharves, warehouses, banks, stores, yards, theatres and pubs, most of whom lived outside Poplar, were footing a large part of the bill for the policies operated by the Poplar councillors and Guardians.

Before 1919, when the majority on the council and on the Board of Guardians had been controlled by the Poplar Muncipal Alliance, the rates had always been kept as low as possible. In Sir Alfred Warren's words, the Alliance at that time 'was able to control the tendencies and actions of the Extremists and was the means of effecting large economies and materially reducing the capital indebtedness of the Borough'.[1]

In the cause of keeping down local rates the Alliance had urged that some measure be introduced for pooling the rate burden over the rest of London. But the people who had actually achieved such a measure and a consequent reduction in rates had turned out to be the very extremists denounced by Warren. The immense sums of money thus saved to Poplar firms did not reconcile their owners to Labour rule. True, the new MCPF arrangement had stopped the rates soaring which they would otherwise have done. But thereafter they appeared to be stabilised, and even to move upwards marginally, at a time when many councils were actually reducing rates as a result of the fall in prices and wages.[2] Warren and his colleagues were convinced that Poplar's rates could be brought down also, given the right policies. These would include the economies in Poor Law relief recommended by Cooper and reductions in the level of wages paid by the borough council to its employees to bring them into line with the wage cuts being generally implemented.

Throughout 1922 Warren bombarded Mond with demands
for action against the Poplar councillors and guardians and
betrayed a growing exasperation when no real action was taken.
He urged that when the guardians were surcharged they should
not be forgiven and the surcharge cancelled by the Minister, as
had happened in the past; he demanded that the Minister
should refuse to sanction further loans for the guardians; he
proposed that the Minister should pass a law so as to take over
the guardians' functions himself; also that he should bring the
Poor Law under one London authority as recommended by the
Royal Commission. He repeatedly urged the repeal of Section
nine of the 1918 Representation of the People Act which had
for the first time given the vote to those on Poor Law relief,
contending that what was known as the 'pauper disqualification' should be reintroduced. The 1918 Act, claimed Warren,
meant that the Guardians were able to win votes from 'nearly
14,000 people on outdoor relief together with the votes of their
friends and sympathisers . . . We feel that the inclusion of this
section was an unfortunate oversight on the part of the legisla-
ture and that its retention in the Act will go a long way towards
rendering nugatory the Authority and direction of the Ministry
of Health.'[3]

Another solution put forward at the time, though not as yet
among the proposals made by Warren to Mond, was to give
local firms votes in proportion to the value of the capital
locally employed.

Already in 1921 the Municipal Alliance had begun its campaign to force the Poplar councillors to reduce the wages of
council employees. As noted earlier, the Poplar Council had
decided in May 1920 to introduce a minimum wage of £4 for
both men and women in their employ. In the months following
this action, prices continued to rise until about November 1920,
after which they began to fall. And as at the same time unemployment rose and trade declined, so one section of employers
after another was able to demand and enforce reductions in
wages. The export trade had collapsed; it could only be revived,
so it was argued, if prices were more competitive. This meant
cutting costs, particularly wage costs, which had been artifici-
ally inflated during the post-war boom.

For the industrialists, the financiers and their spokesmen in
Parliament and in the civil service this argument seemed

unanswerable. There was a tendency to look back nostalgically to the pre-war level of wages and to assume that if only pre-war conditions could return, prosperity would come back too. In pursuit of this goal, there took place within the space of less than three years the sharpest fall in wages and prices known to British history. Yet right to the end the prosperity that politicans and company chairmen had predicted with such confidence was to elude them.

Meanwhile one section of workers after another including miners, engineers and workers in ship building and ship repair tried to resist, but bit by bit they were beaten back and defeated. Under pressure of mass unemployment among their members and indeed loss of members, trade union leaders were obliged to accept wage reductions which in some industries were very steep.

It was in this context that the battle over the wages paid to Poplar's employees was fought. The original £4 minimum fixed in 1920 had been designed to prove that a Labour authority was a model employer. But its preservation was later seen as a contribution towards the general struggle to resist wage cuts. Precisely because it was a Labour council, it must do its utmost to act in solidarity with the trade unionists who were fighting against wage cuts in every industry, or so the Poplar councillors believed. Their belief was the opposite of that of Herbert Morrison who, as we have seen, was in favour of municipal wage levels rising and falling with those outside.[4]

The Poplar employers had begun to complain in 1921 that the pay of workers in private employment locally compared unfavourably with that of borough council employees, and was arousing discontent. They stressed the fact that if the council's wage bill could be reduced, their own rates could also be lowered, thus lightening an unnecessary burden which was itself inhibiting recovery.

Towards the end of 1921 the Poplar Municipal Alliance sent a resolution to the council protesting at the fact that 'notwithstanding the gradual reduction in the cost of living and the agreement arrived at between employers and trade unions as to the lowering of salaries, wages etc, in accordance with such agreement, no steps have been taken by the council and guardians to give effect to same.'[5] This resolution was of course ignored by both council and Guardians and, at the beginning of 1922, the Municipal Alliance issued a public declaration denouncing the 'disproportionate payment of wages by the Borough Council and Guardians compared with private firms'.

> This unequal and unfair treatment in the payment of wages, etc., naturally breeds discontent amongst men engaged in similar occupations and trades under private control – not that the men employed by private undertakings are dissatisfied with their agreed scale of wages, but it is in the nature of things for them to make unfavourable comparison between themselves and the various artizans and workmen of the Borough Council and Guardians. . . . The Borough Council's and Guardians' workmen in their daily encounters make no secret either of their shorter hours, their higher remuneration or the more easy conditions of their labour.[6]

The statement alleged that a bricklayer working for a private contractor earned 2s 0½d an hour, whereas one working for the borough council was paid 2s 2½d; builders' labourers got 1s 7½d an hour while the council paid them 1s 10d. Moreover, the National Council for the Building Industry had recently agreed that the pay of building workers should go down by a further halfpenny.

The Municipal Alliance further pointed out that labourers working on roads, drains and sewers were shortly to get 1s 5½d per hour (which, though the statement did not say so, meant £3 8s 6d for a 47-hour week). But, it said, the labourers employed by the borough council 'receive £4 per week for 47 hours, equalling practically 1s 8½d per hour'. And, it went on, 'a Dustman is receiving £4 a week and a convenience attendant, married to the Dustman, also receives £4 a week – £8 per week going into one household'.

Shortly afterwards there were questions in the House of Commons. Sir Alfred Mond was asked whether he was aware of the resentment caused by the maintenance of Poplar's wages 'above the rates ruling under trade union agreements and in accordance with the scale based upon cost of living, and whether he can take any action to remove this cause of unrest'? Mond replied that he had no power to take any action.[7]

By July 1922 the Poplar councillors felt obliged to reconsider the position. They were faced with a difficult problem. On the one hand they believed that wage cuts should be resisted and they had done their best to fortify such resistance. On the other hand, they had to consider their electors, many of whom were very poor, and for whom increases or reductions in rates were reflected in their weekly rent books. They decided that some reductions must be made, and the resolution to do so was moved by John Scurr who said that they considered that members of the working class were entitled to a much higher standard, but at the same time they had to face certain economic facts and compromise between their real views and the actual conditions prevailing.[8] However, the reductions decided upon turned out to be marginal. It was agreed to implement only half of the reductions accepted by the JICs and trade unions concerned, and then only those which came above the minimum. This minimum – £4 for the unskilled, £4 5s for skilled workers – was to remain untouched.

The decision infuriated the local employers, and a former councillor, Frederick Thorne of Messrs Fred and T. Thorne – builders with premises on the Isle of Dogs – decided to challenge the council on the issue. It so happened that his firm wanted to have a drain relaid and connected to the council's sewer. The firm asked to do the work themselves, but the council refused to grant them a licence, and instead used their statutory right to carry out the work by direct labour, after which they sent a bill to Thorne for £30 0s 9d for work done. But Thorne offered payment of £25 only, since this was the amount that would have been due had the labour been paid at 1s 4d an hour instead of at the council rate of 1s 10d. Thorne refused to settle the bill and early in 1923 the council sued him. When it came up at Thames Police Court the magistrate, Mr J. A. R. Cairns, sided with Thorne.[9] In giving his decision he said that the question turned on whether the council was entitled to pay wages substantially above those fixed by agreement between employers and operatives and pass on these wage costs to the person for whom they had done the work. The only matter in dispute was whether the rate paid was reasonable. He thought that the wages accepted by the trade union on work of that kind must be taken as reasonable. 'Suppose the council had decided to embark on a social experiment to pay its labourers and carmen 20s or some such fanciful figure per hour, would I be compelled to accept the resolution of the council as final?' he asked. He dismissed the summons and awarded twelve guineas costs against the council.[10]

It was the first sign of the difficulties the Poplar council might face if it persisted in its wages policy. The next attack was a much more formidable one: in May 1923 the District Auditor threatened to surcharge the councillors with £17,000 paid in wages in excess of the trade union rate for the year ending March 1922. The case which arose out of this action and which was not finally settled for several years had repercussions far beyond Poplar.

At the time the growing powers of the District Auditor had already been a subject of controversy and, indeed, complaint from both Guardians and councillors. The District Auditors owed their origin to the 1834 Poor Law Amendment Act which empowered the appropriate government department to appoint officers to audit the accounts of guardians, to disallow any unlawful payments and to surcharge individual Guardians with the amounts involved in such payments, compelling them to repay it personally or risk distraint upon their goods and chattels. In the decades that followed the audit system was extended to include the accounts of other local councils, and every year the number of surcharges and disallowances ran into many hundreds. In 1921–2, for example, there were 1,680 disallowances in England and Wales. Most of the surcharges were trivial in amount and were repaid without argument by those responsible. But any councillors surcharged had the right to appeal either to the courts or to the Minister of Health, and every year some of them did so. The Minister of Health could reverse the Auditor's decision or he could uphold it, but in either case he could relieve the person surcharged of the liability to pay. In practice the majority of those who appealed against surcharge were so relieved. Thus in 1921–2 there were 198 appeals but in only seven was cancellation of the surcharge refused. In eight other cases the Auditor's decision was reversed, but in no less than 183 though the Auditor's decision was confirmed, the surcharge was remitted. It was in effect a method of ensuring that those who were surcharged did not repeat their offence.

If the Auditor had confined his disallowances to cases involving corruption, fraud, misconduct or even negligence, there would have been small cause for complaint. The controversy had arisen because throughout the nineteenth century, as a result of various legal cases, the powers of the Auditor had been gradually extended outside these areas. In the first place he could surcharge for items of expenditure which were 'unreasonable' or 'excessive' and the judge of this was not, it seemed, the elected councillors but the non-elected Auditor, backed up, if put to the test, by the Minister of Health on the one hand and the judges on the other. In the second place, items which the Auditor could disallow as 'contrary to law' had been continually added to by the development of the doctrine of *ultra vires*, whereby the judges had decided that it was illegal for a local authority to spend money on any purpose which had not been specifically authorised by Parliament. All in all the District Auditor was devoting an increasing proportion of his attention not to the accuracy of the accounts but, as the Webbs put it, 'to what is complained of as an "audit of policy"'.[11] More and more the Auditor was being used as a device to insist on policies which the Minister of Health thought desirable, but which he had no other legal powers to enforce.

The Poplar wage case now involved the extension of the Auditor's powers in a new direction. For on this occasion he was challenging the right of the councillors to exercise a power actually conferred on them by Parliament. Section 62 of the Metropolis Management Act of 1855 empowered the council to employ such servants as might be necessary and to pay them such salaries or wages as it (the council) might think fit.[12] The Auditor was thus attempting to stop the council doing something which by law it was specifically entitled to do.

All this was not yet quite clear when the District Auditor, Mr Carson Roberts, summoned the Poplar Borough Council to show cause why they should not be surcharged £17,000 in respect of excess wages paid in the year 1921–2. The hearing took place on 31 May 1923 in the council chamber.[13] The councillors were anxious to discover the legal grounds for the surcharge and had therefore intended that the hearing should be held in private. However, half an hour before the proceedings began, a large crowd assembled outside the building singing 'The Red Flag' and trying to get in. After finding that some of their supporters had already gained access, the councillors decided to allow as many as could be accommodated into the public gallery, where, despite efforts by Lansbury and others to restrain them, they did not hesitate to applaud the councillors and shout rude remarks at their opponents.

The councillors' attempts to discover the legal basis of the Auditor's proposed surcharge failed at this hearing. John Scurr, who had been elected mayor for that year, asked the Auditor to point out where they had committed an illegal act. The Auditor merely replied that he was there to listen to any case for or against. Pressed further by George Lansbury, he admitted that the legal question at issue appeared to be whether the council had complete discretion as to the wages it paid, or whether there was a point where the government Auditor had a right to step in. George Lansbury said that they could not answer a charge before it was made, but no clearer indication of the Auditor's legal grounds emerged. John Scurr then submitted a statement on behalf of himself and the other members of the council in which he claimed that the Auditor was going beyond his jurisdiction, and he had no power to surcharge in respect of wages which were above the trade union minimum rate, because Section 62 of the Metropolis Management Act of 1855 placed the matter definitely within the jurisdiction of the council, which was authorised to pay such salaries and wages as it might think fit. He went on to claim that the £4 minimum had been confirmed by the electors in the November 1922 election.

One of the functions of the Auditor was to examine the complaints of aggrieved ratepayers, and on this occasion the Poplar Ratepayers' Association (with which the Poplar Municipal Alliance had amalgamated) engaged a well known KC and local government expert, Edward Naldrett, to question the legality of the £4 minimum. He said that he represented some two hundred ratepayers and maintained that the council was not entitled to pass a resolution such as that establishing the £4 minimum. He referred to the case of Thorne and quoted the opinion of the magistrate in that case. Ex-councillor F. Thorne then spoke up and was continually interrupted from the gallery, after which, in reply to further questions by Lansbury, the Auditor said he had received letters of complaint about the wages and that exception had been taken to the council's attitude by an association of manufacturers.

The Auditor did not make his final decision known at the hearing, but a few days later the councillors received it in writing. He had decided to enforce a surcharge in respect of the wages paid, but instead of the original sum of £17,000 had reduced the amount to £5,000.

The response of the councillors was to call a special meeting of the borough council on 12 June 1923 and on this occasion no attempt was made to restrain the crowd which packed the gallery and the body of the hall to its utmost capacity and spent the time before the meeting singing not only 'The Red Flag' but a song currently popular called 'I want some money'.[14]

On behalf of the finance committee, J. J. Rugless explained that the council had two alternative courses of action: they could appeal to the courts, or they could appeal to the Minister of Health. In view of the importance to local government in general of obtaining a ruling on the points of law involved, the committee believed they should go to the court. Charles Key pointed out that the question at issue was whether a local authority was to carry on in the way it had been elected to do or whether the central government was to be allowed to step in and stop it. He contended that the £4 minimum had been justified by the 1922 election and that the Auditor was trying to prevent them carrying out a policy which had the electorate's support.

Sumner said that although the London County Council did not agree with Poplar's policy, they were very much surprised at the Auditor's ruling. And indeed, as the case went on its implications were to cause consternation in local government circles far removed from Poplar. George Lansbury observed that the councillors' crime was that, when they got the power, they did what they had said they would do.[15]

The resolution to appeal to the court was carried, after which the matter was handed over to the lawyers. As in earlier cases the council's solicitor, W. H. Thompson, engaged Henry Slessor and the case came up in November before the Lord Chief Justice, Lord Hewart, and Judges Sankey and Salter who gave judgement against Poplar on 21 November, apparently on the grounds that the words in the Metropolis Management Act did not mean what they said. Section 62 of the Act had laid it down that the council could pay such wages 'as they think fit'. But the judges said: 'We cannot think that the words "as they think fit" entitled a council to pay any sum that they like to any of their employees.' And they went on to argue that the council was in a 'fiduciary position', not merely to the majority who elected them but to all the ratepayers. 'A councillor', the judges said, 'is not entitled to be unduly generous at the expense of those on whose behalf he is a trustee.' And they added: 'We think that a payment to a servant . . . may be of so excessive a character as to go beyond the limits of legality and become an illegal, or *ultra vires* payment.'[16]

At this, the councillors decided to take the matter to appeal.

NOTES

1. THL, Poplar Box 880. Letter to Mond dated 26 June 1922.
2. 1922–3: 22s 8d; 1923–4: 23s.
3. THL, Poplar Box 880. Letter to Mond dated 26 June 1922.
4. According to Herbert Morrison's autobiography, the £4 minimum (which was first introduced by Bermondsey Borough Council) 'placed the union leaders in difficulties'. He added: 'Ernest Bevin in particular did not like it. The increase had been simply bestowed on the members of his union, and the negotiating machinery had been ignored. Bevin and his fellow trade union leaders then took the view that if Labour majorities were going to do that sort of thing, there was no point in having unions or collective bargaining' (*Herbert Morrison. An Autobiography* by Lord Morrison of Lambeth, 1960, p. 89). Ernest Bevin was the first general secretary of the Transport and General Workers' Union, formed in 1922.
5. EEN, 31 January 1922.
6. ibid.
7. House of Commons, *Hansard*, 15 February 1922.
8. ELA, 5 August 1922.
9. John Arthur Robert Cairns, Metropolitan Police Magistrate from 1920 onwards. Stood as a Liberal candidate in the 1928 general election.
10. ELA, 17 March 1923.
11. Sidney and Beatrice Webb, *English Poor Law History*, part 2, *The Last Hundred Years*, vol. 1, p. 215.
12. The power under the Metropolis Management Act was actually conferred on Boards of Works and Vestries; when the metropolitan borough councils came into existence they took over the powers of these bodies.
13. ELA, 2 June 1923 and EEN, 5 June 1923.
14. The words of this song ran as follows:
    > I want some money,
    > Gimme some, gimme some, gimme some, gimme some, do.
    > Isn't it funny
    > What a lot of difference money makes to you.
15. EEN, 15 June 1923.
16. *The Times*, law report, 22 November 1923.

12

The Guardians and the Dock Strike

The Poplar Order which declared that any relief in excess of the Mond scale was illegal had been issued in June 1922. From that month onwards, throughout the rest of 1922 and the whole of 1923, the Poplar Guardians deliberately violated the provisions of the order. Week after week they paid out relief on a level higher than the scale prescribed. In particular, they failed to enforce Mond's maximum for large families or to obey the rules on the treatment of the resources of relatives. And regularly every week, they reported such cases to the Ministry as 'excep tions'.

For most London boards of guardians the Mond scale was by mid-1923 a thing of the past. Devised as a method of pooling relief costs, it was soon replaced by a simpler scheme which required the London guardians to calculate their claims on the Common Poor Fund by means of a flat rate of 9d per day per person relieved. Only in Poplar did the Mond scale have any application, and here it was a maximum scale which the Poplar Guardians deliberately disregarded.

It was constantly suggested that the rest of London was footing the Bill for Poplar's illegal overpayments. This was in one sense a misleading allegation and always had been. For under the new 1923 Act, Poplar could only draw on the Metropolitan Common Poor Fund for expenditure of 9d per day per person relieved, a total which worked out rather lower than the cost of the Mond scale and a good deal lower than the cost of Poplar's scale. All the rest of their relief expenditure was paid for out of Poplar's local rates. But in another sense the charge that others were paying for Poplar's generosity was not unfounded, since the numbers on relief would have been fewer had Poplar treated the resources of relatives as expected of them, fewer still had it adopted the severely deterrent policy of some London Boards. This was one reason why the numbers on relief in Poplar were so high; by this time they amounted to nineteen in every hundred, or nearly one person in five.

The Guardians knew, of course, that one day they would be

called to account for their disregard of the Poplar Order. Even
if the Ministry took no other steps, the District Auditor would
declare the expenditure illegal when the time came and they
would all be surcharged. Unless they could persuade the Minister of Health to let them off these surcharges, they could be sold
up and their furniture and other possessions seized and, indeed,
might all end up in jail again. They knew that this was the
prospect which faced them in the end, but for some reason,
unaccountable to their enemies, the day of reckoning never
seemed to arrive.

True, the Guardians did receive one Auditor's report towards
the end of 1922, but this was for the half year ending March
1922, a period before the Poplar Order had been thought of and
before any maximum scale had been legally imposed on the
Guardians. Thus the border-line between what was legal and
what was not was still blurred for the period in question. In this
report, however, the Auditor, a man named A. G. Twiss, made
charges very similar to those in the Cooper Report. It was
apparent that he was no supporter of the theory that the func-
tion of the elected representatives was to decide policy, that of
the officials to carry it out. On the contrary there was an implied
criticism of the officials for their subservience to the elected
Guardians. He said of the Relieving Officers: 'It would seem
that they are completely dominated by the Guardians and
timorous of exercising any discretion vested in them otherwise
than in favour of the applicant. . . .' And he went on: 'It is
evident that the Relieving Officers no longer consider whether
the case is one of sudden or urgent necessity, but apply the less
stringent test as to whether the case is one in which the Guardians are likely to make an Order.'[1]

Like Cooper, he thought the Guardians' approach was
demoralising the unemployed: 'I am convinced that the lavish
way in which relief is being distributed by the Guardians must
have the effect of destroying any desire on the part of the
recipients to obtain work.'

The Guardians' refusal to operate the household means test
in the approved fashion and take fully into account the resources
of relatives was severely censured. 'The case of JL makes it clear
that the Guardians refuse to recognise the legal and moral
obligations of a single son, earning £4 10s weekly, to maintain
his aged parents,' he commented. And again: 'A large percent-

age of the cases relieved are of young single men out of work. Many of these are members of households of which the weekly income is sufficiently large to preclude any question of destitution.'

In Twiss's view the obligation upon relatives to maintain one another did not only rest with parents and children, brothers and sisters, but also with fathers-in-law and brothers-in-law, as was made clear in the case of AB:

> The case of AB . . . relates to a widow aged 28 with an infant child aged 2. The woman lives with her father-in-law and his single son. . . . The RO reported that both men refused information as to their wages. The father-in-law is an LCC watchman and would earn about 50s weekly. His son is a carman and his wages . . . would be from 50s to 60s weekly. . . . The Guardians granted relief amounting to 21s 0d, readily accepting the suggestion that the men do their own housekeeping and that the woman merely occupies two rooms upstairs. The result is that two able-bodied men without dependants, earning between them at least £5 a week, are provided with a housekeeper at the expense of the rates.

Like Cooper, Twiss strongly disapproved of the extra Christmas relief of 5s for each adult and 2s for each child provided in December 1921, saying that this appeared to him to be 'unreasonable and excessive' and moreover placed the recipients of relief 'in a better position during Christmas week than their neighbours who were so unfortunate as to be endeavouring to support themselves by their own unaided exertions'.

The report was forwarded to the Guardians by the Ministry which asked for their comments, and in February 1923 Edgar Lansbury, as chairman of the Board, made a detailed reply to the Auditor's criticisms.[2] His comment on the allegation that the Guardians were encouraging idleness by their lavish relief was bitter:

> If, rather than studying case-papers (the Auditor), would study the hundreds of unemployed men and women who daily call upon the local Guardians and Councillors begging for work instead of 'lavish' relief the Guardians might be more impressed with his opinion. The actual fact is that whenever there is any work to do, there is the keenest competition to obtain it amongst those who are

on relief, and much resentment and jealousy is engendered between the few who get the work and those who do not. Let the Auditor come to Poplar and tell the men and women themselves that they are fortunate in having no work and being on Parish Relief.

Edgar condemned the 'slanderous and callous attacks upon those who are forced by circumstances to seek relief', and ended by saying that they intended to go on with their work as Guardians of the Poor since 'they do not accept the view that they were elected to be Guardians of the old and discredited Poor Law principles which animate the present Auditor's report'.

In the end, despite his detailed criticism, the Auditor only disallowed one item of expenditure, namely, half the Christmas relief. For this he imposed a surcharge of £1,778 on David Adams and Charlie Sumner who had been the mover and seconder of the resolution to give this extra help. Perhaps conscious that it was not the best possible ground on which to engage Poplar in combat, the Minister of Health cancelled this particular surcharge a few months later.

Meanwhile everyone was aware that it was not this but the next Auditor's report which would matter. For it was during the subsequent half year – April to September 1922 – that the Poplar Order had come into operation and the deliberate violations of the law had commenced. But the time when this report should have appeared, i.e. spring or summer of 1923, passed without any sign that it was on its way. The process of audit had often been conducted in a somewhat leisurely fashion but on this occasion those responsible appeared to be gripped by some kind of paralysis. So for a period the Poplar Board of Guardians ceased to make national news headlines. But it was to become the target once more in August 1923 during an unofficial dock strike.

The origin of this strike was a demand by the Port employers at the beginning of 1922 for a reduction of three shillings a day in dockers' pay so that the minimum would go down from 13s to 10s a day. Most of the dockers were in the Transport and General Workers' Union which had first come into existence on New Year's Day 1922 as result of the amalgamation of a number of dock and transport unions. The general secretary of this giant organisation was Ernest Bevin and the one thing he wanted to avoid while the new union was finding its feet was a major industrial dispute. However, good generals do not wait for their opponents to signal their readiness for combat. On the contrary, if the enemy is regrouping and quite unprepared that is the moment to mount an offensive. This is what the dock employers did in January 1922.

At the time work in the docks was scarce, and most trade unions were in process of conceding wage reductions, so it was not surprising that Bevin surrendered one shilling immediately and promised that the remaining two shillings would be discussed within six months. By September 1922 he had signed a compromise agreement for the second shilling to go, on the understanding that the third shilling reduction was not to come into force until June 1923, and then only if the official cost-of-living index fell ten points below the level of September 1922. Bevin secured the endorsement of a delegate conference of the docks group of the union for this agreement soon after it was made in the autumn of 1922. He stated, among other things, that the employers had been trying to lengthen the working day, but that the union had successfully protected the existing hours and conditions of work which were much more important than wages. 'It must not be assumed that this acceptance (of the wage cut) represents any weakness,' stated the T&GWU *Record* in September 1922: 'It is merely an appreciation of the economic circumstances of the moment.'

No doubt those who endorsed this agreement thought that the second shilling cut was inevitable but that the third might never happen. Even so the agreement was a dubious one. Bevin himself had attacked the practice of tying wages to the cost-of-living index at the famous transport inquiry in 1920, and this particular agreement was a bad bargain even on paper.[3] When mass meetings were held in the autumn of 1922 in the East End of London to explain its terms there was much opposition. The *Record* (August 1923) later claimed that the proposed settlement had been sent to dock branches in London, but of these 'only 47 took the trouble to vote, 26 voted in favour of acceptance, and 21 against, the other 29 did not bother'. This, on the face of it, was hardly an overwhelming vote of confidence. It was not the last time that Bevin was to misjudge the mood of his members, to underestimate their will to resist attacks on their standards, and then to blame them for the subsequent anger and disarray.

In June 1923 the inevitable happened. The official cost of living index fell to 169 (it went up again immediately afterwards and did not resume its downward course until after 1926); by July the Port employers were trying to enforce the third shilling wage cut and Bevin had a vast unofficial strike on his hands which, starting in Hull on 2 July, spread rapidly to other ports including London.

For many of the dock labourers the prospect of a further wage cut was intolerable. Work was so scarce that many could only expect two or three days' work a week. This meant trying to live on half wages – about 33s a week – eked out with a few shillings unemployment benefit for idle days. Now even this wretched remuneration was to be lowered. Among other things, the men argued that prices had not really fallen as implied by the official cost of living index. 'Shopkeepers in West Ham, Woolwich and Wapping are not responsive to charts compiled in Westminster' was the ironic comment of the London un-official strike committee.[4] 'The officials have always been great guys for sliding agreements – they slide one way, and that is the employer's way' wrote an indignant reader to the *Daily Herald*.[5] But since Lansbury had left the *Daily Herald* and the TUC had made itself responsible for the paper, its tone had changed. Now it was publishing leaders which stressed the moral obligation of workers to abide by agreements arrived at by their leaders.

The annual conference of the Transport and General Workers Union took place on 9 July and, after an unsuccessful attempt by some dock worker delegates to obtain union support for the strike, a resolution was carried by a large majority requesting the men to call it off and honour the agreement for a cut in pay. As a result, the strikers at most ports returned to work within a few days, though Hull remained out until the end of July. But in London the strike went on and on; at its peak there were said to be 60,000 men idle, and resistance only finally collapsed on 19 August.

One factor which helped prolong the strike was the action of the Stevedores' Union in declaring it official. The Stevedores' Labour Protection League was a small union which had declined to amalgamate with the T&GWU. Its headquarters were in Poplar and its membership came overwhelmingly from East London. The stevedores were skilled men; when in regular work they might earn as much as £6 a week. Strikers from

another skilled section, the lightermen, who, unlike the stevedores, had been parties to the T&GWU amalgamation, now
announced their intention of leaving that union and forming a
new one together with the stevedores and any dock labourers
who would join. Thus Bevin was faced not only with an
unofficial strike but with an attempted breakaway. Bevin's
reaction was one that became familiar in the inter-war period.
Utterly convinced of the correctness of his own judgement, he
sought for ulterior motives among those who opposed him. Thus
he presented the affair as an attempt by communists to smash
the T&GWU. In fact, the strike leaders had publicly dissociated
themselves from the communists, and the communists in turn,
though actively supporting the strike and denouncing Bevin for
his acceptance of a wage cut, had nevertheless made clear their
total opposition to the formation of a breakaway union.

Poplar, being one of the main waterside boroughs, was
inevitably the centre of strike activity, indeed, the unofficial
strike committee's headquarters was in Poplar Town Hall. For
the councillors it was a situation of great difficulty. Three of
them, Hegarty, Sloman and O'Callaghan, were active members
of the Stevedores' union. On the other hand, Petherick and
Adams were in the T&GWU. Petherick went on working
throughout the strike and his family was the target of so much
hostility that as a result he moved temporarily into Tottenham.
David Adams was a full-time T&GWU official; his office was
occupied by members of the unofficial strike committee for use
as a committee room, a situation which he seems to have
accepted; certainly he remained on the premises himself.

In such circumstances it was not surprising that the Poplar
councillors should keep quiet about their attitude to the strike;
only O'Callaghan, one of the stevedores, was provoked into
making a reply to Bevin's allegation that the Stevedores' Union
was trying to separate the waterside workers from their fellows
in the provinces. 'Mr Bevin is doing the separating by his foolish
attacks on a union which is far better organised than his own,'
O'Callaghan told the *Daily Herald*.[6] George Lansbury expressed
the feelings of a number of them when he wrote to *The Times*: 'I
deplore the present dispute more than I can say, not at all
because I am on the side of the employers, but solely because of
the disunity and destruction of trade union loyalty and discipline which has ensued.'[7]

Whether they liked it or not, the Poplar Guardians became embroiled in the strike because after it had been on for a while some of the strikers began to apply to them for relief. They comprised some 1,700 to 1,800 men who had previously been working only part of the week and had been signing on at the employment exchange and drawing benefit for idle days. When the strike took place they not only stopped receiving any wages, but the employment exchange cut them off unemployment benefit, as it was against the law to pay benefit to anyone involved in a trade dispute. The men concerned had appealed against this disallowance, arguing that they should not be classed as strikers. Since they worked on a daily contract, they were unemployed men who were refusing to make contracts at a lower rate. Not surprisingly this appeal failed. As it was an unofficial strike, the men were getting no strike pay and after trying to hold out for a little they came to the Guardians for relief. The same thing was happening in other waterside boroughs and in every one the Guardians were faced with a difficult decision.

The legal position was ostensibly governed by what was known as the Merthyr Tydfil judgement of 1900 which held, in effect, that it was illegal for guardians to give any form of poor relief to strikers themselves, but *not* illegal to relieve their wives and children.

This general ruling applied not only at the beginning of the century, it has applied to the law governing social security ever since. The trade union movement has never officially demanded that strikers should be maintained out of public money; at the same time governments have not seriously tried to prohibit the relief of strikers' children. It has, however, always been a sensitive area of debate. Those who look on strikes as manifestations of bloody-mindedness are apt to be driven into a frenzy if they think their rates and taxes can be used to support them. And it cannot be denied that if wives and children are given relief, they are likely to share it with the breadwinner. On the other hand, those who see a strike as an unequal contest between exploiter and exploited have argued (as Edgar Lansbury did) that if the workers are to be defeated it must not be by starvation, since the employers are not going to starve, whatever happens.

When the dock strikers began to apply for relief, the response of the boards of guardians in London differed according to the political outlook of those in charge. Woolwich, Lambeth, East Ham, Camberwell and Southwark took a hard line in keeping with the Poor Law tradition; they were reported to be refusing relief except to strikers who produced a doctor's certificate stating that they were starving. In Bethnal Green and Stepney, relief was given to dependents of strikers only, which was the most the law permitted. The West Ham Guardians, known to be controlled by left-wingers, managed to get round the law. They treated the men as though they were unemployed and put them on their usual scale of out-relief, but they said it was 'on loan', knowing perfectly well that they would never see a penny of it back. But in Poplar and in Bermondsey, dockers on strike were treated exactly as though they were unemployed, with no pretence that relief was 'on loan'. There was no doubt in anyone's mind that this action was illegal.

Ironically enough, one of those in Poplar most actively engaged in seeing to it that strikers got relief was Councillor David Adams, the T&GWU official, whose office had been occupied by strikers but who was himself a Guardian. The applications for relief were so numerous that the members of his particular relief committee were obliged to divide up the interviewing. Adams himself averaged 400 interviews a week, but one week they touched 800. His average was only surpassed by the two women Guardians, Julia Scurr and Helen McKay, who dealt with an even greater number.

Inevitably, as the strike came to an end in ports outside London, the Bermondsey and Poplar Guardians came under attack; it was their action alone, argued writers to *The Times*, that was prolonging the strike. Day after day news of the strike was conveyed under headlines such as 'Strikers on the Rates', or 'The Rate-Aided Dock Strike'. Once more the hunt was up, the newshounds were in full cry on Poplar's trail.

In retrospect it seems doubtful whether the actions of Poplar and Bermondsey Guardians influenced the duration of the strike. Its moving spirits were the stevedores and lightermen, skilled workers, many of whom were in a position to live off savings for a short while. After the strike was over John Scurr firmly denied that Poplar's policy had kept the men out. 'Years ago when there was an official strike and the Board did not give relief it lasted many more months than in this case,' he said. 'The majority of strikers never came either to Poplar, West Ham or Bermondsey Guardians, but buckled their belts a little tighter, and did the best they could living on their savings.'[8]

However, as chairman of the Guardians, Edgar Lansbury was not inclined to equivocate. He had always claimed that one of the objects in keeping relief scales as high as they could was to discourage the reduction of wages. When the newspapers now accused them of giving relief which, in certain cases, was higher than the wages dockers could earn, Edgar did not reply, as he might have done, that only large families received relief which was higher than a normal wage and that most people were much better off if they were working than on relief. Instead, he entirely accepted the charge that some strikers were getting relief above what they had earned, and emphasised that this did not apply only to dockers but to other workers as well. The Guardians had to relieve destitution, and that adequately, he said, and if in so doing they were paying more in relief than some of the men got in wages, 'well, so much the better for relief and so much the worse for wages'. For the first time in any dispute he could remember, the workers 'had been able to stand up to the employers with a full belly. The employers had not been used to that.' This time the workers had not been compelled to starve as they did in the past when there had been an industrial struggle, with the result the press had been filled with 'blackguardly remarks'.[9]

Despite these words, made shortly after the strike collapsed on 19 August, support for the strikers had precipitated a financial crisis for the Board of Guardians. For it had pushed up the cost of out-relief from £11,000 a week at the beginning of July to £14,500 by mid-August,[10] with the result that the Guardians found themselves by September faced with the need to reduce expenditure.

They did consider asking the borough council for a higher rate contribution as an alternative but were reluctant to do this since the rates had already been raised that year. Their only other course was to reduce their scales of relief and this in the end they decided to do.

It was not only the financial crisis which had brought about this retreat. The fact was that after two years, during which their scale had not been varied while prices and wages had fallen very substantially, they had found, despite Edgar's brave words, that the scale for the larger families was indeed higher than many people's wages and was beginning to cause divisions. Already at the end of December 1922 they had held a special joint discussion with representatives of the local Trades Council and of the local unemployed organisations on the whole issue of the relationship between wage levels and relief scales. At the time they postponed action, now they could do so no longer. They had fought their prolonged rearguard action believing that if every public authority did likewise the drive for wage reductions could be halted. But they had not succeeded in persuading other Labour authorities to take such a stand, and wages had been forced down willy nilly. In their own area, dry dock labourers were now getting only £2 6s 11d for a full week's work, the docker was getting £2 13s 10d, the railway goods yard man £2 8s and the road labourer £2 10s 10d.

In this situation it had become harder to justify a scale which, if rent and fuel were included, gave £2 8s to a man with wife and three children and much more to families with four or more children. Increasingly there were signs that the continued maintenance of the scale, now worth far more than it had been when introduced, was creating dissension among their own followers. In an interview with the local paper Edgar said: 'The Guardians decided – in fact the Labour people of Poplar decided – that the time had come when it was necessary to consider the scale and to see whether we were justified in maintaining it, especially in cases where there were large families and where the scale exceeded the ordinary rate of wages very largely.'[11]

The guardians accordingly lowered their scale by reducing the allowance per child where there were two or more children. They ceased to publish any scale rate for families with more than six children. Allowances for the small families with only one child, and for single people, remained untouched, as did the method of treating the resources of relatives. The combined result was a new scale still above the Mond scale.

The reductions were preceded by an exceedingly unpleasant event. At a meeting on 26 September the Guardians were visited by a deputation from the Unemployed Workers' Organisation with a request for higher allowances for single people. As chairman, Edgar Lansbury replied, explaining with regret that a reduction in allowances was to be recommended, though not those of single people. After closing the meeting, he found his way blocked by a crowd of some two hundred unemployed at the foot of the stairs who had locked and bolted the front door. After a scuffle, Edgar returned to the boardroom where the Guardians all sat down again, and for an hour and a half rude remarks were shouted from the gallery while George Lansbury engaged in a heated exchange with some of the demonstrators. One of the officials had meanwhile phoned the police who turned up in large numbers outside the building. It was proposed they should be authorised to break in. Edgar Lansbury opposed this, believing that they should sit it out as before, but this time he found himself in a minority. After some argument between the Guardians the police were authorised to enter. Thereupon Edgar's misgivings were justified. The police smashed the windows to get in and once inside used their truncheons on the demonstrators in such a fashion that twenty had to be treated in hospital.

Part of the background to this affair was the resentment felt by the Guardians at attacks from people who they thought should be their allies. The Unemployed Workers' Organisation (UWO) which was responsible for the demonstration was a body set up as a rival to the Communist-led National Unemployed Workers' Movement. The UWO was under the influence of Sylvia Pankhurst who had been expelled from the Communist Party and who was an 'anti-parliamentarian', in other words, she believed that socialists should not participate in parliament or in borough council or Guardian work. This brought her into conflict with the Poplar councillors including a number of people who had once collaborated with her in struggles for women's rights and against the war.

Though not herself present at the UWO demonstration she now wrote an article about it in her paper, the *Workers' Dreadnought*, based on reports from UWO members present. It appeared on 6 October; in it she accused A. A. Watts of proposing that the police be brought in, but her main target was George Lansbury. 'The result of working-class representatives taking part in the administration of capitalist machinery is that working-class representatives become responsible for maintaining capitalist law and order and for enforcing the regulations of the capitalist system itself,' she wrote. This assertion, valid in some areas, hardly fitted the facts in Poplar where the Guardians still had the threat of surcharge and possible prison hanging over them because of their refusal to operate the regulations and, moreover, were soon to be taken to court for their defiance of the law over the dock strike.

However, the local leader of the UWO was at long last able to express some satisfaction that his theory had been proved right. 'The policy of the UWO is definitely anti-parliamentary, and we can claim victory for our defeat by being able to prove the fallacy and futility of the local governing bodies in their endeavour to abolish poverty and distress,' he wrote in the *Workers' Dreadnought* on 13 October.[12]

Meanwhile, the local employers in Poplar were a long way from believing that the Guardians were 'assisting in the maintenance of the capitalist system' as alleged by Pankhurst. On the contrary, for them, the Guardians' stand over the dock strike had been the last straw. They were by no means mollified by the reductions in the scale of allowances subsequently announced, and their anger at the failure of the Government to deal with Poplar had been mounting. Indeed, the behaviour of the Conservative Ministers who had taken office at the end of 1922 had been the opposite of what was expected in this respect and, in particular, had been a grave disappointment to Sir Alfred Warren, now secretary of the Poplar Ratepayers' Association, which had amalgamated with the former Poplar Municipal Alliance.

Warren had been irritated enough with the Lloyd George Government and Mond's failure to deal with Poplar; shortly before that Government's fall he had had an interview with one of Mond's officials at the Ministry of Health, during which he had denounced them as an 'inveterate body of jelly-fish administrators' and had blamed them for their 'shilly-shallying policy or want of policy'.[13]

But ever since the arrival of the Bonar Law Government and Mond's departure, Warren and his friends had been cold-shouldered in a fashion they had not anticipated. Initially this was partly the result of a political vacuum at the Ministry of Health itself. In the temporary Government formed by Bonar Law in October 1922, Arthur Griffith Boscawen had held the post of Minister of Health. He, however, had lost his seat in the subsequent general election. He had then remained in the Cabinet as Minister of Health while a convenient by-election was sought; this seemed to have emerged early in 1923 with the safe Conservative seat of Mitcham, Surrey. But when the contest took place, Boscawen lost this seat too. It was not until 7 March, very late in the day, that Bonar Law accepted the inevitable and made Neville Chamberlain (up till then Postmaster-General) Minister of Health.

Warren had meanwhile written to the Ministry in January 1923 asking the Minister to receive a deputation to discuss action against the Poplar Guardians. In the circumstances it was not surprising that he had no reply. So after Chamberlain had been made Minister he wrote again on 1 May saying: 'We have been waiting since your official appointment to receive an answer to our communication of Jan 10.' He again asked the Minister to receive a deputation.

Any expectation that a Conservative administration would be more accommodating than the previous one was, however, swiftly dispelled. One day Chamberlain would prove himself a much more formidable opponent of Poplarism than anyone else. But at the time he had other things on his mind, with the result that he brushed aside Warren and his friends with an indifference which seemed to them humiliating. He did this all the more easily since Warren was no longer an MP. Twice in May and again in July and August they received letters explaining that Chamberlain could not receive a deputation from Poplar owing to the heavy calls on his time.[14]

At last on 9 August, while the dock strike was in progress, Warren wrote to Chamberlain complaining that the Poplar Guardians were illegally 'expending large sums of money weekly in relief of the strikers' and sent a copy of his letter to the newspapers, which published it. They also published a reply from the Ministry which came like one more slap in the face to Warren and his friends. For it simply stated that, if relief was being given unlawfully, there were two remedies. First, any ratepayer could apply to the High Court for an injunction to restrain the Guardians. Secondly, the District Auditor could disallow any expenditure which in his opinion was unlawful and surcharge the amount on the Guardians. However, since the Guardians were entitled to appeal to the Minister of Health against any such surcharge it was incumbent on the Minister to refrain from expressing a premature opinion.[15]

It was after this letter which conveyed such lofty disinterest that Percy Squires, chairman of the Poplar Ratepayers' Association and a manufacturer of printers' ink, began to discuss with Warren the possibility of direct action in the form of a rates strike by Poplar firms. Meanwhile the suggestion that a ratepayer could apply to the Court for an injunction against the Guardians was looked into. The employers in the Timber Trades Federation met at the London Chamber of Commerce and decided to take legal advice on the possibility of action against both the Poplar and the Bermondsey Boards of Guardians.[16] But since the strike ended a few days later the proposal to seek an injunction was dropped.

In actual fact, when Warren wrote to the Ministry on 9 August, Neville Chamberlain was fishing in Scotland and a Cabinet reshuffle was in progress. Stanley Baldwin had succeeded Bonar Law as Prime Minister and, after an unsuccessful attempt to install Reginald McKenna as his Chancellor of the Exchequer, he offered the job to Chamberlain who once more accepted a post for which he was merely the second choice. The Ministry of Health was in turn filled on 27 August by Sir William Joynson-Hicks.

To the new Minister, Sir Alfred Warren wrote yet another letter listing his attempts to lead a deputation to Chamberlain and the response he had received.

> You will therefore see that men having a very considerable interest in the affairs of Poplar have been endeavouring by every constitutional means to get before the responsible Minister so as to cogently state their case and to ascertain what measure of remedy, if any, the Government propose to take in dealing with the acute problem of socialist administration. We have been striving for nearly 9 months to obtain a hearing, but up to the present without avail. There is very acute feeling in the minds of men who in this Borough are having to bear very heavy responsibilities in respect of Rates at what they regard as scant courtesy on the part of the Ministry in not affording them an opportunity of an interview.[17]

Joynson-Hicks ('Jix' as he was nicknamed) was a very different character from either of his predecessors. No one could ever say of him that he shirked confrontation; indeed he welcomed it. He wrote to Warren saying that he would be pleased to meet his deputation on 4 October.

On meeting the Minister at last, the deputation produced its familiar list of complaints and asked him to take immediate action by withholding loans from Poplar, by disenfranchising those on poor relief and, if necessary, by superseding the local Poor Law Guardians altogether.

Joynson-Hicks seemed anxious to impress those present with the strength of his resolve to deal with Poplar once and for all. 'When I came to the Ministry a month ago, I knew that the question of Poplar was one of the difficult problems that was bound to come to my notice,' he said. 'Therefore I called for a report on conditions in Poplar'. Suggesting that Poplar's endeavour to provide 'full maintenance' for those on relief was 'a distinct challenge to the authority of Parliament', he nevertheless pointed out that if he were to take over administration of Poor Law in Poplar, as the deputation proposed, he would have to ask Parliament for new powers. 'I do not say that I shall not do that,' he observed, and went on: 'It is a question for me to weigh carefully, whether the time for action has or has not come, whether I should take any steps, and if so what steps.' He continued: 'You will realise that if I begin to take any steps whatever, those steps have got to go right through to the end. . . .' 'I am quite certain' he added, 'that any step I take will involve a very serious conflict with the Poplar Board of Guardians, they will be fighting for a principle – and one honours them for fighting even if one does not agree. It may be, if I decide upon it, a very stern, a difficult and a long fight.' Perhaps to emphasise that he was not of the same vacillating temperament as others, he ended the interview by once more insisting that, if he took the first step, he would 'go on to the end'.[18]

These portentous words were reported in the newspapers and were taken by them to mean that at long last Poplar was to be put down; one of them remarked that it was 'the writing on the wall' for the Poplar councillors.[19]

Curiously enough, those whom Joynson-Hicks intended to reassure were dissatisfied. When, on 11 October, a report was given on the deputation to a meeting of the Poplar Ratepayers' Association, those present were so exasperated by Hicks's references to a 'long fight' that they pledged themselves to withhold payment of the next quarter's rates and to continue to withhold payment till assured 'that sound and careful administration will be effected'. The meeting was chaired by Percy Squires and representatives of most of the largest firms were present. Guidance was promptly dispatched to all the firms concerned, making it clear that those who participated in the action and withheld their rates need not expect to go to prison; it was envisaged that the borough council would distrain upon their goods and put them up for auction, whereupon the firm concerned should step in and buy back its property at 'a figure not higher than the sum required to satisfy the Council's claim, plus a small sum for costs'.

This elaborate plan was never carried out. When Joynson-Hicks heard about it he wrote Warren a furious letter, denouncing them for 'preparing to follow the line of action which they so strongly criticise in the local authorities, and themselves to infringe the law of the land'. Two wrongs did not make a right, he said, and he could not countenance unconstitutional attempts to redress grievances. After which the organisers of the protest decided somewhat tamely that the proposed action should be called off.[20]

Joynson-Hicks had good reason to be annoyed, since he was not only determined to act, but to act fast. He raised the question with the Cabinet on 22 October 1923, proposing to revive the draft Bill which had been approved by the previous government and then abandoned. This draft Bill gave the Minister of Health power to dissolve a local board of guardians and appoint people to take over its duties. Joynson-Hicks proposed to expand it to enable a Minister to do the same with a borough council which defaulted. In other words it would give the Minister power to abolish both the Poplar council and the Poplar Guardians.

Joynson-Hicks outlined his case to the Cabinet in a lengthy memorandum.[21] He pointed out that the Poplar Guardians had been for many years 'acting in defiance of the general methods of poor law administration'; that when Sir Alfred Mond had issued an Order limiting the amount of relief which could be paid to the able-bodied, the Guardians had simply declined to obey it. 'This condition of affairs is not one which has ever been contemplated by the law, and the remedies provided by law are entirely inadequate and inappropriate.'

The memorandum went on to list four existing remedies and to explain why they were useless. First, an aggrieved ratepayer could get an injunction from the court restraining the Guardians from granting illegal relief. But 'the Guardians would not obey such an injunction and ask nothing better than to become martyrs by being committed to prison for their principles'. Second, the District Auditor had power to surcharge for illegal expenditure. But surcharges of thousands of pounds upon men such as the Poplar Guardians would be 'almost ludicrous'.

The third possible remedy was the power of the Minister to alter the boundary of any Poor Law union. The memorandum explained that this remedy had in fact been explored. A proposal to constitute one large Poor Law union to cover Poplar, the whole of Stepney and the City of London had been examined. 'At one time there were hopes that an agreement of this kind could be made, but I fear that the City of London would not now be prepared to concur in the arrangement unless allowed a representation on the new Board of Guardians based upon their rateable value. This is an impracticable suggestion, and without their active concurrence action cannot be taken.'[22]

The fourth remedy was one which had already been applied without success by Mond: that of withholding advances of money to be repaid out of the MCPF. Joynson-Hicks showed why this remedy would not work. Poplar would simply go on as at present until they had no money left and then, with the cooperation of the council, would again intercept the moneys due to the LCC and other central bodies 'and we shall be back in the position of 1921, with the Guardians and council again going to prison as martyrs on behalf of the distressed poor of the borough'. He urged the Cabinet to consider whether Poplar should be allowed to go on as at present. 'Poplarism is an infectious disease,' he said, 'the infection is already obvious in London Unions such as Bermondsey and in West Ham, and it is also, though less obviously, at work in many of the large industrial Unions in the country.'

He concluded that his Bill enabling him to take over the duties of both Guardians and councillors should be pushed through in the coming autumn session of Parliament. 'I am convinced that sooner or later the Government will have to deal with Poplar', he said, and ended: 'I am satisfied that the Government cannot safely further postpone action in the matter.'

The Cabinet agreed that the proposed Bill should be carried through in the autumn session. However, on the very next day, 23 October 1923, came the first hint of a possibility that there might not be an autumn session at all. Baldwin addressed the Cabinet at length on the subject of unemployment, told them that the only way to deal with it was to protect the home market and said that he proposed to take the verdict of the country on the matter within six months. A few days later, to the dismay of most of Baldwin's colleagues, his time table had been much speeded up and on 13 November he told them that 'the march of events' compelled an immediate dissolution.

Joynson-Hicks had got his Bill ready, indeed it had been approved by the Cabinet Committee of Home Affairs. But that was as far as it went. When the General Election took place on 6 December 1923 the Conservatives lost their overall majority. So Joynson-Hicks never got the chance to demonstrate his firmness of purpose; the Bill which had been designed to bring about Poplar's downfall was once more shelved. Saved by the bell, Poplar would live on to fight again.

NOTES

1. For this and ensuing extracts from Twiss's report see BGM, 28 February 1923.
2. For Edgar Lansbury's comments, see BGM, 28 February 1923.
3. The cost of living index stood at 179 in September 1922 and a fall of ten points to 169 constitutes a reduction of only 5 per cent, whereas the shilling off pay from 11s to 10s would be more than 9 per cent.
4. DH, 9 July 1923.
5. ibid., 28 July 1923.
6. ibid., 14 August 1923.
7. *The Times*, 15 August 1923.
8. ELA, 25 August 1923.
9. ELO, 25 August 1923. DH, 24 August 1923.
10. BGM, 25 August 1923.
11. ELA, 6 October 1923.
12. Edgar Lansbury's account of the event appeared in an interview with the *East London Advertiser*, 6 October 1923. Another version, together with a report of the ensuing altercation between George Lansbury and one of the leaders of the deputation, appeared in *East End News*, 28 September 1923 and 2 October 1923. There were frequent references to Sylvia Pankhurst and the UWO in Home Office Memoranda to the Cabinet on 'Revolutionary Organisations'. See PRO Cab 24:

CP 407 (27 September 1923); CP 412 (4 October 1923); CP 415 (11 October 1923).

13. THL, Poplar Box 880. Letter from Warren to Percy Squire, 4 August 1922.
14. THL, ibid.
15. ELA, 18 August 1923.
16. ibid., and *The Times*, 15 August 1923.
17. THL, Poplar Box 880. Letter dated 13 September 1923.
18. EEN, 9 October 1923.
19. ELA, 13 October 1923.
20. THL, Poplar Box 880. Letter dated 19 October 1923.
21. PRO, Cab 24 CP 416 (23) dated 15 October 1923 and Cab 23/46. Meeting 22 October 1923.
22. Since the City of London's rateable value was nearly three times that of Poplar and Stepney put together, the scheme would have given the City a permanent and overwhelming majority over the other two.

13

The First Labour Government

The general election in December 1923 resulted, after some weeks of uncertainty, in the installation of the first Labour Government. The Conservatives had lost their overall majority but were still the largest party in the House with 258 seats. The Liberals were once more united behind Asquith and their seats had risen to 159. But Labour's gains had been greater still; there were now 191 Labour MPs in the House. Two more exponents of Poplarism now joined March and Lansbury: John Scurr, elected for Mile End, Stepney, and Susan Lawrence represent ing East Ham North.

Not one of the three parties could command a majority in the House without the support of another, so political manoeuvring began directly the election was over. And although, on 11 December, Baldwin announced that he was not going to resign, it was clear that without allies his Government could not last many days. So those who were greatly alarmed at the prospect of a Labour Government hoped that the Liberals might be drawn into a coalition with the Conservatives.[1] Asquith demolished such hopes in a speech to Liberal MPs on 18 December when he jeered at those who suggested that their first act should be to 'go over bag and baggage to the enemy'.

In point of fact, the similarity of view between Liberals and Tories by now appeared more marked than their differences. Both parties emphasised their belief in private enterprise in face of the new socialist challenge. However Liberal MPs remained convinced that their turn in office must come again; they had not yet grasped the fact that, as George Lansbury put it, 'people had had enough of Tweedledee and Tweedledum'.[2]

All the same, by making protection the key issue in the election, Baldwin had attacked one of the few remaining principles which now separated Liberals from Tories: the preservation of free trade. The Liberals had spent the election campaign denouncing the Tories for failing to cure unemployment, attributing this to their incompetent foreign policy, and bitterly opposing Baldwin's protectionist programme. So on 18 December, when it was all over, Asquith suggested that the situation offered the Liberals an opportunity of a new kind:

> Neither the Tory Party nor the Labour Party has the chance to retain or obtain even a short lease of office unless it abandons for the time being the principal position on which it fought the election . . . whoever may be for the time being the incumbents of office, it is we, if we understand our business, who really control the situation.[3]

And he observed: 'If a Labour Government is ever to be tried in this country, it could hardly be tried under safer conditions.'

For some weeks it looked as though everything would flow smoothly the Asquith way. The House of Commons met; a motion that the Government had not the confidence of the House was carried on 21 January 1924, and Baldwin resigned the following day. Ramsay MacDonald became the first Labour Prime Minister and on the same day published the names of his new Cabinet. These names were on the whole reassuring to the Liberals. Moreover, MacDonald had gone out of his way during the debate to deprecate any suggestion that Socialism was a hard and fast doctrine, with a great gulf between it and the doctrines of other parties. More and more it seemed that the Liberals would be able to do as Asquith had foretold and control the situation. They were full of hope. 'The sole condition of success is that the Labour Government should be willing – as, so far, it shows signs of being – to turn its back on socialism and proceed on lines that will secure Liberal support.' This was the comment of the *Liberal Magazine* which, in an editorial, expressed pleasure at the changed prospects ahead.[4]

But then came an event which, in one stroke, demolished the Liberal edifice of self-congratulation and which showed, moreover, that the Liberals were far from being 'in control of the situation.' Inevitably, this event concerned Poplar.

On the evening of 23 January 1924, the day after the formation of the Labour Government, a meeting of the Poplar Board of Guardians was in progress. The circumstances were unusual, even for them, for the bailiff was in possession of the Guardians' office and was threatening to sell up the furniture within five days. He had been put in by Brentwood Asylum because the Guardians had refused to pay £34 for the maintenance of a patient, an ex-serviceman named Damien. The origin of this quarrel was a government decision in 1922 to transfer the cost of caring for mentally-ill ex-servicemen from the Ministry of Pensions to the local boards of guardians. The Labour Party had unsuccessfully opposed this move and it had been the subject of numerous protests from boards of guardians. So, some months earlier, the Poplar Board had decided not to pay for any case of this kind.

Now, as chairman of the Board, Edgar Lansbury proposed that both the new Ministers of Pensions and of Health should be asked as a matter of urgency to receive deputations. He went on to express confidence in the new Minister of Health, John Wheatley, in terms rather disturbing to those who looked forward to a period of Liberal-Labour harmony.

During the whole time that they had had a Labour and socialist majority on the Poplar Board of Guardians, said Edgar, they had been 'hindered, badgered and browbeaten' by successive Ministers of Health. But now at last he believed that they had a Minister who would see things from their point of view. Up to now they had been a voice crying in the wilderness; now they were coming into their own, and he believed the new Minister of Health would put his seal and sanction on the work they had done. 'It's not nice,' he said, 'to feel that at any moment we might individually or collectively be sold up, seized, or made bankrupt.' However, the Guardians were 'not people to let the grass grow under their feet'. He was well aware that Mr Wheatley would be faced by his permanent officials, but if Mr Wheatley had as much gumption as he believed, he would put those officials in their places.[5]

The Guardians agreed that both the Ministers should be asked to receive deputations. F. O. Roberts, the new Minister of Pensions, was visited first, and a few days after the interview it was announced that ex-service mental patients would be a charge on the Exchequer. That particular battle had been won.

Much more important was the interview between the Guardians and John Wheatley, the new Minister of Health. It took place on 5 February. Unlike most of his Cabinet colleagues, Wheatley, one of the Clydeside MPs, was known as a left-winger, and the Guardians had good grounds for believing that he would share their point of view. Indeed Wheatley later said that he had known when he first entered the Ministry that he would have to deal with Poplar and had made up his mind what to do before he ever met the deputation.[6]

The Guardians explained to Wheatley that they were asking for three things. Firstly they wanted the Poplar Order rescinded. Secondly, they wanted remission of any surcharges made on the grounds that in calculating the relief of an applicant they had given insufficient weight to the resources of other members of the family. Thirdly, they asked for cancellation of any surcharges arising from the £4 minimum wage.

Replying, Wheatley pointed out that he could not say any-anything about the £4 minimum since legal proceedings were involved. And he said he would have to look into the legal position concerning the liability of families to support those on relief. But on the main question at issue, he told them without hesitation that he had already decided to rescind the Poplar Order and to cancel any surcharges made under it. Not only this, he made his decision public immediately in a statement to the press.

For the Guardians it was indeed a cause for celebration. For twenty months they had defied the Poplar Order week after week in order to support the unemployed at an adequate level. They had tried to preserve the self-respect of those who came to them, insisting that relief for those for whom there was no work was a right and not something for which they should be forced to cringe and beg. In doing this they had acted illegally and over the whole period had risked prosecution, bankruptcy and possibly jail. A long-drawn out threat is in many ways more difficult to withstand than a short sharp conflict with authority, such as had taken place when they had gone to prison during the rates dispute. The theory of Joynson-Hicks and others that they did not mind going to prison, and even aimed to be martyrs, had always been wide of the mark. They had been under a considerable personal strain for a long time. But now their ordeal was over and it had proved worth while.

True, as Edgar Lansbury put it to a meeting in Bow Baths that weekend, Wheatley's action had merely cleared the ground; the present law still stood and they could be taken to court by the auditor if they paid more in relief than he judged reasonable. But there was no mistaking the sensations of triumph which gripped the meeting as Charles Key told them that if the workers in other districts were alive to their interests, they would not only copy Poplar, but even try to do better. And George Lansbury suggested that the more the Government got 'Poplarised' the more popular it would be. They were building better than they knew in Poplar, he said, they were fighting for human life and happiness which were worth more than money.[7]

Elsewhere, Wheatley's action in summarily cancelling the Poplar Order was received with consternation. Those who had been lulled in the belief that Ramsay MacDonald's new Cabinet consisted of 'moderate' men were jolted out of their complacency. A *Times* leader described the move as a 'dangerous and costly error of judgement' and went on to say:

> When the new Government came into office it was freely predicted that the people most likely to give them trouble would be found in the ranks of their own avowed supporters. The Poplar Guardians without, in the language of Mr Edgar Lansbury, letting the grass grow under their feet, seem bent on proving that the prophets were right.[8]

Among the most enraged were of course the Poplar employers. Percy Squires, chairman of the Ratepayers' Association, alleged that the complete breakdown of Poor Law administration was now threatened.[9] Sir Reginald Blair, former Poplar MP and chairman of the London Municipal Society, Sir Alfred Warren and Joynson-Hicks himself were among those who joined the chorus of denunciation.

One person utterly taken aback by the decision was the Prime Minister, Ramsay MacDonald. For Wheatley had deliberately avoided consulting him before making his decision known. Two days later, on 8 February, the subject came up at a Cabinet meeting 'as a matter of urgency'. At the end of the discussion, according to the official minutes, 'The Prime Minister made a strong appeal to all his colleagues not to make public announcements or take administrative action on questions of great public interest, particularly when they were of a controversial character, without previous consultation with the Prime Minister, who would consider whether it was necessary to consult the Cabinet.'[10]

MacDonald was in a quandary. To put Wheatley's decision into reverse was politically unthinkable even if it had been technically feasible. It seemed he had only two courses open to him. One was to support the cancellation of the Poplar Order on principle, to argue that Guardians who were trying to put Labour's programme into practice deserved support not persecution. Yet such a course would be entirely contrary to his own beliefs and, even more important, would risk losing the support of the Liberals on whom his continuation in office depended. The alternative course was to pretend that the cancellation of the Poplar Order had no significance, and this was the one he took. The Cabinet decided that Wheatley must issue a statement, 'preferably the same evening',[11] in consultation with the Lord Chancellor, Viscount Haldane, a Liberal. In this statement, which appeared on the following day, Wheatley said that the Poplar Order was obsolete and unworkable and that rescinding it 'does not involve or imply any alteration in general Poor Law policy'.[12]

This statement did not appear to make any difference to the hostile attitudes taken by Conservatives, Liberals, the newspapers and what was regarded as 'responsible opinion'. MacDonald was about to address the House of Commons for the first time as Prime Minister; in the circumstances he judged it necessary to deal with the Poplar affair at the outset of his speech to the newly reassembled House. 'I am told,' he said, 'that the cancelling of a certain Order by my Right Hon Friend the Minister of Health was the signal that the red flag was to be flown by every Board of Guardians from John o' Groats to Land's End. I was amazed at it. Every one knows perfectly well that that Order had ceased to operate. Everybody knows perfectly well that the cancellation of the Order had been again and again under consideration in the Department concerned.' He went on to say that the rescinding of the Order was 'nothing but a merely mechanical operation'.[13]

Asquith, however, was not mollified. He refused to accept MacDonald's defence and said that Wheatley's action was inciting other boards of guardians to follow Poplar's example. He insisted that unless the Government reconsidered its action there was not the least chance of it receiving the approval of the House of Commons. 'I, and many of my Friends – all my Friends I think – regard this as a matter of capital importance,' he said.[14] After which the new Prime Minister was obliged to set aside a day for the affair to be debated.

Before that day arrived, however, the Liberals found themselves in an awkward position. The Government showed no sign of reconsidering its action, as Asquith had demanded; moreover, no moves had been made towards finding an alternative method of controlling Poplar. Now it was clear that if the Liberals tabled a motion censuring the Government on the Poplar issue, the Conservatives would be bound to support it which would mean a Government defeat of such magnitude that MacDonald might be forced out of office before he had been there a month. This could mean another general election in which the Liberals would be attacked for having combined with the Conservatives to stop Labour rule before it had even begun. This might not be to the Liberals' electoral advantage. All in all, Asquith's previous assumption – 'it is we, if we understand our business, who really control the situation' – seemed increasingly wide of the mark. Asquith, it appeared, was as much the prisoner of MacDonald as MacDonald was of Asquith.

As the days passed, uneasiness grew. This was reflected in newspapers such as *The Times* which began to put matters in a different light, asserting that the Cabinet had not been consulted by Wheatley before he cancelled the Poplar Order and that the men dominating it were far from being extremists. By 25 February, the day before the crucial debate was to be held, there was a *Times* leader which revealed concern lest the Government be brought down on the issue. Even before this, Edgar Lansbury was commenting on the Liberal change of heart. 'The Government is not to be sacked after all,' he wrote sardonically in the *Workers' Weekly* on 22 February.

And so it proved. On the day of the debate, 26 February, a Liberal motion criticising the action of the Minister of Health in cancelling the Poplar Order was moved, the Conservatives, led by Joynson Hicks, tabled an amendment in more extreme terms; this was defeated by the combined vote of Labour and Liberal MPs. The Liberals then announced that they would not press their own motion to a division on the grounds that the Government had given satisfactory assurances.

This episode was significant for two reasons. The failure of the first Labour Government (and for that matter of the second Labour Government) to implement election promises was, between the wars, customarily attributed by people in the labour movement to the fact that having no overall majority, they could only carry out those measures which commanded

Liberal support. The Poplar incident showed that, in the early stages at least, this was by no means the case.

The other significant aspect of the affair was the method of handling it in debate. Liberal and Conservative speakers attacked in terms which had now become familiar, i.e. Poplar Guardians encouraged the work-shy and were undermining the sense of responsibility and the sanctity of home life. Yet no Government speaker challenged these allegations, no Government speaker defended the actions of the Poplar Guardians, though Poplar was, after all, attempting to implement the very principles for which Labour was supposed to stand. At the end of the debate, the Prime Minister was able to comment with satisfaction: 'The Minister of Health in the course of the admirable speech which he delivered, did not offer a single sentence in defence of the Poplar administration.'[15]

Wheatley, indeed, had been tied down by a Cabinet decision taken on 18 February that he 'should make it clear that the rescission of the Order was never intended in any way to encourage or condone slack administration'.[16] This Cabinet discussion virtually obliged him to argue the case on grounds of expediency rather than principle. He therefore adopted the time-honoured device of politicians in office, of attacking his predecessors and alleging that when in office they had been even more incompetent. It is a device which is very effective in the debating chamber, but its use has perhaps contributed to the growth of cynicism about politics and politicians in the minds of others.

On this occasion, Wheatley certainly used the method to great effect. He taunted his opponents with the whole long history of the Poplar Order, and showed how, from the very beginning, Poplar had ostentatiously defied it and week by week had sent in the record of cases in which they had exceeded the legal amount permitted by amounts totalling £2,000 a week, so that within twelve months the illegal expenditure had added up to £110,000, and was now probably not less than £160,000. 'And here is a remarkable thing,' jeered Wheatley; 'although the Ministry of Health were aware that Poplar was breaking the law, no attempt whatever was made by the Ministry of Health to enforce the law. I do not know what excuse can be presented to this House by our predecessors for their conduct.' Remarking that the Poplar Board was the only one in London whose audits had not been completed, he said: 'I had to emancipate my Department from this state of degradation.'[17]

In response to this attack, Joynson-Hicks denied suggestions that he or his predecessor, Neville Chamberlain, had told the officials to delay closing the Poplar audits. He argued that it was the sheer volume of work involved in examining each case reported that had defeated the auditors. 'It was the greatest audit of the Department,' he said. 'There were about 30,000 cases receiving relief in Poplar during the whole of that period, and a very large number of those cases were debatable points. It is impossible to conceive that any auditor could get through the enormous work of dealing with 30,000 cases, with £2,000 in dispute every week over a period of, now, a year and a half.'[17]

The implications of Joynson-Hicks's speech were far-reaching. If Labour boards of guardians could no longer be controlled by the traditional method of audit and surcharge, some other form of administration would have to be introduced. The reform of the Poor Law, long advocated by those who deplored its inhumanity, began to assume importance for quite other reasons.

Meanwhile, the Poplar Guardians had received official notification that the Order had been rescinded. Commenting a little ruefully at a Guardians' meeting the following day, Edgar Lansbury said that the House of Commons had spent eight hours discussing Poplarism, and though there were many expressions of sympathy, there was very little real sympathy. Explaining the principles for which Poplar stood, he said he had never heard such a mess as one speaker after another had made of it.[18] He pointed out that they still had to fight on two issues. One was the Ministry's rule that the maximum relief for a family must be 10s a week less than the pay of a grade A labourer, no matter how many children there were. The other was the rule that children at work should shoulder the whole burden of the family's destitution.

A few weeks later Wheatley was guest of honour at the annual dinner of the London Labour mayors. He said amid laughter that the word 'Poplar' would be found inscribed on the hearts of Ministers of Health by future explorers of their tombs. He added that the position he filled might well be included in the category of 'dangerous occupations' since no fewer than five

Ministers had occupied the position before him though the
Ministry had only been formed in 1919.[19]

In May the right of the Council to pay a £4 minimum wage
to its employees came again before the court. The District
Auditor had surcharged them £5,000 on the grounds that the
wage was excessive and therefore unlawful. Poplar had taken
the matter to the Divisional Court which had upheld the
Auditor. Now came the appeal.

Unlike their stand on poor relief, for this contest they had
wide support, not only from the labour movement but from
broader local government circles, including many Liberals.
This was not because there was approval for a £4 minimum
wage, far from it. But the case was seen as a fight against the
further extension of the powers of the District Auditor over
elected councillors. Freedom to decide the level of wages had
been conferred on local authorities by Parliament. Now the
auditor and the judges were combining to deprive them of that
freedom.

The barristers briefed for either side were well-known
political figures. The Poplar councillors were represented by an
eminent Liberal MP, Sir John Simon, and the District Auditor
by Conservative MP, Sir Douglas Hogg, who had been Attorney
General in the Baldwin Government.

Sir John Simon argued that the amount of wages paid was a
matter for the borough council's discretion. It was admitted
that they had acted honestly and there had been no misconduct;
how then could it be said that what they had done was contrary
to law? The proposition before the court would 'extend to a
remarkable degree the powers and functions of a district
auditor.'[20]

Sir Douglas Hogg, for the Auditor, said the payments were
unreasonable, and that the test was whether any prudent or
reasonable man would have paid so much. He took up the
argument of the councillors that so long as the wages paid were
those approved by the electors there could be no complaint, and
countered with the argument of the Municipal Alliance that in
Poplar there were a number of ratepayers, people who lived
outside the borough, and public companies, who had no votes
at all.[21]

The upshot of the appeal was that the councillors won their
case by a two to one majority. But the reasons for their victory

gave no grounds for rejoicing. For only one of the three judges concerned held that the Auditor had no power to interfere with the wages paid. The other two judges both found that the Auditor had such a power. But one of them thought he should not have interfered in the year 1921–2, since at that time the £4 was not so unreasonable as to be contrary to law. Thus, though the councillors had been saved on this occasion, the decision meant that in future years, when the discrepancy between the £4 minimum and the prevailing wage rates had become greater, they could almost certainly be surcharged.

Despite this, the councillors greeted the judgement with relief and, at George Lansbury's suggestion, they had a party to celebrate. However, it was announced almost immediately that the Auditor was in turn going to appeal to the House of Lords. This would take months. Meanwhile, by July, events had begun to repeat themselves. Members of the Council were summoned by the Auditor to show cause why they should not be surcharged £45,000 for the wages which had been paid in the subsequent year, 1922–3. As before, large crowds assembled and the 'Red Flag' was sung, the whole performance was re-enacted, the same arguments deployed.

A few weeks earlier another case, this time against the Poplar Guardians had come before the courts. It arose from the dock strike of the previous summer. As recounted in the last chapter, Warren of the Municipal Alliance, who had been driven almost beyond endurance by the refusal of successive Ministers of Health to deal with the Poplar Guardians, had actually proposed a rates strike by Poplar firms in the autumn of 1923. This had been abandoned after expressions of disapproval from Joynson-Hicks; moreover, when the dock strike ended the proposal to seek an injunction against the Guardians had been dropped. But another proposal – that the Guardians be taken to court for granting relief to strikers – had been carried through. Representations on behalf of eight local Poplar firms[22] had been made to the then Attorney General, Sir Douglas Hogg who, just before the general election, had applied to the courts on their behalf for a declaration that payment of relief to able-bodied men who could obtain work must be disallowed by the Auditor. The men referred to were 'Labourers engaged in the Port of London in or about the actual handling of cargo in or on ship, quay, warehouse or craft'.

Though a new Attorney General had replaced Hogg since the Labour Government took office, the case went ahead and came before the court in June. The chief witness for the defence was David Adams who, as already said, had been closely involved as a Guardian in dispensing relief to the strikers, despite his position as a local official of the Transport and General Workers Union whose general secretary had done his best to break the strike. On this occasion the Guardians did not try to fight the issue on principle; they merely defended their action on the grounds of expediency, saying that men had not been able to get work because of the mass pickets and that, in any case, there was not enough work to go round. Not surprisingly, the judge granted a declaration in favour of the Attorney General that the payments had been unlawful.

Soon after, the Auditor notified them that he was imposing a surcharge of £1,843 for relief given to the dock strikers. The surcharge was not divided equally; the largest share was assigned to those who had handled the most cases. These were Julia Scurr, Helen McKay and David Adams. The Guardians decided on 23 July to appeal to the Minister of Health to relieve them of the surcharge.

John Wheatley, however, had not much longer in office. A blunder had been committed by the Labour Attorney General, Sir Patrick Hastings. He had prosecuted the editor of the Communist *Workers' Weekly* under the Incitement to Mutiny Act 1795 for an article urging soldiers not to turn their guns on their fellow workers, and had subsequently withdrawn the prosecution following questions from Labour MPs initiated by John Scurr. This had resulted in a Conservative move for a vote of censure and a Liberal demand for a committee of inquiry. MacDonald decided not to try and ride out the storm, and the Government resigned early in October.

Paradoxically, Poplar had gained more from the nine months' existence of the Labour Government than anyone else. Denounced by the Conservatives and Liberals as Bolshevik extremists, repudiated by the dominant Labour leadership as an electoral liability, the Poplar Guardians had nevertheless received, in Edgar Lansbury's words, 'seal and sanction' for their deliberate violation of the law over a long period.

As an area of heavy unemployment, Poplar also gained from improvements to the unemployment insurance scheme introduced by the Government, including an increase in benefits, easing of conditions for receiving it and the abolition of the 'gap.'

But apart from this, the only really significant achievement of the first Labour Government was Wheatley's Housing Act, which laid the basis for the great growth in municipal house-building over the next few decades. In most other respects, Labour's impact appeared to have been no more than marginal. A year earlier Charles Key had prophesied that soon the movement would have to face the question: 'You now have power – what are you going to do with it?' Poplar had given its answer: 'We have come to make a change.' The first Labour Government had no such perspective and, so far as the majority of citizens were concerned, any change was not very apparent.

It would be untrue to suggest that the leading activists in Poplar were disappointed, since the attitude of the dominant Labour leaders to their own activities over the previous three years had taught them what to expect. 'I don't think it matters much how long the Government is in,' had been George Lansbury's comment just after it took office. 'What does matter is not what we say, not what we talk about, but what we propose to do at a given moment.'[23] In the *Workers' Weekly* at about the same time, Edgar Lansbury had put his view. Suggesting that the Poplar Guardians and councillors had the confidence of the Poplar workers because they had 'never fallen down at the Capitalist trumpet,' he went on:

> The Labour Government will get the confidence of the workers of Great Britain only so far as they make an effort to do the major things in their programme. And just so soon as they try to do the major things set out in their programme they will meet the same kind of lies and slander, hatred and malice, as we get in Poplar now. If the Labour Party sits still it will die. If it goes forward to the attack on the Capitalist system, it may lose a whole world of Liberal and Liberal-Labour supporters, it may lose its whole representation in the Upper Chamber, but it may find its soul.[24]

But in the months that followed it transpired that one of the chief objectives of Cabinet members was, precisely, to sit still, so as not to rock the boat. Indeed the first Labour Government demonstrated that those who shrink from the mass movement and who believe that the struggle for Socialism should be confined to parliamentary processes are often the most reluctant to use Parliament for that purpose when the opportunity arises. Towards the end of the Labour Government's term of office, John Scurr expressed his concern about the direction in which events were moving. 'Are the leaders of the Labour movement looking forward or backward?' he wrote in *Socialist Review*: 'Are they content with patching, or do they wish to transform society?'[25]

To go further than patching is not easy for those who are simultaneously anxious to preserve continuity. In *Lansbury's Labour Weekly*, a journal started by George soon after the Labour Government's fall, the frustrations on the left found expression:

> There has been a Labour Government and it has not challenged Capitalism at a single point. It has followed, in foreign affairs, in dealing with unemployment, indeed on every vital issue, a policy of 'continuity' with its capitalist predecessors. Certain of its leaders have even lauded that 'continuity' as a blessed principle of British political life.[26]

John Scurr was expressing similar views in *Socialist Review*. 'I do not care a brass farthing whether we have a Labour Government or not if the game is to be played under the present rules,' he wrote in September 1925.

But leaders like Ramsay MacDonald envisaged the way forward through an endless series of minor modifications of the existing system. 'The Socialist transforms by the well-defined processes which a living social organisation allows,' he wrote in June 1924. 'He rejects everything of the nature of violent breaks and brand-new systems. He is an evolutionist par excellence.'[27]

He was as much averse to the aims and tactics of people like George Lansbury and the other Poplar activists as were his Conservative and Liberal opponents:

> It cannot be over-emphasized that public doles, Poplarism, strikes for increased wages, limitation of output, not only are not Socialism, but may mislead the spirit and policy of the Socialist movement. . . . The Socialist, therefore, looks with some misgivings upon some recent developments in the conflicts between Capital and Labour. They are contrary to his spirit; he believes they are both immoral and uneconomic and will lead to disaster.[28]

Lansbury and his friends had never equated Poplarism with Socialism. What they did believe was that so long as capitalism lasted, they must fight to alleviate its injustices. In so doing they would be demonstrating to the workers that Labour had something new to offer. 'The issue that is raised by Poplar is larger than an issue of local government', George Lansbury had written earlier. 'It is the whole question whether the Labour Movement means business. Are we going to attempt to carry out what we say on the platform, or are we to be misled and side-tracked by considerations of "statesmanship"?'[29]

John Wheatley was alone in MacDonald's Cabinet in his belief that Poplar, far from 'misleading the spirit and policy of the Socialist movement', as MacDonald had suggested, was showing the rest of the movement the way forward. Some months after the resignation of the MacDonald government, Wheatley came to Poplar to open a block of flats, and said that he did not think that Poplar owed nearly so much to him as he owed to Poplar. Acknowledging his 'great joy and pride in being associated with Poplarism', he expressed the belief that 'the Poplar Borough Council in many respects was a great pioneer in the work of social emancipation, and it was only as the policy of Poplar permeated the country that they would march towards a different order of society'.[30]

But those who thought like Wheatley were outnumbered in the leadership of both the TUC and the Labour Party by others who talked endlessly of the promised land, but seemed anxious to avoid any action which would bring them into conflict with the existing social order.

NOTES

1. Or even, as suggested in a letter to Baldwin from the chairman of the City of London Conservative and Unionist Association, that a Liberal Government could be formed with Conservative support to keep out Labour (see *Liberal Magazine*, February 1924, p. 125).
2. DH, 28 January 1924.
3. *Liberal Magazine*, January 1924.
4. ibid., February 1924.
5. EEN, 25 January 1924.
6. ELA, 6 June 1925.
7. *The Times*, 11 February 1924.
8. ibid., 7 February 1924.

9. EEN, 12 February 1924.
10. PRO, Cab 23/47. Cabinet 11, 8 February 1924.
11. ibid.
12. *The Times*, 9 February 1924.
13. House of Commons, *Hansard*, 12 February 1924.
14. ibid., 13 February 1924.
15. ibid., 26 February 1924.
16. PRO, Cab 23/47, Cabinet discussion 18 February 1924.
17. House of Commons, *Hansard*, 26 February 1924.
18. EEN, 29 February 1924.
19. ELA, 29 March 1924.
20. *The Times*, Law Report, 16 May 1924.
21. ibid., 21 May 1924.
22. The eight firms involved as 'relators' were Lock, Lancaster; W. W. and R. Johnson and Sons; British Oil and Cake Mills; Fletcher and Son and Fearnall; N. J. Fenner; H. B. Alder and Co.; R. and H. Green and Siley Weir; Wilkinson, Heywood and Clerk.
23. *The Times*, 11 February 1924.
24. *Workers' Weekly*, 15 February 1924.
25. *Socialist Review*, September 1924.
26. *Lansbury's Labour Weekly*, 11 April 1925.
27. Preface to new edition of *Socialism: Critical and Constructive* by J. Ramsay MacDonald (1924).
28. ibid.
29. See article on 'Poplar and the Labour Party' by George Lansbury in *Labour Monthly*, July 1922.
30. ELA, 6 June 1925.

14

The Last Phase

In the general election of October 1924 a Conservative Government backed by a huge majority took office. It was to stay in power for the next four and a half years, and the new Minister of Health was once more Neville Chamberlain.

The period when Poplar could expect any help from the Government was gone. However, the mood of Poplar's inhabitants remained as before. In April 1925, when the Guardians' elections took place, the Municipal Alliance lost its three remaining seats and twenty-four out of twenty-four went to Labour. 'POPLAR GUARDIANS NOW ALL RED' was the headline in a local newspaper, and 'POPLARISM VICTORIOUS'. But in that same week Poplar Borough Council finally faced defeat in the long drawn out struggle for the right to pay a £4 a week minimum wage.

Following the decision of the Divisional Court the previous June quashing the surcharge imposed by the District Auditor for paying wages that were in his opinion unreasonable, the District Auditor had appealed to the House of Lords. After three days of legal argument, the five Law Lords concerned (Lords Buckmaster, Atkinson, Sumner, Wrenbury and Carson) found in favour of the Auditor.[1]

The borough councillors had contended that the wages were a matter for their own discretion and not that of the Auditor. The five Law Lords thought otherwise; unanimously they found against the councillors, though the reasons they gave for their judgement varied.

Lord Buckmaster said the councillors had not exercised their discretion properly because they had agreed to pay £4 for labour irrespective of what that labour might be. Lord Atkinson said the councillors would fail in their duty if they 'allowed themselves to be guided . . . by some eccentric principles of socialistic philanthropy or by a feminist ambition to secure equality of the sexes in the matter of wages'. He referred at length to the payment of £4 a week to charwomen and said: 'What has been given to the women as wages are really to a great extent gifts and gratuities disguised as wages and are therefore illegal.'

Lord Sumner, dealing with the councillors' contention that no adult employee should in any circumstances have less than £4 a week said the borough council had no authority to 'give practical effect, at the ratepayers' expense, to such an abstract resolution'. He thought that the councillors had exercised their discretion 'upon principles which are not open to the Council and for objects which are beyond their powers'.

Lord Wrenbury thought that 'wages in a particular service are such sum as a reasonable person, guiding himself by an investigation of the current rate in fact found to be paid in the particular industry. . . . It is a figure which is not to be based upon, or even increased by, motives of philanthropy nor even of generosity stripped of commercial considerations'.[2]

Lord Carson agreed with Lord Buckmaster.

Lansbury's Labour Weekly had a good laugh at their lordships' expense. The following open letter appeared on 11 April:

My Lords – I see you have forbidden the Poplar Borough Council to pay its labourers £4 a week. . . . None of you (except poor Wrenbury who drags out a hungry existence on about £55 a week – often when I see a man shivering at a street corner, I say "That may be poor Wrenbury") take less than £120 a week, not counting your savings from past 'emoluments'. It needed high moral courage to announce to the world your profound conviction that any one of you was worth thirty ordinary men. Except of course poor Wrenbury who is only worth fourteen ordinary men.

But it wasn't really funny. For five years the Poplar councillors had adhered to their £4 minimum while all around them wage levels had crumbled. They had wanted to play their part in defence of working-class standards at a time when these were under attack. But the employers' offensive had been relentlessly pursued; one section of workers after another had been defeated, so that Poplar's £4 was now some 40 per cent above the pay of labourers who worked for other local authorities and some 78 per cent above that of female employees. It was as though they stood on a narrow promontory while the advancing tide engulfed the shore on either side, as far as the eye could reach.

Ever since 'Black Friday' in April 1921 they had seen trade

union leaders giving in, or compromising even at times, when the rank and file were in the mood to fight. Worst of all, they had seen other Labour-controlled authorities fail to make any serious stand on the issue.[3] Indeed, Herbert Morrison had argued that Poplar's whole approach to the wages' question was wrong.

Could they have defied the court and gone on as they had done over the issue of outdoor relief? George Lansbury made clear some of the arguments against this in the *Labour Weekly*, saying that if the councillors had determined to continue the payments 'their officers, whose signatures are necessary on cheques, would refuse to sign, and even if they signed, any ratepayer could get an injunction ordering the bank not to pay'.[4] This was true enough, but it was not the kind of consideration that had deterred the councillors from breaking the law in the past.

But there were other factors in the situation which made some retreat inevitable. It was clear that on this issue they could not hope to win an outright victory as in their previous contests. And this in turn was linked to the change in the political climate. The belief that 'the workers are coming into their own', as the *Daily Herald* had put it in the heady days of 1919, was fading; 'direct action' was out of fashion except with such bodies as the National Unemployed Workers' Movement and the Minority Movement, both of which were shortly to be outlawed by the Labour Party, a process which had already begun in the case of the Communists. True, the old spirit would revive again briefly during the 1926 General Strike, but after that it would disappear for a long, long time.

Ruefully the Poplar councillors decided that they would have to give way on the £4 minimum. At a special meeting on 9 April 1925 they adopted a resolution proposed by Charles Key:

'That this Council, under protest and with great reluctance, proposes to consider the whole question of wages with a view to bringing them into conformity with the decision of the House of Lords.'

They sent this resolution to Neville Chamberlain as Minister of Health with a request that he would cancel the surcharge of £5,000.

At the same time they referred the new wages to a special wages sub-committee which spent some time considering how small a wage cut was feasible, and finally drew up a list of reductions varying from 2s 6d to 7s 6d a week to be introduced gradually over ten weeks. The reductions meant that the pay of the lowest grades which included male and female convenience and baths attendants would go down from £4 to £3 12s 6d a week. At this level they remained more than 20 per cent above the prevailing rate for men and more than 50 per cent above that for women. Moreover, in terms of purchasing power they were worth much more than the original £4 when first introduced.

The new wage rates were not, however, adopted without some grumbling when they came before the council on 28 May. Councillor O'Callaghan objected, saying that he 'thought the Council would have put up a better fight before knuckling under'.[5]

Neville Chamberlain, however, was far from satisfied with these reductions. He wrote to say that he was not unwilling to remit the surcharges since the court proceedings were in the nature of a test case, provided he received an indication that the council would put their wages on to a footing which would prevent the constant recurrence of similar surcharges in the future. But, he pointed out, the new wages were 13s 8d above the JIC rates for men and 26s 4d above those for women.[6]

The response of the councillors was to go into negotiation with the Ministry and to spin it out for many months during which it gradually became clear that they did not intend to retreat any further. Half way through, in December 1925, they were notified that summonses had been granted against thirty-nine of them to recover the £5,000 surcharged together with £1,198 costs. 'Couldn't we have a whip round?' asked George Lansbury to laughter.[7] The councillors' negotiators were Charles Key and Edgar Lansbury. Back they went to the Ministry and the summonses were postponed.

What could Chamberlain do in the face of this obduracy? If he refused to cancel the surcharges it would doubtless mean some sort of confrontation with Poplar, and he might find himself in the kind of situation which had so embarrassed his predecessors. Unlike the previous conflicts in which Poplar had been engaged, the councillors had not ostentatiously broken the law when they stuck to their £4 minimum. On the contrary, it had been widely assumed, even by many of their bitter opponents, that they had been within their legal rights. The judges had, in effect, suddenly made a new law. Persecution for actions in the past which had been widely thought to be legal at the time would arouse sympathy.

Chamberlain had hoped to use the threat of the surcharges to persuade Poplar to reduce wages much further. The attempt had failed, and the result would be that, even if he cancelled past surcharges, the District Auditor would inevitably surcharge them for their present and future wage scales. However, that was something for the future; decisions on it could be postponed.

In the end a settlement was reached in March 1926 under which Poplar made a further gesture. They agreed that after August 1926 their present wage scale could be varied up or down according to the cost of living sliding scale used by the JIC for local authority employees. In other words, the margin between their own wage scales and those of other local authorities would be permanently maintained. As was pointed out in *Lansbury's Labour Weekly*, 'The net effect is that employees of the Poplar Council and Guardians will always be better paid and work under more favourable conditions than most other districts in London.'[8]

In return for this decision, Chamberlain agreed to cancel not only the £5,000 surcharge for 1921–2 over which there had been the legal fight, but all later surcharges arising from the £4 minimum. These had been mounting; for the council alone they totalled £11,500 for 1922–3; £22,000 for 1923–4; £24,600 for 1924–5. There were also surcharges levelled on the Guardians for operating the £4 minimum for their staff.

The settlement was accepted at a mass meeting of 700 employees with only two voting against; it was felt to be a satisfactory outcome in the circumstances.

Neville Chamberlain also had reason to congratulate himself. Although he knew that Poplar would be surcharged all over again for the year 1925–6 despite their wage reductions – this in fact happened, the Auditor made a surcharge of £23,000 – he had postponed the necessity of handling a tiresome crisis. There was always the hope that Poplar could be dealt with as part of a general local government reform.

Yet ironically enough, Chamberlain was not destined to

avoid embarrassment over the Poplar affair. Indeed, in the end he was obliged to go to considerable lengths to extricate himself from an awkward situation. This was created by the Poplar Municipal Alliance whose members were by this time in savage mood. For years they had protested to one Minister of Health after another without avail. They had been forced to contribute more money in rates than they considered just or necessary; they had watched this money being paid out in wages and out-relief which were so high as to be illegal. They had stood by helpless while the councillors and Guardians had repeatedly broken the law and defied the auditor. They had watched with mounting incredulity the failure of successive governments to bring the council to book and enforce the law. Now, despite court decisions against them, Poplar's wages were to continue on a much higher level than elsewhere. To crown everything, these same councillors and Guardians were to escape all the penalties of the law and the consequences of their actions. They would get off scot-free.

The last straw had been the discourtesy shown them by Neville Chamberlain himself. Other Ministers of Health, such as Mond and Joynson-Hicks, had treated them as persons of some importance, allies in the struggle against Poplarism. They had listened to them, had seemed to welcome their views, had appeared anxious to accommodate them. But not Neville Chamberlain. Time and again he had rebuffed them, never trying to hide his disdain. Now they took their revenge.

They decided to challenge Chamberlain in the courts, claiming that once there had been a court decision he had no legal right to cancel the surcharges. A fund of £5,000 was raised from local firms and a member of the Alliance and former councillor, John Dore, applied on their behalf to the High Court to quash the Order of the Minister of Health remitting the surcharges. The case began in July 1926; judgement was not delivered until February 1927. And it went against Chamberlain.

For fifty years it had been assumed that any councillor or Guardian whose expenditure had been disallowed could test the validity in the courts, but that, if the judgement went against him, he could still appeal to the Minister to remit the surcharge. Now the judges had ruled that no such remission could be allowed and that Chamberlain had acted illegally in granting it.

Chamberlain had taken office as Minister of Health with an

ambitious programme for sweeping changes in social policy, many of which would have merited the approval of the Poplar Municipal Alliance and other employers. Thus he planned a total reform of the Poor Law which, though it would do little to meet the criticisms of humanitarians, would abolish boards of Guardians altogether and put their responsibilities into the seemingly safer hands of county council and county boroughs. (In Poplar this would mean that the powers of the local Board of Guardians would be transferred to the London County Council.) At the same time Chamberlain was planning a reform of local government finance involving, among other things, the de-rating of industry, so that firms like those in the Poplar Municipal Alliance would be relieved of three-quarters of their rates.

Such measures were coming very soon but, in the meantime, to his annoyance, Chamberlain had found himself constantly facing unforeseen crises which necessitated emergency bills of a miscellaneous character. Thus the behaviour of certain boards of guardians – notably that in West Ham, which defied the Minister over the issue of relief during and after the 1926 General Strike – forced his hand. No one was more ruthless if up against it than Chamberlain, and his answer to West Ham was to introduce the very Bill he had wanted to avoid and which had been before the Cabinet in earlier years. Under the Boards of Guardians (Default) Act he took power to unseat recalcitrant Guardians and put his own appointees in their place. This Act, originally devised as an instrument to put down Poplar was, in the event, never used against Poplar, but only against other Guardians.

Now the judgement over the Poplar wage case faced Chamberlain with another crisis which he would have preferred to sidestep. It had arisen because the judges had altered the law in a way never contemplated by Parliament. They had now done it twice in connection with Poplar, first depriving the council of its right to fix its wages and next depriving the Minister of his right to waive penalties, a right which he had exercised for half a century. They had, in short, filched the power of policy-making from elected representatives and put it in the hands of non-elected officials and judges.

Not only Poplar was now involved; Bethnal Green and Woolwich had also been surcharged for paying wages above those the auditor thought fit. On inquiry, Chamberlain found that unless the law was quickly changed no less than ninety-seven people from these areas might go to prison.

Chamberlain was hardly the man to aim at the restoration of former democratic rights to his political enemies. But he could have introduced an emergency Bill legalising his action in remitting the surcharges. However this he was loth to do. For it was clear to him, as to previous Cabinet Ministers, that the law on surcharging no longer worked. It had been effective enough in the case of councillors and Guardians before the war when only small irregularities and little illegalities were involved, sometimes committed inadvertently by the councillors and Guardians concerned. It had worked, too, as a check on corruption. But as soon as Labour-controlled authorities began to emerge and to act on principle, to pursue deliberate policies which would benefit their poorest constituents in defiance of the intentions of the central government, it became clear that the weapon of disallowance and surcharge had become ineffective. For one thing, the very size of the sums involved was out of all proportion to the means of those surcharged. For another, there were, among the new breed of Labour councillors and Guardians, people who seemed quite prepared to risk penalties for the sake of their principles. True they were in a minority. But if Poplar went on winning, more and more other local authorities might follow suit and defy the Government. Some other way of curbing the activities of such people had to be found.

Chamberlain found it in a drastic measure: the Audit (Local Authorities) Bill, which provided that all those surcharged for sums of more than £500 would be automatically disqualified from holding office for five years. There would be no right to ask the Minister for remission; the only remedy would be an appeal to the High Court on legal grounds. The Minister's power to cancel surcharges was retained only for those of less than £500.

To George Lansbury it was obvious that the sole purpose of this Bill was to make it more difficult for Labour-controlled authorities to carry out Labour's programmes. 'Baldwin, Chamberlain, Churchill, Birkenhead and the rest do not mind Labour or Socialist majorities that are content to keep things as they are,' he wrote in a special article in *Lansbury's Labour Weekly*. 'They do not object to a Labour Government if it is a nice Pleasant Sunday Afternoon Government that is content to leave untouched the sacred ark of the covenant of Capitalism. . . . Our governing class, with the ingenuity and cunning they know so well how to exercise, allow the workers to retain all the outward signs and symbols of democracy. We elect municipal councils and other authorities, but after election if they dare to put Socialist principles in operation, then the "artful dodgers" who rule us scheme and plot to overthrow Labour majorities.'[9]

The Bill received its Second Reading on 15 June 1927. Naturally the Labour opposition opposed it on the grounds that it enormously increased the powers of 'bureaucratic officials independent of popular control', and established the principle that elected representatives of the people could be disqualified for reasons that had nothing to do with corruption, misconduct or negligence. George Lansbury, John Scurr and Susan Lawrence were among those who spoke against the Bill, the last dwelling on the narrow-minded attitude of the District Auditor who, she alleged, had actually attempted to surcharge the London County Council for furnishing the ponds in the London parks with ducks. But the Labour amendment was, of course, defeated and the Bill became law.

Ironically enough, among those who were angry with Chamberlain over this measure was the Poplar Municipal Alliance who had brought it about. They had already tried unsuccessfully to persuade Chamberlain to unseat the Poplar Guardians under the Guardians Default Act, as he had those of West Ham, but he had refused. Now they contended that the Audit Act was insufficient protection, since if one lot of councillors was disqualified, another lot with similar ideas could always be elected in their place.

But the thing that annoyed them most was Chamberlain's announcement that he intended 'wiping the slate clean'. The new Bill provided that all those who had been surcharged in the past were to be relieved of their liability. Whatever might happen to councillors in the future if they chose to rebel, all past surcharges, now running into many tens of thousands of pounds, were to be cancelled outright. The idea that after all this the Poplar councillors and Guardians would escape any penalties could not fail to infuriate their enemies.

And what of the Poplar councillors and Guardians themselves? It would be wrong to suggest that the final cancellation of the surcharges did not come as a personal relief to them, though they had shown their usual fortitude in face of the threat that had hung over them and had never in public betrayed the smallest anxiety on this score.

They were not of course by this time precisely the same people as those who had decided to challenge the powers that be in 1921. To their distress Charlie Sumner had died in 1925, O'Callaghan and Rugless in 1926, Julia Scurr early in 1927. Ill-health had caused Joe Banks to resign; Edgar Lansbury had not stood again for the council in November 1925; Susan Lawrence and John Scurr were no longer there since they were now MPs for other constituencies. And some others among the original band had dropped out. But George Lansbury himself was still there and so were Charles Key and David Adams, the Cressalls, Albert Baker, T. J. Goodway and Jack Wooster, to name only a few.

There was little sign that they had changed very much, but the situation in which they found themselves was totally different from that of 1919 when they had been elected so full of hope. They had sought to live up to George Lansbury's guiding principle for socialists in office: 'What matters is not what we say but what we do.' They had done their best to raise the living standards of the people who had elected them and had, indeed, succeeded in doing so against extraordinary odds. But they had failed to persuade the rest of the labour movement to take the same path. To some of them, at least, it seemed that the forward march of Labour had long since taken a wrong turning.

NOTES

1. *Roberts* v. *Hopwood* (1925), Law Reports. A.C. 578.
2. ibid. See also article *Poplar and the Auditor* by W. H. Thompson, LRD Monthly Circular, May 1925.
3. The main exception was Bethnal Green which had a minimum rate of £4 for men and £3 10s for women, and which had been surcharged at the same time as Poplar.
4. *Lansbury's Labour Weekly*, 18 April 1925.
5. ELA, 6 June 1925.
6. Letter dated 14 July 1925, reprinted PBC, 23 July 1925.
7. ELA, 19 December 1925.
8. *Lansbury's Labour Weekly*, 6 March 1926.
9. ibid., 11 June 1927.

15

In Retrospect

For many years, the word 'Poplarism', which still appears in the Addenda to the *Shorter Oxford English Dictionary*, was defined censoriously as 'the policy of giving out-relief on a generous or extravagant scale practised by the Board of Guardians about 1919 and later any similar policy which lays a heavy burden on the ratepayers.' But later the definition was significantly modified and now reads: 'The policy of giving generous or (as was alleged) extravagant outdoor relief, like that practised by the Board of Guardians of Poplar in 1919 or later.' There was good reason for the alteration. For most of the immediate aims for which Poplar councillors and Guardians fought and for which they were denounced as Bolshevik extremists have long since been officially recognised as desirable. At the time their attitudes were thought to offer a threat to society. But now society has to some extent adopted these attitudes, or at least claims to do so.

Thus the action for which they were imprisoned was aimed at a redistribution of wealth from rich to poor; it raised the issue of whether the poor areas should support the poor or whether the burden should be shared by the rich areas. This 'revolutionary movement for the equalisation of wealth', as *The Times* put it, was denounced by the organs of orthodox opinion; yet since that time equalisation of London's rates has become a normal feature of local government finance, while Rate Support Grants from the Exchequer are specifically designed to give most to the poorest areas in order to raise them to the level of the richer ones.

Poplar campaigned for what *The Times* defined as 'the Communist doctrine of full maintenance for the unemployed.' But this 'Communist doctrine' was enshrined in the Beveridge Report in 1942, and governments have since accepted that anyone for whom there is no work has the right to maintenance, despite occasional bouts of sniping from the right who, whenever jobs are scarce, can be heard to complain that the unemployed are too well off on the dole.

Poplar fought for adequate child allowances for all unemployed families and refused to be bound by the rule that a large family with many children must live on an amount less than that earned by the lowest paid labourer. With the introduction of Family Allowances in 1946 came official recognition at last that children should entitle the parents to more money whether at work or not. The theory is at least accepted by society as a whole, even if in practice the actual level of child benefits has often failed to keep pace with rising prices.

The Poplar Guardians were attacked for refusing to operate the household means test on the families of the unemployed. The struggle against the household means test went on all through the thirties; it was virtually done away with in 1941 and, though far too many people's weekly income still depends on a personal means test, the process of assessing the sons and daughters, parents, grandparents, mothers and fathers-in-law of the claimant in determining his or her entitlement has never reappeared except in a form so modified as to be unrecognisable.

The Poplar councillors tried to put into effect the principle of equal pay for women. They were denounced by the Law Lords for so doing. But equal pay is now incorporated in an Act of Parliament; in law, if not yet in fact, posterity has vindicated Poplar's stand.

Attitudes and behaviour have thus changed much over fifty years, largely as a result of the spread of ideas generated by the labour movement. Towards the growth of these ideas the Poplar councillors and Guardians made a notable contribution.

When it comes to the wages front, a fundamental shift in the relation of forces can be discerned. Fifty years ago the trade unions were weak and employers were able to force down wages. The Poplar councillors fought a long defensive battle against this process. Nowadays the strength of the trade unions is such that no employer attempts to enforce reductions in money wages. Instead, while the value of wages is eroded by inflation, governments step in to stop them rising, sometimes on a voluntary basis by agreement with the trade unions, sometimes by Act of Parliament. The last time that a local authority challenged this process was in the nineteen-seventies when Clay Cross Urban District Council introduced increases in pay for its employees in defiance of a pay-freeze imposed by a Conservative Government. The Poplar councillors escaped retribution; not so those of Clay Cross who suffered the full penalty of the law.

And this reveals a curious paradox. While many of the immediate aims for which the Poplar pioneers fought have been won,
the drastic legal sanctions devised by Neville Chamberlain to
discipline rebellious local authorities have changed little since
they were introduced in 1927. They were last re-enacted in the
1972 Local Government Act under which, when an auditor
certifies that a loss or deficiency of more than £2,000 is due to
the wilful misconduct of a councillor, the latter is automatically
disqualified for five years. Those disqualified can appeal to the
court only; the Minister has no power to cancel the surcharge,
let alone remove the disqualification.

The results of this curtailment of the Minister's powers to
remit a surcharge were illustrated in the case of the Housing
Finance Act, introduced by a Conservative Government in the
nineteen-seventies, which directed all local authorities to raise
the rents of their council dwellings by certain uniform amounts.
A number of local councils refused, and though subsequently
they gave way, some four hundred councillors faced eventual
surcharge and disqualification. The Clay Cross councillors
meanwhile persisted in their refusal to raise the rents and were
subjected to a special audit, surcharge and disqualification.
When the 1974 Labour Government was elected it proceeded
to carry out its election pledge to repeal the Housing Finance
Act, and also took steps to exonerate those councillors who had
defied it. This required special legislation, and the upshot was
that the threat of surcharge and disqualification was withdrawn with some difficulty from the four hundred councillors
concerned; however, the House of Lords insisted on an amendment to ensure that the disqualification of the Clay Cross councillors should remain, an amendment subsequently narrowly
accepted by the Commons. Such is the legacy of the 1927 Act.

As in the nineteen-twenties, judges continue to reinterpret
the law from time to time in a fashion not intended by Parliament, but to the disadvantage of the underprivileged. Thus the
courts in the nineteen-fifties decided that the Birmingham
Corporation, authorised by Act of Parliament to operate a
transport undertaking, and to charge such fares 'as they may
think fit', were acting illegally when they adopted a scheme for
free travel passes for pensioners; later, special legislation had to
be put through Parliament to reverse this judge's decision. In
contrast, when, in the nineteen-seventies, a Conservative

council, Tameside, refused to change over to comprehensive education, as required by an Act of Parliament, their challenge to the law was upheld in the courts.

Though the law may not have changed very much, the machinery of local government has been greatly altered over fifty years. For one thing, local authorities have lost some of their most important functions. For example, social security is no longer in the hands of locally elected boards of guardians but in those of national agencies of various kinds. Municipal gas and electricity undertakings have all been nationalised. Health and hospital services have been transferred to the National Health Service. Whatever may be said in favour of this process of centralisation it has meant that directly-elected representatives no longer play a part in managing these services, and the people in charge feel themselves answerable to those above them rather than those below.

At the same time, central control of local government activities is, in most respects, tighter than formerly. Control is largely exercised by a hold over finance, made possible because local government lacks an independent source of revenue other than rates, and these have proved inelastic. The tendency has been for central directives to become more numerous and detailed, while the councillor's scope for decision-making becomes more limited. This, it is sometimes argued, has led to the erosion of public interest and public participation in local government affairs.

A glance at the situation fifty years ago reveals, however, that there is nothing very new about the indifference with which local government affairs are commonly regarded. In the nineteen-twenties public interest was, in most areas, also very limited, judging by the low turnout at elections and the small attendance at council meetings. Poplar was an exception, mainly because Lansbury and his friends combined an unusually strong determination to change the world as they found it, with an ability to involve others and stir them to action.

In conclusion, it should not be forgotten that, though some of the Poplar councillors' immediate aims have been achieved, their long-term one has not. They looked on their endeavours as part of a struggle to abolish the capitalist system. But the Socialism on which they set their sights is still far off, and socialists as divided as ever on how to reach it.

Appendix A

Outdoor Relief Scales in 1922

	Mond Scale (including winter fuel allowance of 3s a week)		Poplar scale (including winter fuel allowance of 3s a week and a rent allowance based on actual rent up to 10s)	
	s	d	s	d
Man and wife	28	0	33	0*
Man, wife and child	34	0	39	6
Man, wife and 2 children	39	0	44	6
Man, wife and 3 children	44	0	49	6
Man, wife and 4 children	48	0	54	6
Man, wife and 5 children	54	0†	59	6
Man, wife and 6 children	54	0†	64	6
Man, wife and 7 children	54	0†	69	6
Man, wife and 8 children	54	0†	74	6

* This figure of 33s for a man and wife was given in the Cooper Report but in fact it seldom rose to this amount, since the rent allowance was based on the *actual* rent up to 10s and this was unlikely to be more than 5s to 6s in the case of a man and wife without children. A more realistic example of the Poplar scale would have been 28s or 29s made up of 20s scale rate, plus 3s winter fuel allowance plus 5s–6s rent. The figure for a single person is not given in the above table since, as explained in the text, it was incorrectly set out in the Cooper Report. Excluding the winter fuel allowance the Mond scale provided 15s for a single person living alone; the Poplar scale was 12s 6d plus rent allowance up to 5s, or 17s 6d.

† The maximum chargeable to the Metropolitan Common Poor Fund (and later the maximum legally allowed under the Poplar Order) for any family was 10s below the standard rate of wages for workpeople of Grade 'A' under the Agreement of the London District Industrial Council for non-trading services (manual). At the time of the Cooper report this wage was 64s which means that the maximum in out-relief was 54s. In June 1922 the wage was reduced and the maximum became 50s 6d.

Appendix B

Biographical Notes on the Thirty Councillors who went to Jail in 1921

The author would be glad to receive any corrections or additions to these notes, particularly in cases where the entry is short.

Adams, David Morgan (1875–1942) Born in Poplar. Moved to Wales and at age twelve became a coal-miner. Later a seaman, then a soldier serving three years with Welch Regiment in India. Returned and became a docker. Secretary, Export Branch, Dock, Wharf, and Riverside Workers' Union, 1911–20; later became full-time official of Transport and General Workers' Union. Poplar Guardian, 1913–30. Poplar councillor, 1919–42. Mayor, 1934. Member of Parliament for South Poplar, 1931–42.

Baker, Albert (1887–1956?) Born in Poplar. Started work on railways at age 14. 1911 joined Amalgamated Society of Railway Servants, later National Union of Railwaymen. Member Poplar No. 1 Branch NUR. Poplar Trades Council Executive, 1911–13. Poplar Guardian, 1919–30. Poplar councillor, 1919–37. Mayor, 1933–4.

Banks, Joseph Henry (1871–1938) Born in Poplar. Started work on railways. Joined ASRS in 1894; later a member of Poplar No. 1 Branch NUR. Secretary to Poplar Trades and Labour Representation Committee (Headquarters, 6 Campbell Road) which in 1909 was made up of forty-five trade union branches, the ILP, the SDF and the Christian Socialist Fellowship. Later, secretary of Poplar Trades Council until 1922. In 1910 dismissed by Great Eastern Railway for taking leave without permission to act as agent for George Lansbury in election. Remained Labour agent for Bow and Bromley Division of Poplar until 1922. First elected to Poplar Borough Council in 1903; continued as councillor until he resigned on grounds of health, December 1922. Poplar Guardian, 1911–22.

Cressall, George Joseph (1880–1951) Born in Stepney. Worked as a general labourer at Hubbucks Paint Works. Joined

Liberal Party, 1902. Became dissatisfied when local Liberal councillor on London County Council refused to support a wage of 30s for employees. Left Liberals, 1907 and helped form Limehouse Branch, Independent Labour Party. Moved to Poplar, 1912. Member, Bromley East Branch, General Municipal Workers Union and delegate to Trades Council from 1912. Spoke for ILP at dock gate meetings. 1918 became full time Labour agent and secretary South Poplar Labour Party. Founder member of National Union of Labour Organisers. Poplar councillor, 1919–49. Mayor, 1931–2. Poplar Guardian, 1922–5; 1928–30. Received OBE, 1949.

Cressall, Nellie Frances (1882–1973) Born in Stepney, name of Wilson. Father a carpenter, mother a parlourmaid. Worked in a laundry in Whitechapel Road. Married George 1904. Eight children born between 1904 and 1927. Joined Limehouse ILP, 1907. 1912 suffragette and colleague of Sylvia Pankhurst. Addressed meetings at Blackwall Tunnel Dock Gates. During 1914–18 war served on Food Control Committee. Poplar councillor, 1919–65. Mayor 1943. Made Freeman of the Borough, 1959.

Farr, Albert Victor (1872–1941) Born in Bethnal Green. Postman. Member of Union of Post Office Workers. Poplar councillor, 1919–22.

Fleming, Benjamin (1879–1965) Labourer, later a hospital porter. Poplar Guardian, 1919–31. Poplar councillor, 1919–31.

Goodway, Thomas John (1870–1947) Born in Chelsea, came to East London age of ten. Postman. Dismissed by Post Office in 1890 for taking part in a strike. Reinstated, 1893. Secretary, Bow Branch Postmen's Federation during first world war (later Union of Post Office Workers) Poplar councillor, 1912–47. Mayor, 1926–7. 1939 Elected to London County Council for Bow and Bromley Division.

Green, Walter Henry (1871–1957) Born in Bethnal Green. Dock labourer. Poplar councillor, 1919–22.

Heales, James Joseph (1873–1955) Born in Bethnal Green. Journeyman bootmaker. Poplar councillor, 1919–22.

Hopwood, Robert John (1877–1964 ?) Engineer. Worked for Bryant and May before 1914–18 war. Secretary Bow Branch

Amalgamated Society of Engineers during First World War.
Succeeded Joe Banks as Secretary Poplar Trades Council,
1923–4. Poplar alderman, 1919–25.

Jones, James Horatio (1861–1946) Born Portsea. Appren-
ticed to boat-builder; left and started own business. In 1889 one
of founders of No. 4 Branch London Carmen's Union. Became
railwayman with Midland Railway. Member Poplar No. 1
Branch NUR. Churchwarden. Poplar councillor, 1917–45.
Mayor, 1939–40.

Kelly, Thomas Edwin (1873–1941) Grocer and provision
dealer. 1902 secretary of Bow and Bromley Branch National
Amalgamated Union of Shop Assistants. Member Independent
Labour Party, 1906. Unsuccessful candidate in borough
council elections, 1906 and 1912. Poplar councillor, 1919–28.

Lansbury, Edgar Isaac (1887–1935) Son of George.
Brought up in Poplar, trained for Civil Service. Left it and went
into partnership with his brother in a timber merchant business
in 1910. Married, 1st, Minnie Glassman, 1914. 2nd, Moyna
MacGill, 1924. Member of Communist Party and in May 1924
elected as substitute member of its central executive committee.
Poplar councillor, 1912–25. Mayor, 1924–5. Poplar Guardian,
1920–7. Chairman Board of Guardians, 1922–5.

Lansbury, George (1859–1940) Born in East Anglia. Came
to London age seven. At sixteen became a coal-heaver. Married
1880. Emigrated to Australia, 1884. Returned 1886 and went
into father-in-law's timber business. Active for Liberals from
1886. 1892 joined Social Democratic Federation, later joined
ILP. 1889 joined Gasworkers' Union. Stood as Socialist for
Walworth, 1895. First elected to Poplar Board of Guardians,
1892 and to Poplar Borough Council, 1903. Christian pacifist.
Elected member of Parliament for Bow and Bromley Division
of Poplar in 1910 but resigned his seat in protest at Parliamentary Labour Party's attitude to suffragettes. Editor of *Daily
Herald*, 1912–22. Poplar Guardian, 1892, 1904–30. Poplar
councillor, 1903–40. Mayor, 1919–20, 1936–7. Member of
Parliament for Bow and Bromley, 1910, 1922–40. Leader of
Opposition in Parliament, 1931–5.

Lansbury, Minnie (1889–1922) Born in Stepney of Jewish
parents named Glassman. School teacher. Married Edgar,

1914. In 1915 committee member of East London Federation of Suffragettes of which Sylvia Pankhurst was secretary, in 1916 became its assistant secretary and continued in this position, being last re-elected in May 1918 when the organisation changed its name to the Workers' Socialist Federation. Member of Communist Party as soon as it was formed in 1920. During 1914–18 war was appointed to War Pensions' Committee. Poplar alderman, 1919–22.

Lawrence, Arabella Susan (1871–1947) Solicitor's daughter. 1895 entered Newnham College, Cambridge, to study mathematics. 1900 elected as 'moderate' (i.e. Conservative) to London School Board. 1910 elected as 'municipal reform' (i.e. Conservative) candidate for West Marylebone to London County Council. Concerned with wages and conditions of school cleaners, she came to know Mary MacArthur and in 1911 joined Fabian Society; in 1912 joined ILP. Became an organiser for National Federation of Women Workers. 1913 elected to London County Council as Labour candidate for South Poplar. Served on LCC until 1928. Poplar alderman, 1919–24. Member of Parliament for East Ham North, 1923–4, 1926–31. Junior posts in first and second Labour Governments. See also *Dictionary of Labour Biography*, vol. III.

Mackay, Jennie (1872–1955) Connected with trade union movement from 1901. First woman member in the area of what later became National Union of General Municipal Workers. She and her husband (a baker's vanman) were in the Social Democratic Federation; 1913 both were arrested during disturbances surrounding arrest of Sylvia Pankhurst during suffragette campaign. Served on school care committee and as school manager. Poplar councillor, 1919–45.

March, Samuel (1861–1935) Born Romford. Father an agricultural labourer, victimised for joining Joseph Arch's union. One of fifteen, Sam became a part-time farm-worker at age of nine. From twelve to fourteen, part-time bakehouse job. At eighteen came to Poplar and became a 'carman' (i.e. driver of horse-drawn vehicles). 1889 joined London Carmen's Union and was chairman of his branch. 1896 became full time secretary of the union, which changed its name to National Union of Vehicle Workers in 1912. Joined Poplar Labour League, and stood unsuccessfully for Poplar Borough Council in 1900. When union amalgamated with others to form T&GWU in 1922, he became national secretary of Commercial Road Transport section of that union. Poplar councillor, 1903–27. Represented South Poplar on London County Council, 1919–25. Member of Parliament for South Poplar, 1922–31.

Oakes, John Edward (1876–1961) Born in Poplar. Toolmaker. Poplar councillor, 1919–25.

O'Callaghan, Joseph Thomas (1879–1926) Stevedore. After 1921 obliged to seek other work owing to Depression, and took post as assistant relieving officer. Poplar councillor, 1919–26.

Partridge, Alfred (1864–1940) Born in Ely. Blacksmith. Leading member of Congregational Church. Poplar councillor, 1903–34. Poplar Guardian, 1919–22, 1925–31.

Petherick, Charles (1883–1965) Born in Stepney. Dock labourer; later foreman for Port of London Authority. Secretary South Dock Branch, Dock, Wharf and Riverside Workers' Union during First World War. Poplar councillor, 1919–31. Poplar Guardian, 1925–30.

Rugless, James John (1873–1926) Born in Bethnal Green. Leadworker. Poplar councillor, 1919–26.

Russell, Josiah (1882–1943) Born in Stepney. Railway carman (i.e. van driver). Poplar councillor, 1919–31.

Scurr, John (1876–1932) Born in Australia, but brought up in Poplar by his uncle who adopted him when his mother died. Roman Catholic, of Irish descent. Started work in an office in 1892; later carried on his own small retail hardware store; after 1912 had employment on *Daily Herald*; in 1924 became editor of *Socialist Review*. 1897 joined Poplar Labour League, and later became its secretary; also joined Social Democratic Federation and later British Socialist Party; was also active for ILP. President of Poplar Trades and Labour Representation Council, 1911. In 1912 during dock strike acted as chairman of London District of the Dockers Union. Executive Committee of United Irish League, 1900–6. Supporter of suffragette movement and was arrested for speech on subject in Norwich. Pacifist in 1914–1918 war. Poplar alderman, 1919–25. Mayor, 1922–3.

Poplar Guardian, 1922–5. Member of Parliament for Mile End, Stepney, 1923–32. See also *Dictionary of Labour Biography*, vol. IV.

Scurr, Julia (1871–1927) Daughter of John O'Sullivan from County Cork, Ireland, but brought up in Limehouse. Active in Irish Movement. Married John in 1900. In early 1900s helped organise deputation of women on unemployment to Prime Minister Balfour. Active in East End Federation of Suffragettes. In 1914 led demonstration on sweating to Prime Minister. Did care committee work. First elected to Poplar Board of Guardians in 1907; became well known in this capacity. Served as a Guardian until her death. Member of Poplar and Stepney Sick Asylum, later St Andrew's Hospital. Poplar councillor, 1919–25.

Sloman, Henry William (1879–1957) Stevedore. Member of Stevedores' Labour Protection League, later Amalgamated Stevedores and Dockers. Union branch secretary, 1925, 1928. Poplar councillor, 1919–31. School manager.

Sumner, Charles Edwin (1867–1925) Labourer. Worked for twenty years for Pearce's Chemical factory. Active in building Bromley East Branch of Gasworkers Union in the 1890s; associated with Lansbury in SDF. Elected to Poplar Board of Works before 1900 and first became a councillor in 1900. Unsuccessfully contested Bow and Bromley in LCC election of 1913, sponsored jointly by Bow Branch of British Socialist Party and Bromley East Branch of National Union of Gasworkers. Poplar councillor, 1900–25. Poplar Guardian, 1907–25. Chairman of Board of Guardians, 1919–22. Represented Bow and Bromley division on London County Council, 1919–25. In last few years of his life was a paid organiser for the NUGMW.

Williams, Christopher Edward (1885–1966) Born in Poplar. Labourer. Joined Gasworkers and General Labourers Union in 1905. In 1912 nominated as borough council candidate by local union branch and stood unsuccessfully on behalf of Poplar Trades and Labour Representation Committee. Three years serving soldier during 1914–18 war. On his return member of War Pensions Committee. Poplar councillor, 1919–31. Poplar Guardian, 1925–30.

Some of the Councillors who did not go to Jail but helped to secure the release of those who did

Blacketer, Thomas John (1881–1953)   Engine driver. Poplar councillor, 1919–34. Poplar Guardian, 1922–31. Mayor, 1930–1. Secretary Bow and Bromley Division Labour Party after resignation of Joe Banks.

Hammond, Joseph Arthur (1874–1938)   Railway signalman. Secretary Poplar No. 1 Branch NUR in 1918. Poplar Guardian, 1914–30. Poplar councillor, 1919–38. Mayor, 1925–6.

Hubbart, Peter (1875–1956) Corn porter. Joined dockers union, 1892. Executive of Poplar Labour Protection League 1907, later its general secretary. Poplar Guardian, 1919–31. Poplar councillor, 1919–48. Mayor, 1929–30.

Key, Charles William (1883–1964)   Schoolmaster. Poplar councillor, 1919–40. Mayor, 1923–4. Poplar Guardian, 1925–31. Member of Parliament for Bow and Bromley, 1940–50.

Watts, Alfred Augustus (1862–1928)   Compositor. Member of Social Democratic Federation, later British Socialist Party. Founder member of Communist Party in 1920. Poplar Guardian, 1904–28. Poplar councillor, 1925–8. Represented North Battersea on London County Council, 1919–25.

Wooster, John Thomas (1862–1947)   Bricklayer's labourer. One of 25. Left school at eleven and went into Simpson & Payne's candle factory, working 12 hours a day for 5s a week. Joined Social Democratic Federation, later ILP, later Poplar Labour League. Poplar councillor, 1919–47. Mayor, 1927–8.

Index